THE TYPOLOGY
AND DIALECTOLOGY
OF ROMANI

Edited by

YARON MATRAS
University of Manchester

PETER BAKKER
Aarhus Universitet

HRISTO KYUCHUKOV
University of Shumen

JOHN BENJAMINS PUBLISHING COMPANY
AMSTERDAM/PHILADELPHIA

The paper used in this publication meets the minimum requirements of American National Standard for Information Sciences — Permanence of Paper for Printed Library Materials, ANSI Z39.48-1984.

Library of Congress Cataloging-in-Publication Data

The Typology and dialectology of Romani / edited by Yaron Matras, Peter Bakker and Hristo Kyuchukov.

    p.   cm. -- (Amsterdam studies in the theory and history of linguistic science. Series IV, Current issues in linguistic theory, ISSN 0304-0763 ; v. 156)

  Includes bibliographical references and index.

  1. Romany language--Grammar. 2. Romany language--Dialects. I. Matras, Yaron. 1963- . II. Bakker, Peter. III. Kichukov, Khristo. IV. Series.

PK2897.T97   1997

491.4'975--dc21   *1 8⊃2076796*   97-42187

ISBN 90 272 3661 5 (Eur.) / 1-55619-872-8 (US) (Hb; alk. paper)   CIP

John Benjamins Publishing Co. • P.O.Box 75577 • 1070 AN Amsterdam • The Netherlands
John Benjamins North America • P.O.Box 27519 • Philadelphia PA 19118-0519 • USA

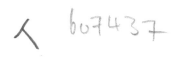

THE TYPOLOGY AND DIALECTOLOGY OF ROMANI

Volume 156

Yaron Matras, Peter Bakker and Hristo Kyuchukov

The Typology and Dialectology of Romani

CONTENTS

INTRODUCTION

PETER BAKKER
University of Aarhus
and
YARON MATRAS
University of Manchester

1. Romani linguistics: a very brief history

Romani is a minority language in all societies where it is spoken, but in terms of numbers of speakers Romani actually ranks among the more widely spoken languages of the world. With an estimated number of between five and ten million, it has more speakers than Catalan or Danish. This volume deals with two central topics in the study of the Romani language in which significant progress has been made in recent years: typology and dialectology. Recent descriptions of hitherto unknown or only sparsely documented dialects have broadened the database for both comparative and typological work on varieties of the language. Insights from this work have in turn begun to serve as input for more general typological studies, with Romani figuring both in larger language samples and in studies of single phenomena. The position of Romani as a *Balkanized Indic language* (Matras 1994a) and its hybrid patterns of morphosyntax are of special interest in this context.

Romani dialects were being documented as early as the sixteenth century. In 1542 Andrew Boorde published a short sample of British Romani in his *Fyrst Boke of the Introduction of Knowledge*, and the first Romani vocabulary, based on a northern continental dialect, was published by Bonaventura Vulcanius in 1597 (Kluge 1901:91, 113-114). An Italian theatre play from 1646 contains some dialogues in Romani (Piasere 1994); in 1668 the Ottoman writer Evliya Çelebi presented samples of Balkan Romani (Friedman & Dankoff 1991), and Job Ludolf followed in 1691 with a German Romani wordlist (Kluge 1901:172-173). It was not until the second half of the eighteenth century, however, that the grammar and the origin of the Romani language became the subject of intensive scholarly discussion, leading ultimately to the wholesale dismissal of various speculations that had flourished earlier (cf. Hancock 1988).

Between 1760 and 1785 various persons were engaged in Romani-related research — among them William Marsden and Jacob Bryant in England, the Hungarian Istvan Vali in the Netherlands, Christian Büttner, Johann Rüdiger, and Heinrich Grellmann in Germany, and H.L.C. Bacmeister, Simon Pallas and even Catherine the Great in Russia. They discovered, partly in cooperation and partly independently of one another, similarities between Romani and living Indo-Aryan languages. Grellmann is usually credited with the discovery of the Indic origin of Romani, probably since he devoted to this topic an entire chapter in his book on Gypsies (Grellmann 1787), a work which was subsequently translated into English and other languages. While Grellmann not only made use of his colleagues' materials, but also plagiarized other sources extensively (cf. Ruch 1986), it was Rüdiger whose original essay on Romani (Rüdiger 1782) in fact constituted the breakthrough.

Rüdiger was critical both of society's treatment of the Gypsies and of the contemporary scholarly discussion concerning their language and origin. Relying on wordlists collected mostly by Büttner, he first noticed lexical similarities between Romani and Hindustani, which he went on to explore empirically. With a short description of the Hindustani language written by a missionary in hand, Rüdiger sought the help of a native speaker, a Romani woman of the Sinti group named Barbara Makelin (cf. Adelung 1815:30). He thus obtained both Hindustani and Romani translations of phrases and paradigms and was able to show that the two languages shared not only some basic vocabulary, but also the essentials of inflectional morphology and some syntactic features. As a typologist, Rüdiger's achievement is not only illustrating the shared origin of the two languages, but also explaining the differences between them (cf. Matras 1994a:1; Haarmann 1989). He described the emergence of the definite article in Romani, for example, as a case of the functional reanalysis of an Indic demonstrative following the model of the contact language, and noted the heavy impact of language contact in areas such as word order and indeclinable particles. Thus, as early as the late eighteenth century data on Romani was already providing scholars with insights into the mechanisms of contact-related grammatical change and the principles of areal linguistics.

By the time August Pott had begun his voluminous work consisting of a grammar and a comprehensive dictionary (Pott 1844-1845) several dozen published sources on various Romani dialects had become available. It was Pott, nowadays considered the founder of Romani philology, who concluded on the basis of these sources that, despite variation and the strong influences of foreign contact languages, Romani dialects clearly form a linguistic unity. Empirical

Romani dialectology on a large and comprehensive scale can be said to have started with the work of Franz Miklosich. His twelve-part opus on the *Speech Varieties and Migrations of the Gypsies of Europe* (Miklosich 1872-1880) is not only a comparative study of the most important Romani dialects, but also a meticulous historical and typological study of the language as a whole. On the basis of a comparative study of Indo-Aryan languages and their various stages of development, relying especially on evidence for the formation of the nominal paradigm, Miklosich concluded that the ancestors of the Roma must have left India around the tenth century, following the transition from Middle to New Indo-Aryan and the collapse of the ancient case inflection system. Miklosich also recognized various strata of lexical borrowings in the language, which he regarded as evidence for the migration route which the Gypsies had taken on their way to Europe and for the pathways of dialectal dispersion within Europe thereafter. Perhaps his most important observation pertained to the significance of the Greek component. Its presence in all dialects of Romani led Miklosich to conclude that a Greek-speaking area had been the European homeland of all Gypsies before their dispersion across the continent. It is only in the last decade that Miklosich's observations and their implications for an areal-typological classification of Romani have again become the focus of linguistic research and that Romani has been dealt with in the context of Balkan *Sprachbund* phenomena (see e.g. Friedman 1985; Matras 1994a and 1994b).

The first three decades of the twentieth century saw significant achievements in the description of single Romani dialects, the most outstanding one being John Sampson's grammar and etymological dictionary of the dialect of the Gypsies of Wales (Sampson 1926). A thriving discussion also emerged surrounding the origins of Romani in India (see de Goeje 1901; Sampson 1907; Turner 1926) as well as the connection between the European Gypsy dialects and the Indo-Aryan varieties spoken by the Dom and the Lom in the Near East and Armenia respectively (see Macalister 1909-1913; Finck 1907; also surveyed in Hancock 1988). Modern Romani-related research has since been mostly concerned with the following problems: 1) The unity and diversity of Romani dialects and their implications for both dialect classification and linguistic origins; 2) The impact of language contact on linguistic change, including grammatical borrowing and contact-induced internal innovation, as well as the retention of Romani vocabulary in instances of language shift; 3) The sociology of the language, in particular questions of status, codification, and standardization; and finally, more recently, 4) Romani in the context of current theoretical issues in general linguistics.

It would be beyond the scope of this Introduction to take an inventory even of the main studies published in the past few decades (but see Bakker & Matras, forthcoming). Noteworthy however is the unprecedented upsurge of publications, especially monographs, during the 1990s. This latest period has seen extensive work in all four domains named above. As a representative sample of dialect descriptions we mention Boretzky's (1993) study of the Balkan dialect Bugurdži, Boretzky's (1994) outline of the Vlach dialect Kalderaš, Hancock's (1995a) Vlach grammar, Igla's (1996) study of the Vlach variety of Ajia Varvara, Halwachs' (1996) outline of the Central dialect called Roman as spoken in the Burgenland, and Cech & Heinschink's (1997) description of the Balkan Sepečides variety. Language contact surfaces in numerous case-studies, and we note in particular Boretzky & Igla's surveys of loan morphology (1991) and loan phonology (1993) as well as the collections by Bakker & Cortiade (1991) and Matras (1995 and forthcoming). Advances in the codification of Romani for both descriptive and applied purposes are represented by the appearance of the dictionaries by Demeter (1990) for Kalderash Vlach, by Hübschmannová et al. (1991) for the Central dialect of the Czech and Slovak Republics, and by Boretzky & Igla (1994a) for the Vlach and Balkan varieties of southeastern Yugoslavia. Finally, attempts to discuss Romani dialects in the context of current theoretical frameworks are best represented by Holzinger's (1993) study of Sinti as well as Matras' (1994a) study of Kelderaš/Lovari, both applying discourse-based functionalist methodologies. But general linguistic typology has also recently taken an interest in specific features of Romani, as exemplified by Plank (1995; also Payne 1995), Van der Auwera (in press), and others.

2. Core typological features and the unity of Romani

Despite over two centuries of research on the origin of Romani and its European dialects, ignorance of the fact that Romani constitutes a distinct and easily definable linguistic entity is still widespread. A superficial indication of speakers' own awareness of linguistic unity is the term *romanés* (occasionally also *rómnes, romanéh, romanó* or *róman*) which they use to designate their language. In the light of all that has been written on Romani in the past two centuries it is no longer necessary to argue the case for the structural unity of the language; we choose nonetheless to scan some of the core structural features of Romani in this section. This is intended primarily to facilitate access by non-Romanologues to the more specific contributions to this volume, but may also prove useful to those seeking additional confirmation of a well-defined, structural linguistic entity.

While diversity is doubtless most extreme at the lexical level, Romani dialects share a basic lexical core comprising the most frequently occurring items. This core is itself composed of various historical layers, showing some 700 Indic roots, around 70 Iranian, 40 Armenian, and perhaps 230 Greek items (cf. Boretzky & Igla 1994a). This composition is constant, not random, and is subject to little variation, and so it is taken to reflect an inherent shared origin rather than superposed convergence. But beyond core vocabulary, which in Romani is admittedly small, the language undoubtedly constitutes a grammatical unity.

Romani morphology is best characterized by a delicate balance of inflective features inherited from Older Indo-Aryan, agglutinative features which parallel some of the later developments in Modern Indo-Aryan and in Modern Indo-Iranian as a whole, and a more recent tendency towards analytic formation characterized by structural renewal and the grammaticalization of items of Indo-Aryan stock. These processes which involve inherited Indo-Aryan morphology partly overlap with grammatical borrowing of unbound, semi-bound, and in some cases even bound morphemes from the European contact languages. On the whole, different morphological formations may be found within the same grammatical categories, though some areas of Romani grammar may typically resort to specific patterns (for an extensive discussion see Elšik's contribution to this volume).

Romani has two genders (masculine and feminine), and two numbers (singular and plural). The expression of gender can be regarded as an inflective feature of nominal declensions, though a degree of agglutination is apparent in the regularity of the suffixes -o for masculine and -i for the feminine in the nominative singular of nouns, adjectives, and demonstratives, in participles including the active participles often used for past-tense formation of unaccusative verbs (predominantly expressing change of state; cf. Matras 1995b), in subject clitics, and reflected finally in the nominative definite articles o and i (alternating with e in some dialects) respectively. Number partly shares this regularity, with -e marking the plural in some nominal declensions, in adjectives and demonstratives, in participles, clitics, and in the definite article of some dialects. Number and gender agreement thus appear across all these categories, though there are nominal and adjectival declensions which do not take overt gender marking, and the rules for gender marking are typically different in thematic and athematic paradigms (see below). Agreement also extends to the genitive case, which agrees with the head noun of a possessive construction through 'Suffixaufnahme' (see Plank 1995:11-13; Payne 1995:288-289).

Internal inflection stands out in the system of demonstratives, which is typically quadripartite, encoding the source of knowledge about a referent (context vs. situation) as well as its accessibility or 'discreteness' (Matras, in press).

Derivation of both nouns and verbs however typically involves agglutinative suffixing procedures. Thus *-ni* forms feminine animates, *-to* ordinal numerals, etc.. In addition, the genitive case is used for derivational purposes in some dialects. Compounding is rare, and the use of verbal roots such as *ker-* 'do' or *d-* 'give' in complex formations can be regarded as a case for grammaticalization rather than as lexical compounding. There are a number of productive category-changing suffixes such as *-alo* and *-ano*, which derive adjectives from nouns, or *-ipen/-ibe* and variants, which derive nouns from adjectives and verbs. With verbs, agglutination is particularly outstanding in the formation of the causative by means of the infixes/suffixes *-av-*, *-ar-*, *-ker-* etc. (see contributions by Hübschmannová & Bubeník and by Cech & Heinschink to this volume), while passivization on the other hand involves inflective procedures including a change in the root of the verb, often with palatalization accompanied by a shift in stress (*dikh-él* 'sees' > *díčh-ol* 'is seen'). On the whole, the regular patterns allowing for causativization and passivization lend themselves to an interpretation of transitivization/de-transitivization as the central axis underlying verb derivational processes in the language.

Romani verbs are inflected for person/number by two series of inflective personal endings, correlating with the presence vs. absence of infixed extensions of the verbal stem. These extensions (*-d-*, *-l-*, *-t-*) are sensitive to phonological environment and show some dialectal variation. They have been interpreted as 'aorist' suffixes (Hancock 1995a), or alternatively, regarded as expressions of aspect rather than tense (see Holzinger 1993; Matras 1994a). Tense in the strict sense is expressed in most dialects by an agglutinating suffix-*as* which is external to aspect and — a typological rarity — to person marking. Renewal and consequent dialect variation is typical of the formation of the future tense. This is also an area where in some dialects analytic formation in the verb system may be encountered, with auxiliaries such as *l-* (lit. 'take') or particles such as *ka* (derived from *kam-* 'want' modelled on the Balkan future tense). Analytic formation may also encompass other areas of the verb in some dialects. Thus an analytic passive, based on the use of the copula as an auxiliary with a passive participle, is in use alongside a middle voice, based on the inflected passive (de-transitive) followed by the reflexive pronoun *pe(s)*. In a number of dialects, some unaccusative verbs will employ the copula auxiliary and a past participle rather than finite forms of the main verb in both past and present tenses.

Nowhere is the interplay of inflective, agglutinating, and analytic features as clearly represented as in the formation of nominal case (see the contribution by Matras to this volume). Romani preserves traces of the Old Indo-Aryan noun inflection in the nominative, the accusative, and the vocative. The accusative, which is based on the Old Indo-Aryan genitive, is the most productive non-nominative case and is sometimes designated 'oblique', for two main reasons: Firstly, it forms the basis for further case formations. Secondly, it co-occurs with the oblique case of adjectives, adjectival demonstratives, possessives, and definite articles, where a nominative/non-nominative two-way distinction prevails. The accusative figuring as an oblique hosts a series of agglutinative suffixes expressing the dative, locative, genitive, instrumental/sociative, and ablative cases. While the inflective cases encode gender and number (see above) and occasionally declension class (though differentiation here is minimal, compared to Old Indic, Latin, or contemporary Slavic), the agglutinative markers are isomorphic and highly regular; they vary only to the extent to which they are subjected to partial phonological assimilation with the preceding oblique ending, rendering alternate forms such as locative *-te/-de* reminiscent of case agglutination in Turkic or other language groups. Analytic case formation with prepositions (usually gramaticalized Indic adverbs of location) generally co-exists with the inflective/agglutinative pattern, but often substitutes for the latter. Indeed, for the language as a whole analytic prepositions may be said to be gaining ground at the cost of case endings.

Suppletion is on the whole rare in Romani. It is best represented in the system of third person pronouns (though not pronominal clitics), where nominative stems differ from non-nominative (oblique) stems, a differentiation which in some dialects is mirrored by the system of definite articles as well. In addition, suppletion is often found in the present/future and indicative/non-indicative formation of the copula (see Boretzky's contribution to this volume) and in the present/past of the verb 'go' (*dža-/g-*). To those one might add the negated copula in some dialects, as well as verb negation on the whole, which often shows indicative/non-indicative suppletion. A weaker case for 'semi-suppletion' in contemporary Romani could be made for reflections of the Old Indic present/past stem alternations which are still present in some verbs such as *sov-/su-* 'sleep', *mer-/mu-* 'die', *per-/p-* 'fall'.

Morphosyntax is more strongly influenced by contact phenomena than morphology proper, though some Indic features are preserved, in particular the non-nominative possessor, usually marked by the accusative/oblique (rather than the dative) in a possessive construction with the copula. Word order within the noun phrase only partly resembles Indo-Aryan patterns. For adjectives and demonstratives the dominant order is Det-N, with N-Det as an occasional though highly marked variant. Numerals always precede the noun, as do genitive attributes (though N-Gen may appear in lexical compositions). The definite and indefinite articles, a Romani innovation, precede the noun and thus conform to the earliest significant European contact language, Greek. Word order in the clause is often subject to variation and innovation through contact influences (see Boretzky 1996b), though in overall basic terms Romani word order can be classified as Balkan. Thus, thematic elements precede the verb while rhematic elements follow. This leads to an alternation of SV and VS as 'establishing' and 'connected' respectively (Matras 1995c). In addition, SV prevails in indicative complements while VS prevails in non-indicative complements. Romani has a striking tendency towards finiteness. Clause combining is consequently carried out almost entirely by unbound conjunctions. Subordinating conjunctions are partly derived from interrogatives or deictics, and partly borrowed. There is a strong tendency to borrow adversatives and sentential particles from contemporary contact languages (Matras 1996).

The most salient syntactic Balkanisms in Romani are the lack of an infinitive, the use of separate conjunctions with factual and non-factual complementation, the spread in some dialects of object doubling (see Bubeník's contribution to this volume), the use in some dialects of a future particle derived from the verb 'want', and perhaps some of the rules of lexical case assignment, the emergence of a middle voice, as well as the development of past tense evidentiality in some unaccusative verbs (Matras 1995b). Some of these features have been reversed or altered in some dialects, though traces of the Balkanized core structure remain. For example, a 'new infinitive' (Boretzky 1996a) is introduced in some Romani dialects based on the finite form of the third person singular present, though it is still introduced by the non-factual complementizer *te*.

Language contact plays an important role both in specific dialects of Romani and with regard to the character of the language as a whole. All varieties of Romani have distinct inflectional and partly derivational paradigms for vocabulary (nouns, verbs, adjectives) pre-dating the contact with Greek and for that acquired thereafter, labelled 'thematic' and 'athematic' repectively (see Bakker's contribution to this volume; Hancock 1995a; cf. also Boretzky 1989). While the thematic paradigms are Indic in origin, the athematic ones are typically a combination of Indic inflection and derivation with borrowed affixes of apparently Greek origin (Bakker, this volume), though other contact languages may occasionally contribute to the athematic morphology of single dialects as well, as in the case of plural endings on the noun. Borrowing of linguistic material is strongest in the area of unbound sentential and connective particles, including for example phasal adverbs, indefinites pronouns, and adversatives. Dialects affected more intensely by a particular contact language may show borrowed semi-bound items, such as prepositions or verbal particles from German in Sinti, or even bound morphemes, as in the case of Slavic aspectual markers and conditionals in some Northern, Central and even Balkan dialects, Slavic evidentials in some Balkan dialects, and Rumanian plural endings in Vlach.

The presence of significant layers of lexical and grammatical loans in Romani and the re-occurring tendencies of Romani dialects to undergo at least partial syntactic convergence with their co-territorial contact languages have led some researchers — mainly social scientists (for example Okely 1983; Willems 1995; Lucassen 1996), but recently also linguists (Wexler, forthcoming) — to express scepticism with respect to the existence of Romani as a coherent linguistic entity of Indic origin. Instead, the Indic component is seen as part of an Asian vocabulary collected along trading routes and markets, in other words as a trading slang, functionally akin, perhaps, to the secret vocabularies of itinerant groups in Europe (Cant, Shelta, Rotwelsch, Jenisch, Bargoens etc.) or to a pidgin. However, Romani comparative dialectology and a typological approach to Romani (analyzing it in the light of what is known about universals of language) provide us with tools to assess contact in its real dimensions and true impact on the language.

Romani as a unity is firstly characterized by a hybrid structure, owing its inflectional and derivational morphology and some patterns of morphosyntax to Indo-Aryan, and its sentence-level syntactic organization to the convergent development it underwent as part of the Balkan area during its early European phase (see Matras 1994a). Thus, Indic and non-Indic elements in the core structure that characterizes all varieties of Romani are not randomly distributed, but reflect the tendencies of languages in general to follow categorial differentiation in processes of language change and structural renewal. Moreover, Indo-Aryan morphology in Romani is not simply a fossilized remnant accompanying a random heap of Asian vocabulary, as suggested. Rather, its productivity can be seen at two levels: First, Indo-Aryan morphology is incorporated even into the inflectional paradigms applied to 'new words' (athematic elements). The Indic-derived markers for case, person, aspect, and tense are in fact equally used for thematic and athematic elements, and the systematic differentiation is reflected merely in their mode of attachment to the respective root. Second, and of no less importance, inherited Indic morphology constitutes a reservoire for creative processes of grammaticalization which accompany both internal and contact-motivated syntactic renewal. Thus the great majority of prepositions derive from Indo-Aryan adverbials (and have cognates among postpositions in Modern Subcontinental Indo-Aryan); adverbial conjunctions are recruited from among the class of Indic-derived interrogatives; Balkan complementational configuration is enabled through reanalysis of an Indic correlative particle as a non-factual conjunction (see Matras 1994a); the Balkan-type future particle is a de-lexicalized Indic-derived verb; etc. etc..

Not only is the distribution of the Indo-Aryan grammatical component very far from being random (or indeed marginal), but borrowing of actual grammatical elements is also regular. Romani may be unique in its thematic/athematic morphological split, but when it comes to incorporating grammatical items from contact languages it follows the universals of grammatical borrowing attested in numerous contact settings (cf. Moravcsik 1978; Thomason & Kaufman 1988; also Harris & Campbell 1995): Superficial contact will result in occasional borrowing of unbound particles; dialects with more intense contact show borrowing of semi-bound elements and some phonemes; prolonged contact will lead to the adoption of some bound morphemes, and perhaps to some changes in word order, though not to a radical change in typological structure. It is clear, when comparing Romani dialects, that the major change in typological structure which distinguishes Romani as whole from Modern Subcontinental Indo-Aryan can be attributed to the process of language convergence in the Balkans and so to a prolonged and extremely intense contact with Greek in particular; in this respect, Miklosich's claim made more than a century ago of a Greek-speaking territory as the European homeland of the Gypsies can still be maintained on the grounds of contemporary methodology. (We return to the issue of language contact and its reflection in the present volume in section 4 below).

3. Dialectal diversity in Romani

Two language groups are not considered in the present context of variation within Romani. First, the so-called Para-Romani languages or dialects. The term relates to the preservation of a Romani-derived vocabulary within a non-Romani grammatical framework in Gypsy communities where language shift has taken place (see Boretzky & Igla 1994b; Bakker & Cortiade 1991; Matras, forthcoming). Para-Romani varieties are relevant to a discussion of dialect classification insofar as their lexical and partly phonological features allow some insights into earlier connections among the underlying dialects of Romani proper. English Para-Romani, also known as Angloromani, plays a marginal role in Hancock's contribution to this volume.

The other grouping that is excluded from this discussion are the Indic languages of Gypsies outside Europe, with the exception of course of the Romani dialects of out-migrants in Iran (see Windfuhr 1970; Djonedi 1996) or the Americas (e.g. Hancock 1976), specifically Near Eastern Gypsy or Náwari (also Nuri or Domari; see Macalister 1909-1913). Despite a striking affinity with Romani, Náwari is also quite distinct, both in parts of its Indic-derived morphology as well as in the impact of subsequent changes and contact layers (cf. Hancock 1995b). Comparisons of Romani with Náwari are drawn in this volume by Boretzky for the copula and by Bubeník for object clitics.

A detailed framework for Romani dialect classification is still lacking, and no comprehensive discussion of documented dialects is yet available. We will therefore restrict ourselves here to naming the major dialect branches, following the classification common in most recent studies and also applied in this volume, and to pointing out some of the types of isoglosses encountered. The reader is also referred to the list of dialect designations mentioned in the volume in the appendix to this Introduction, as well as to the Index of Subjects, where dialect names are included.

Romani can be divided into four main groups called Balkan, Vlach, Central, and Northern. The Northern branch constitutes a somewhat weaker entity, and its sub-branching into British Romani (now virtually extinct), Finnish Romani, Sinti-Manuš (German Romani), Polish-North Russian-Baltic, and sometimes Iberian Romani (now extinct) is often preferred. For all major dialect groups the geographical labelling takes into account the constitution of separate groups between the fifteenth and nineteenth centuries. Subsequent migrations have since resulted in various shifts in distribution as well as in interdialectal contacts and possibly in the emergence of new sub-divisions.

The Balkan dialects are spoken in the central and southern Balkan regions, mostly in Bulgaria, former Yugoslavia, Albania, Turkey, and Greece. They are sometimes subdivided into northern and southern Balkan. The subgroups often have names derived from Turkish, such as *Erli* or *Arli*, from Turkish *yerli* 'settled' (hence locally settled Roma), *Sepetči* (Turkish for 'basket-weaver'), or *Burgudži* (Turkish for 'drill-maker'). Muslim Roma in the Balkans often refer to themselves collectively as *Xoraxane* (or *Koraxane*) *Roma* or 'Turkish Gypsies', from *Koraxaj/Xoraxaj* 'Turkey', apparently a term used as a designation for non-Gypsies (cf. *ḳorāxāy* 'foreigner' in the Romani dialect called Romano of eastern Iran, Djonedi 1996; also Sampson 1926:183-184). Orthodox Roma living among Slavic-speaking peoples often refer to themselves collectively as *Dasikane Roma*. Balkan dialects have recently been promoted through publications and other institutional use of Romani especially in Bulgaria and Macedonia (see Friedman's contribution to this volume). Outlines of Balkan dialects are presented in this volume by Cech & Heinschink and by Igla.

The Vlach (also Vlax) dialects emerged in the Rumanian principalities probably during the period of Romani serfdom and slavery, which ended in the second half of the nineteenth century (see Hancock 1987). The distinction between 'Vlach' and 'non-Vlach' was introduced by Gilliat -Smith (1915-1916) as a classification of dialects in northern Bulgaria, but 'Vlach' has been used since to denote those dialects which share a number of structural features, the most obvious being the impact of Rumanian on vocabulary and loan-morphology. Subgroups usually have names derived from Rumanian or Hungarian occupational terms, such as *Kalderaš* (also *Kelderaš*) from Rumanian *căldărar* 'coppersmith', Čurari from Rumanian *ciurar* 'sieve-maker', or *Lovari* from Hungarian for 'horse-dealer'. Vlach dialects are particularly widespread due to the outward migration of Roma following the abolition of serfdom from 1864 onwards, and the largest Romani population of any one country — that of Rumania — is almost entirely Vlach-speaking.

The Central dialects are spoken in the Czech and Slovak Republics, in southern Poland, by a minority of non-Vlach Romani-speakers in Hungary whose dialect is called *Romungro* or 'Hungarian Romani', and by a small group in the Austrian Burgenland and neighboring Slovenia. The Slovak dialect (spoken since the 1950s in the Czech part of Czechoslovakia as well) is represented in a relatively large number of Romani-language publications and provides the corpus for Elšík's contribution to this volume and, along with Hungarian Romani, for that by Hübschmannová & Bubeník.

The Northern dialects are, as mentioned above, probably the most diverse and widespread geographically. They include dialects as far apart as those of Wales and Finland. All documented western European Para-Romani varieties show in their vocabularies traces of this northern group, which is believed to have spread, subsequent to migrations from the Balkans, from southern Germany outwards during the fifteenth century. The group includes the dialects of the *Polska Roma* in Poland and the closely related Baltic and North Russian varieties, which still show traces of German influence in their vocabulary. A distinct entity consists of German Romani or the dialects of the groups whose self-designations are *Sinti* (in Germany, the Netherlands, and parts of Italy), *Manuš* (mostly in Alsace), or *Lalere* (formerly in Bohemia), all showing heavy impact of German on lexicon, morphosyntax, and phonology.

A superficial feature of dialect groups is the self-designation used by speakers. In the Northern dialects, the word *rom* plural *roma* is not used as an ethnonym, as in other dialects, but means only 'man/husband'. Instead, various ethnonyms are used in the Northern dialects including *Kalo* lit. 'black', *Manuš* lit. 'person', *Sinto*, *Romaničel*. On the other hand, only in the Vlach and Balkan dialects do subgroups use names denoting occupations.

There are only few isoglosses in Romani which might possibly reflect underlying subcontinental Indic isoglosses. The alternation of *s*- and *h*- in the copula (Vlach *som* 'I am', Sinti *hom*) is paralleled by the selection of different Middle Indo-Aryan verbs for the copula in subcontinental Indo-Aryan, rendering *s*- alongside *h*- paradigms (cf. contribution by Boretzky to this volume). *s-/h*- in Romani is on the other hand also a regular morpho-phonological alternation affecting person suffixes (*manges/mangeh* 'you want'), interrogatives (*sar/har* 'how'), case (*lesa/leha* 'with him'), and more. Sinti and the Central dialects are considered *h*-dialects, though *h*-forms infiltrate other varieties as well. The inventory of deictic expressions varies somewhat, with the Indo-Aryan stems in *a-/o-, k-, d-*, and *v-* appearing in different combinations, though *(a)dava/(o)dova* for 'this/that' and *adaj/odoj* for 'here/there' are characteristically non-Vlach. The genitive suffix is *-kero* in non-Vlach and *-ko* in Vlach, again mirroring a subcontinental isogloss (Maithili *-ker*, Hindi *-kā*), though phonological simplification on European territory is possible and perhaps even more likely.

Thus in general, dialect differentiation can be taken to represent the result of phonological developments that must have occurred during the past four to five centuries or at any rate following the Europeanization of Romani. These may, as in the case of the *s-/h-* alternation, affect entire morphological paradigms and so constitute superficial grammatical differences. The palatalization of the past infix *-d-/-l-* for example is a general process which is carried out to varying degrees in different dialects, rendering regular paradigm differences as in *(a)rakh-l-om, rakh-lj-om, rakh-č-om, rakh-j-om* 'I found', *phen-d-om, phen-dj-om, phen-gj-um, phen-om* 'I said'. Similarly, there is variation in the copula and past tense personal endings of the first singular (*-om, -em, -um*) and second singular (*-an, -al*) as well as the past tense third singular (*-as, -a*). Interdialectal contact occasionally gives rise to 'contaminated' forms; thus the Central dialect has *sal* for 'you are', cf. neighboring Sinti *hal* and Vlach *san*. Some morphophonological developments of this type must therefore be regarded as secondary to the 'generic' division of dialects outlined above, and so as geographically superposed on them.

More 'generic' features include the distribution of morpheme stems (e.g. as above, for copula formation and deixis) and lexical roots (e.g. Vlach *kor*, Northern, Central, and Balkan *men* 'throat'; Vlach *punro* and Central *pindro*, Northern and Balkan *her* 'leg'). Some derivational formations are more productive in certain dialect groups: the Northern branch typically makes extensive use of genitives as well as of nominalization suffixes (*-ben*) for lexical derivation, while causativization is especially productive in Central and some Balkan dialects (see discussion in Hübschmannová & Bubeník and in Igla, both this volume). In some cases the phonological formation of the root may be said to be 'generic' (cf. Northern and Central *graj*, Vlach and Balkan *gras(t)* 'horse'; Northern, Central, and Balkan *maro*, Vlach *manro/marno* 'bread'). In others, dialect groups appear to have undergone separate secondary developments. Naturally, a complete inventory of dialect-specific sound changes would by far exceed the scope of this section. Some outstanding developments include jotation of initial vowels in the continental Northern dialects (*jamen* 'we', *jaro* 'egg'; cf. Vlach, Balkan, and Central *amen, ar(n)o*), the reduction of affricates to sibilants in Vlach (*šavo* 'boy', *ža-* 'go', Northern, Balkan, and Central *čhavo*, *dža-*), secondary palatalization in Balkan and Vlach dialects spoken in some areas (*kher* > *ćher* 'house') with consequences for the case paradigm (*man-ge*, *tu-ke* > *man-dźe*, *tu-će* 'to me, to you'), and a shift to initial stress and subsequent syllable reduction is characteristic of Sinti (*krik* 'opposite', cf. Vlach *karing*). Some Balkan and Vlach dialects, most notably Kalderaš, retain an opposition [ʀ:r], the uvular reflecting an underlying Indo-Aryan retroflex dental.

To summarize the internal features distinguishing Romani dialects and dialect groups, we may divide isoglosses into 1) distribution of stems, 2) the extent and distribution of a closed set of phonological developments affecting mophological paradigms, 3) productiveness of certain derivational procedures, 4) stem-internal phonological changes, and 5) secondary, geographically restricted phonological changes. Classes 1, 3, and 4 tend to be 'generic' features of the underlying dialect groups, class 2 includes large-scale geographical phenomena, while class 5 accommodates more local phenomena. Alongside these classes of internal features, there are numerous external features deriving from contact with various languages. As stated, a full inventory is not possible here, but we mention again the extensive borrowing of unbound and indeclinable morphemes (sentential and connective particles, phasal adverbs, etc.), the replication of the Slavic system of verbal aspect (*šunel* '(he) hears)', *pošunel* 'he listens') in the Polish-North Russian varieties and the Central dialects, and the use of German prepositions and verbal particles in Sinti.

4. *This volume*

The present collection reflects recent developments in the area of typology and dialectology[1]; Romani being a language with only a very recent written tradition and fragmentary documentation in past centuries, any attempt at interpreting Romani data in an historical depth relies on the comparative study of dialects and structural features. At the same time, the contributions attempt to point out features of Romani which are likely to be of interest to general linguists in the context of studies of universal properties of language.

Peter Bakker's paper is a study of a phenomenon which is rather rare in the languages of the world, but which is present in all Romani dialects to a greater or lesser extent: the paradigmatic-inflectional dichotomy between 'old' and 'new' words. Old words are mostly words from Asian languages (including Byzantine Greek), new words are from European languages. Bakker argues for a Greek origin of the patterns of morphological adaptation of loanwords, although, strangely enough, these patterns are not used for the bulk of the Greek lexical component in Romani.

Victor Elšik's paper focuses on a particular dialect of Romani, a variety spoken mostly in the Czech and Slovak Republics, but draws general comparisons with other dialects as well as with the related Modern Subcontinental Indo-Aryan languages. Elšik's typological classification of Romani is thus of general validity for the language as a whole. Working within the framework of Skalička's Prague School Typology, Elšik defines Romani as a typologically mixed language in almost all aspects of its grammar, showing agglutinative, inflective, and analytic features, though current tendencies show a drift towards stronger analyticity.

Yaron Matras' paper provides a case study which confirms this last point: the drift away from inflectional nominal case-marking and on to an analytic system of prepositions. Matras compares data from all main branches of Romani and postulates three hierarchies which allow to explain (and predict) the structural behavior of a given case form in a given variety. Semantic and pragmatic features play a role here. Some can be related to universal hierarchies and confirm observations made elsewhere, though some particular traits are also apparent.

Vít Bubeník deals with typological aspects of Romani morphosyntax. Drawing on categories developed in the context of Prague School Typology and Dik's Functional Grammar, Bubeník discusses object doubling as a syntactic phenomenon which originates in the grammaticalization of pragmatic functions of noun phrases, and draws a comparison with related structures in the Balkan languages. Areal factors, it is thus argued, play a role in motivating this development, but universal tendencies are involved as well. The question of the trigger behind the Romani structure is further complicated by the existence of a similar phenomenon in Náwari, the Palestinian Gypsy language, though here its appearance could be related to contact with Arabic and so to areal factors, too.

Norbert Boretzky's discussion of the development of the Romani copula is an example of how historical reconstruction in Romani draws on comparative dialectology. Boretzky makes use of the large corpus of data on Romani dialects of both published written sources and recent dialectological fieldwork. Indeed, his endeavor might not have been possible as recently as five years ago due to the little data available at the time. Boretzky posits different roots as the sources for the different verb stems, illustrating the principle of suppletion which Elšik identifies as a feature of inflectional languages. He also discusses the grammaticalization of the copula, its use as an inchoative suffix and a past tense suffix, and the extension of the verb 'come' to mean 'become'.

Milena Hübschmannová and Vít Bubeník also combine descriptive and historical work in their analysis of derivational verbal morphology in Romani. Based on fieldwork undertaken in the Czech and Slovak Republics, they deal with phenomena which are rather a typological oddity in the languages of Europe. Romani is one of the few languages in Europe with regular morphologically formed causatives, passives, reflexives, and inchoatives. The paper also mentions a semantic shift from causative to iterative in Romani, a change also reported from other languages but for which no explanation has yet been proposed. Hübschmannová & Bubeník further show that at least some Romani dialects (namely Hungarian and Slovak Romani) have second causatives. There are clear formal parallels for the phenomenon in older stages of the Indo-Aryan languages, from which the Romani structures in question can be derived. But although causativization is an inherited phenomenon, language contact is seen to play a role in the preservation of causatives, which are more productive in dialects which share the feature of morphological causativization with their coterritorial language; this point is reinforced by Cech & Heinschink in their outline, in this volume, of the Sepečides variety.

Birgit Igla describes a number of properties of Romani as spoken in some communities in the Rhodopes, a mountain range in southwestern Bulgaria. The dialect shows a number of unique features. Case endings appear alongside both prepositions and postpositions. In addition, there are double prepositions, and prepositions which govern the accusative case (whereas other dialects show nominative). Rhodopes Romani is lexically conservative and preserves a number of Indic words which are otherwise hardly known in Bulgarian or Balkan dialects of Romani. It borrows aspectual prefixes from Slavic, a phenomenon also reported from other dialects in close contact with Slavic languages. Some particular phonological developments, which have re-shaped the form of inflectional paradigms, may be the result of phonological convergence with local Bulgarian dialects.

Petra Cech and Mozes Heinschink provide a general outline of the Romani dialect of the Basket-weavers (Sepečides) of Izmir in Western Turkey, a variety now endangered. The dialect is heavily influenced by Turkish in the areas of syntax, vocabulary and idioms, and phonology. On the other hand, the variety is extremely conservative. The verb *therava* 'I have', for instance, which is very rare in Balkan varieties of Romani, is still used here. Particularly striking in this dialect is the number of different causative constructions. The paper reiterates Hübschmannová and Bubeník's conclusion that morphological causatives are especially preserved in areas where the contact language shows similar constructions.

The last two papers deal with written Romani, albeit with two quite distinct aspects of it. Victor Friedman analyzes recent publications in Romani in the Republic of Macedonia, whereas Ian Hancock discusses the Romani language in the novels of the Victorian author George Borrow.

Victor Friedman reported in an earlier paper on the Standardization Conference in Macedonia and its likely implications (Friedman 1995). Romani has enjoyed official recognition in Macedonia for a number of years now, and it is used both in broadcasting and in print. In his present contribution Friedman focuses on features of a bilingual Romani/ Macedonian magazine. The coexistence of several Romani dialects in the same country motivates authors to alternate between single-dialect preferences and dialect mixing. Some of the choices relate to orthography and phonology, others to morphological and syntactic features. Preference is often given to the Arli dialect, which is both widespread and prestigious among the Roma of Macedonia. It is especially noteworthy that the publication appears to follow the proposal adopted at the 1992 Standardization Conference. On the other hand, despite the use of a local dialect the magazine's international orientation is reflected in its choice of the Latin alphabet.

Ian Hancock discusses the individual 'dialect' of a non-Rom who has had an enormous impact on both popular and scientific appreciation of the Romani language during the nineteenth century and thereafter, even to this very day. George Borrow wrote a number of books on the Gypsies of Britain and Spain and had a keen interest in their language. He included in his novels Romani vocabularies, phrases, and texts acquired through personal contacts with Romanichals and Gitanos. Hancock shows that this material is unreliable from a dialectological viewpoint. Borrow was on the one hand fully aware of the unity of the Romani language; he met, and conversed with, Gypsies in Spain, Britain, Russia, Hungary and other places. But his appreciation of this unity allowed him to mix dialectal forms and structures rather freely, which makes his linguistic surveys rather questionable sources.

We return at this point to the issue of contact and its reflection in Romani, and to the point made above that contact is relevant to an appreciation of both the typological features and the dialectal diversity of Romani. Single phenomena discussed by the authors provide several illustrations of this. Bakker shows how contact with Greek led to the adoption of a Greek strategy for loanword incorporation, and how this strategy has since been applied in Romani to cope with ever-changing strata of loan vocabulary. Matras illustrates how the shift to prepositions and the drift towards more analytic case formation relates to the overall re-structuring of the language, particularly in the context of Europeanization and Balkanization. Bubeník considers the case for Balkanization in relation to object doubling. And while causativization in Romani is clearly Indic-derived, it is argued both by Hübschmannová & Bubeník and by Cech & Heinschink that contact with 'morphologically causativizing' languages reinforces the productiveness of these structures. Igla considers the possibility that the unusual vowel shifts in the Rhodopes dialect

mirror sound changes in the local Bulgarian dialect. Finally, Friedman discusses
some of the problems facing the Romani written press in an area where several
Romani dialects coexist, where the technical facilities for the production of written texts can only be accessed via the national (contact) language, but where
writing in Romani is partly, if not significantly motivated by contact with international (i.e. non-Macedonian) varieties of Romani.

So is there a particular insight which Romani dialectology can offer towards
a deeper understanding of universals of human language? We believe there is at
least one such insight, and that is that contact clearly does not necessarily simplify grammatical structure, which is the impression gained for example through
Pidgin and Creole studies, but that contact on the contrary tends to make things
rather complicated. The competing structures in the language, the conditions
under which they are allowed to coexist, and the natural ways by which competition is resolved — all these provide a challenge to the contributors to this
volume, who appreciate Romani in both its unity and diversity.

Endnotes

1.   Earlier versions of the papers by Boretzky, Bubeník, Friedman, Hancock, Igla, Matras,
      and partly Hübschmannová & Bubeník were presented at the Second International
      Conference on Romani Linguistics in Amsterdam in December 1994. The contribution
      by Cech & Heinschink stems from a presentation at the annual meeting of the Gypsy
      Lore Society in Leiden in March 1995, that of Elšik and partly that of Hübschmannová
      & Bubeník from papers given at the Third International Conference on Romani
      Linguistics in Prague in December 1996.

Appendix: Dialects and varieties of Romani mentioned in the present volume

Ajia Varvara. Vlach dialect spoken in a suburb of Athens called Ajia Varvara;
    shows Turkish influence (see Igla 1996).
Arabadži. Balkan dialect close to Bugurdži (see Boretzky 1993).
Arli. Self-designation of a rather diverse group, mostly in former Yugoslavia. The
    name is derived from Turkish *yerli* 'settled'. The dialects of Prilep and
    Prizren (Terzi Mahalla, Yeni Mahalla) seem to be somewhat deviant dialects
    of Arli. The Arli dialects belong to the Balkan group. A grammatical sketch
    has been published by Boretzky (1996c).
Baruči(sko). See Arli. (Arli dialect of a Romani neighbourhood in Skopje,
    Macedonia).
Bašaldo. Self-designation of a Central dialect. See Hungarian Romani.
Bohemian. External name for a Central dialect spoken in 19th century Czechia.
British Romani. Cover term for Welsh, English, and Scottish Romani. The latter
    two are Para-Romani. Lexically Northern. See also English Romani.

Bugurdži. Self-designation of a Balkan dialect spoken in former Yugoslavia (see Boretzky 1993).

Burgenland Roman. A Central dialect related to the *Prekmurje* dialect of Slovenia. The Austrian variant is described in Halwachs (1996).

Burgudži. Alternative name for *Bugurdži*.

Caló. Self-designation of a Spanish-based Para-Romani. See Boretzky (1992), Bakker (1995), and Leigh (forthcoming).

Carpathian. An external label applied to a Central dialect. See Hungarian Romani.

Čurari. A Vlach dialect closely related to *Kalderaš*.

Drindari. Self-designation of a rather deviant Balkan dialect. Described in Kenrick (1969).

Džambaz(i). Self-designation of a Vlach dialect spoken in former Yugoslavia, and sometimes also called *Gurbet*.

English Romani. An English-based Para-Romani, with a Northern lexicon. In earlier stages, however, there were also English Romani dialects with the inherited grammatical system. See Hancock (1984).

Erli. See also *Arli*. Self-designation of a Balkan dialect. *Erli* is usually used for the dialect of Sofia, described by Kostov (1963) and others.

Grekuri. A Vlach dialect reported from Argentina.

Gurbet(i). Vlach dialects of former Yugoslavia, so designated to refer to recent immigrants to the region, in contrast with the 'settled' speakers of a Balkan dialect. See Boretzky (1986).

Hungarian Romani. External label of a Central dialect (but see *Romungro*). See Hancock (1990).

Kalajdži. Self-designation of a Balkan dialect spoken in Bulgaria and Turkey. See Gilliat-Smith (1935).

Kalderaš. Also *Kelderaš*. Self-designation of the Vlach dialect of the Coppersmiths. See Gjerdman & Ljungberg (1963), Boretzky (1994).

Lešaki. Self-designation of a variety of the dialect of the *Polska Roma* spoken in central Poland, and part of the Northern group of dialects. It is related to the North Russian dialect described by Wentzel (1980).

Lovari. Self-designation of a Vlach dialect spoken in Transylvania and elsewhere in central Europe. See Pobożniak (1964).

Mačvano. Vlach dialect originally spoken in Serbia, now mainly in the USA.

Náwari (also *Nuri*, *Domari*). Indic language related to Romani, spoken in the Near East. See Macalister (1909-1913).

Non-Vlach. External cover term usually used to refer to the Balkan branch.

Para-Romani. Cover term for languages which have a Romani lexicon, but a non-Romani grammatical structure. Examples are Caló and most varieties of British Romani. See Boretzky & Igla (1994b), Matras (forthcoming).

Paspatian. A Balkan dialect, called so in the literature as it has been thoroughly described by Paspati (1870). Also called *Rumeli*.

Prekmurje. See Burgenland.

Prilep. A Balkan dialect belonging to Arli, named after the town in which it is spoken.

Rabadži. See *Arabadži*.

Rhodopes. Deviant dialect of Erli spoken in the Rhodopes mountains in Bulgaria. See Igla, this volume.

Romungro. One of the self-designations of a Central dialect spoken in Hungary. The term is also occasionally used by Vlach speakers in central Europe to refer to the Northern dialect of the *Polska Roma*. See Vekerdi (1981).

Rumeli. See *Paspatian*.
Scottish Romani. An English-based Para-Romani, spoken in Scotland.
Sepeči(des). Self-designation of the Balkan dialect of the basket-weavers in Greece and Turkey. Related to Arli. See Cech & Heinschink, this volume.
Sinti. Self-designation of German Romani, a sub-branch within the Northern group of dialects. See Holzinger (1993).
Slovak Romani. External term for a Central dialect, now also spoken in the Czech Republic. See Hübschmannová et al. (1991) as well as Elšik, this volume.
Terzi Mahalla. A Balkan dialect spoken in Prizren, which can be considered a deviant variety of the Arli-type.
Vend. A Central dialect spoken in Hungary. See Vekerdi (1984).
Vlach, Vlax. External cover term for the dialects of Rumania, Transylvania, and adjoining regions, but also widespread elsewhere since the outwards migration from these areas in the nineteenth and early twentieth century. See Hancock (1995).
Welsh Romani. A sub-branch of the Northern group, now though to be extinct. See Sampson (1926).
Xoraxane. External cover term as well as collective self-designation for the dialects of Muslim Roma in the Balkans, usually heavily influenced by Turkish. It refers most frequently to dialects of the Balkan group, though occasional use of the term with reference to Vlach varieties have also been recorded.
Zargari. Self-designation of a (European, probably Balkan) dialect of Romani spoken in Iran by out-migrants. See Windfuhr (1970), cf. also Djonedi (1996).

References

Adelung, Friedrich von. 1815 [1976]. *Catherinens der Grossen Verdienste um die vergleichende Sprachenkunde*. St. Petersburg: Friedrich Drechsler. [Hamburg: Buske].
Bakker, Peter. 1995. 'Notes on the genesis of Caló and other Iberian Para-Romani varieties'. In: Yaron Matras, ed. *Romani in contact. The history, structure and sociology of a language*. Amsterdam: Benjamins. 125-150.
---- & Marcel Cortiade, eds. 1991. *In the margin of Romani. Gypsy languages in contact*. Amsterdam: Institute for General Linguistics.
---- & Yaron Matras. Forthcoming. *An indexed bibliography of Romani linguistics*.
Boretzky, Norbert. 1986. 'Zur Sprache der Gurbet von Priština (Jugoslawien)'. *Giessener Hefte für Tsiganologie* 3:1-4. 195-216.
--- 'Zum Interferenzverhalten des Romani'. *Zeitschrift für Phonologie, Sprachwissenschaft und Kommunikationsforschung* 42:3. 357-374.
---- 1992. 'Romanisch-zigeunerische Interferenzen (zum Caló)'. In: Jürgen Erfurt, Benedikt Jessing & Matthias Perl, eds. Prinzipien des Sprachwandels I. Bochum: Brockmeyer. 11-38.
---- 1993. *Bugurdži. Deskriptiver und historischer Abriß eines Romani-Dialekts*. Berlin: Harrassowitz.
--- 1994. *Romani. Grammatik des Kalderaš-Dialekts mit Texten und Glossar*. Berlin: Harrassowitz.

--- 1996a. 'The "new" infinitive in Romani'. *Journal of the Gypsy Lore Society* 6:1. 1-51.

---- 1996b. 'Entlehnte Wortstellungssyntax im Romani'. In: Norbert Boretzky, Werner Enninger & Thomas Stolz, eds. *Areale, Kontakte, Dialekte. Sprache und ihre Dynamik in mehrsprachigen Situationen.* Bochum: Brockmeyer. 95-121.

---- 1996c. 'Arli. Materialen zu einem Südbalkanischen Romani-Dialekt'. *Grazer Linguistische Studien* 46. 1-30.

---- & Birgit Igla. 1991. *Morphologische Entlehnung in den Romani-Dialekten.* Arbeitspapiere des Projektes 'Prinzipien des Sprachwandels'. Arbeitspaper Nr. 4. Essen: Fachbereich Sprach- und Literaturwissenschaften an der Universität Essen.

---- 1993. *Lautwandel und Natürlichkeit. Kontaktbedingter und endogener Lautwandel im Romani.* Arbeitspapiere des Projektes 'Prinzipien des Sprachwandels'. Arbeitspaper Nr. 15. Essen: Fachbereich Sprach- und Literaturwissenschaften an der Universität Essen.

--- 1994a. *Wörterbuch Romani-Deutsch-Englisch für den südosteuropäischen Raum.* Wiesbaden: Harrassowitz.

---- 1994b. 'Romani mixed dialects'. In: Peter Bakker & Maarten Mous, eds. *Mixed languages. 15 case studies in language intertwining.* Amsterdam: IFOTT. 35-68.

Cech, Petra & Mozes F. Heinschink. 1997. Sepečides Romani. München: Lincom.

De Goeje, M. J. 1903. *Mémoires sur les migrations des Tsiganes à travers l'Asie.* Leiden: E. J. Brill.

Demeter, R. S. 1990. *Cygansko-russkiy i russko-cyganskiy slovar'.* Moskva: Russkiy yazyk.

Djonedi, Fereydun. 1996. 'Romano-Glossar. Gesammelt von Schir-Ali Tehrani-zade'. *Grazer Linguistische Studien* 46. 31-59.

Finck, Franz Nikolaus. 1907. 'Die Grundzüge des Armenisch-Zigeunerischen Sprachbaus'. *Journal of the Gypsy Lore Society* 1. 34-60.

Friedman, Victor A. 1985. 'Balkan Romani modality and other Balkan languages'. *Folia Slavica* 7:3. 381-389.

--- 1995. 'Romani standardization and status in the Republic of Macedonia'. In: Yaron Matras, ed. *Romani in contact. The history, structure and sociology of a language.* Amsterdam: Benjamins. 177-188.

---- & Robert Dankoff. 1991. The earliest text in Balkan (Rumelian) Romani: A passage from Evliya Çelebi's Seyāḥat-nāme'. *Journal of the Gypsy Lore Society* 1:1. 1-20.

Gilliat-Smith, Bernard J. 1915-1916. 'Report on the Gypsy tribes of north-east Bulgaria'. *Journal of the Gypsy Lore Society* 9. 1-55; 65-108.

---- 1935. 'The dialect of the Moslem Kalajdžis (Tinners) of the Tatar Pazardžik district'. *Journal of the Gypsy Lore Society* 14. 25-43.

Gjerdman, Olof & Erik Ljungberg. 1963. *The language of the Swedish coppersmith Gipsy Johan Dimitri Taikon.* Uppsala: Lundequist.

Grellman, Heinrich M. G. 1787. *Historischer Versuch über die Zigeuner, betreffend die Lebensart und Verfassung, Sitten und Schicksale dieses Volkes seit seiner Erscheinung in Europa und dessen Ursprung.* Göttingen: Dietrich.

Haarmann, Harald. 1989. [Introduction to reprint of Rüdiger 1782]. Hamburg: Buske. vii-xxvii.

Halwachs, Dieter W. 1996. *Morphologie des Roman. Basisgrammatik der Romani-Variante der Burgenland-Roma.* Oberwart: Verein Roma.

Hancock, Ian F. 1976. 'Patterns of English lexical adoption in an American variety of Romanes'. *Orbis* 25:1. 83-104.
--- 1984. Romani and Angloromani. In: Peter Trudgill, ed. *Languages in the
British Isles*. Cambridge: Cambridge University Press. 367-383.
---- 1987. *The pariah syndrome. An account of Gypsy slavery and persecution*.
Ann Arbor: Karoma.
--- 1988. 'The development of Romani linguistics'. In: Mohammad Ali Jazayery
& Werner Winter, eds. *Languages and cultures. Studies in honor of Edgar C.
Polomé*. Berlin: Mouton de Gruyter. 183-223.
---- 1990. *A grammar of the Hungarian-Slovak (Carpathian, Bashaldo,
Rumungro) Romani language*. Manchaca: International Romani Union.
---- 1995a. *A handbook of Vlax Romani*. Columbus: Slavica.
---- 1995b. 'On the migration and affiliation of the Ḍōmba: Iranian words in
Rom, Lom and Dom Gypsy. In: Yaron Matras, ed. *Romani in contact. The
history, structure and sociology of a language*. Amsterdam: Benjamins. 25-
51.
Harris, Alice C. & Lyle Campbell. 1995. *Historical syntax in cross-linguistic per-
spective*. Cambridge: Cambridge University Press.
Holzinger, Daniel. 1993. *Das Rómanes: Grammatik und Diskursanalyse der
Sprache der Sinte*. Innsbruck: Institut für Sprachwissenschaft der Universität
Innsbruck.
Hübschmannová, Milena, Hana Šebková & Ana Žigová. 1991. *Romsko-český a
Česko-romský kapesní slovník*. Praha: Státní pedagogické nakladatelství.
Igla, Birgit. 1996. *Das Romani von Ajia Varvara: Deskriptive und historisch-ver-
gleichende Darstellung eines Zigeunerdialekts*. Wiesbaden: Harrassowitz.
Kenrick, Donald. 1969. *Morphology and lexicon of the Romany dialect of Kotel
(Bulgaria)*. Ph.D. dissertation, School of Oriental and African Studies,
London.
Kluge, Friedrich. 1901 [1987]. *Rotwelsch. Quellen und Wörterbuch der
Gaunersprache und der verwandten Geheimsprachen*. Straßburg: Karl
Trübner. [Berlin: de Gruyter].
Kostov, Kiril. 1963. *Grammatik der Zigeunersprache Bulgariens: Phonetik und
Morphologie*. Ph.D. dissertation, Humboldt University, Berlin.
Leigh, Kate. Forthcoming. 'Romani elements in present-day Caló'. In: Yaron
Matras, ed. *The Romani element in non-standard speech*. Wiesbaden:
Harrassowitz.
Lucassen, Leo. 1996. *Die Zigeuner. Die Geschichte eines polizeilichen
Ordnungsbegriffes in Deutschland 1700-1945*. Köln: Böhlau.
Macalister, R. A. Stewart. 1909-1913. 'A grammar and vocabulary of the lan-
guage of the Nawar of Zutt, the nomad smiths of Palestine. *Journal of the
Gypsy Lore Society* 3. 120-126, 298-317; 5. 289-305; 6. 161-240.
Matras, Yaron. 1994a. *Untersuchungen zu Grammatik und Diskurs des Romanes:
Dialekt der Kelderaša/Lovara*. Wiesbaden: Harrassowitz.
---- 1994b. 'Structural Balkanisms in Romani'. In: Norbert Reiter, Uwe Hinrichs
& Jeřina van Leeuwen-Turnocová, eds. *Sprachlicher Standard und Substandard in Südosteuropa und Osteuropa*. Berlin/Wiesbaden: Harrassowitz.
195-210.
---- ed. 1995a. *Romani in contact. The history, structure and sociology of a language*. Amsterdam: John Benjamins.

---- 1995b. 'Verb evidentials and their discourse function in Vlach Romani narratives'. In: Yaron Matras, ed. *Romani in contact. The history, structure and sociology of a language*. Amsterdam: John Benjamins. 95-123.

---- 1995c. 'Connective word order in Romani'. *Sprachtypologie und Universalienforschung* 48:1-2. 189-203.

---- 1996. 'Prozedurale Fusion: Grammatische Interferenzschichten im Romanes'. *Sprachtypologie und Universalienforschung* 49:1. 60-78.

---- In press. 'Deixis and deictic oppositions in discourse: Evidence from Romani'. *Journal of Pragmatics*.

---- ed. Forthcoming. *The Romani element in non-standard speech*. Wiesbaden: Harrassowitz.

Miklosich, Franz. 1872-1880. *Über die Mundarten und Wanderungen der Zigeuner Europas*. I-XII.Wien: Karl Gerold's son.

Moravcsik. Edith A. 'Language contact'. In: Joseph H. Greenberg, Charles A. Ferguson, & Edith A. Moravcsik, eds. *Universals of human language* Vol. I. Stanford: Stanford University Press.

Okely, Judith. 1983. *The Traveller Gypsies*. Cambridge: Cambridge University Press.

Paspati, Alexandre G. 1870 [1973]. Études sur les Tchinghianés ou Bohémiens de l'Empire Ottoman. Constantinople: Koroméla. [Osnabrück: Biblio].

Payne, John R. 1995. 'Inflecting postpositions in Indic and Kashmiri'. In: Frans Plank, ed. *Double case. Agreement by Suffixaufnahme*. New York: Oxford University Press. 283-298.

Piasere, Leonardo. 1994. *Il piu antico testo Italiano in Romanes (1646): una risoperta e une letture etnostorica*. Universita' degli Studi di Verona. Facolta' di Lettere e Filosofia, Istituto di Psicologia, Report 56.

Plank, Frans. 1995. '(Re-)Introducing Suffixaufnahme'. In: Frans Plank, ed. *Double case. Agreement by Suffixaufnahme*. New York: Oxford University Press. 3-110.

Pobożniak, Tadeusz. 1964. *Grammar of the Lovari dialect*. Kraków: Państwowe wydawnictwo naukowe.

Pott, Augustus F. 1844-1845 [1964]. *Die Zigeuner in Europa und Asien. Ethnographisch-linguistische Untersuchung vornehmlich ihrer Herkunft und Sprache*. Halle: Heynemann. [Leipzig: Edition Leipzig].

Ruch, Martin. 1986. *Zur Wissenschaftsgeschichte der deutschsprachigen "Zigeunerforschung" von den Anfängen bis 1900*. Ph.D. dissertation, University of Freiburg.

Rüdiger, Johann C.C. 1782 [1990]. *Von der Sprache und Herkunft der Zigeuner aus Indien. Nachdruck aus: Neuester Zuwachs der teutschen, fremden und allgemeinen Sprachkunde in eigenen Aufsätzen, 1. Stück*. Hamburg: Buske.

Sampson, John. 1907. 'Gypsy language and origin'. *Journal of the Gypsy Lore Society* 1. 4-22.

--- 1926 [1968] *The dialect of the Gypsies of Wales*. Oxford: Clarendon.

Thomason, Sarah Grey & Terrence Kaufman. 1988. *Language contact, creolization and genetic linguistics*. Berkeley: University of California Press.

Turner, Ralph. 1926. 'The position of Romani in Indo-Aryan'. *Journal of the Gypsy Lore Society* 5:4. 145-194.

Van der Auwera, Johan (with Dónall P. Ó Baoill). ed. In press. *Adverbial constructions in the languages of Europe*. Berlin: Mouton de Gruyter.

Vekerdi, Jószef. 1981. *A Magyar Cigány nyelvjárás nyelvtana*. Pécs: Janus Pannonius University.

---- 1984. 'The Vend Gypsy dialect in Hungary'. *Acta Linguistica Academiae Hungaricae* 24. 381-389.

Wentzel, Tatjana. 1980. *Die Zigeunersprache (nordrussischer Dialekt)*. Leipzig: Enzyklopädie.

Wexler, Paul. Forthcoming. 'Could there be a Rotwelsch origin of Romani lexicon?' In: Yaron Matras, ed. *The Romani element in non-standard speech*. Wiesbaden: Harrassowitz.

Willems, Wim. 1995. *Op zoek naar de ware zigeuner. Zigeuners als studieobject tijdens de verlichting, de romantiek en het nazisme*. Utrecht: Jan van Arkel.

Windfuhr, G.L. 1970. European Gypsies in Iran. A first report'. *Anthropological Linguistics* 12. 271-292.

LIST OF ABBREVIATIONS

ABL	ablative	OBL	oblique
ACC	accusative	PART	particle
ART	article	PARTIC	participle
C	consonant	PASS	passive
CAUS	causative	PAST	past
CLASS	classificatory element	PIE	Proto Indo-European
COMP	complementizer	PL	plural
COMPAR	comparative	PLUPERF	pluperfect
COND	conditional	POSS	possessive
DAT	dative	PREP	preposition
DEF	definite	PRES	present
DIAL	dialect	PRET	preterite
DIM	diminutive	PROH	prohibitive
DO	direct object	PST	Prague School Typology
ERG	ergative	Q	question marker
ESR	East Slovak Romani	R	Romani
F/FEM	feminine	REFL	reflexive
FG	Functional Grammar	RG	Romani Gramatika
FUT	future	RS	Romani Sumnal
GEN	genitive	SCR	Slovak-Czech Romani
GERM	German	SERB	Serbian
HR	Hungarian Romani	SG/SING	singular
IA	Indo-Aryan	SOV	subject-object-verb
IE	Indo-European	SUBJ	subjunctive marker
IMP	imperative	T	Turkish
IMPF	imperfect(ive)	TM	Terzi Mahalla
INCH	inchoative	TURK	Turkish
IND	indicative	V	vowel
INDEF	indefinite	VOC	vocative
INF	infinitive	WSR	West Slovak Romani
INSTR	instrumental		
IO	indirect object		
IPF	imperfective		
ITER	iterative		
LOC	locative		
M/MASC	masculine		
N	neuter		
NEG	negator		
NIA	New Indo-Aryan		
NOM	nominative		

ATHEMATIC MORPHOLOGY IN ROMANI: THE BORROWING OF A BORROWING PATTERN

PETER BAKKER

University of Aarhus

0. Introduction

Romani has a particular way of adapting borrowed words. This has the effect that the language formally distinguishes borrowed words from inherited words. The inherited words include Indic, Iranian, Armenian, Caucasian, Greek and unidentified words, and the borrowed words include Slavic, some Greek, and all other words. The division is roughly between European against non-European words. Some of these borrowed words may have entered the language already in the late Middle Ages, shortly after the arrival of the Gypsies in Europe in the thirteenth or fourteenth century. Recently borrowed words, such as those from the host country, are roughly treated in the same way.

In this paper I deal with this linguistic dichotomy in Romani, which splits the lexical component of the language formally into two compartments. These compartments have been called 'thematic' (for the inherited words) and 'athematic' (for the borrowed ones), e.g. in Hancock (1995), following earlier unpublished work by Terrence Kaufman. I will attempt to show that the pattern of adaption was borrowed from Greek, including the morphemes used.

1. Athematic items: The borrowing pattern

The dichotomy between borrowed and inherited words has been noted by students of the Romani language at least since the 19th century (Pott 1844-1845, Miklosich 1872, Paspati 1870), and most grammars of Romani deal with the phenomenon in more or less detail. In recent decades the two components have also been called thematic (inherited) and athematic (borrowed). The athematic items can be words borrowed into Romani five or more centuries ago, but they are still formally distinguishable from the non-borrowed words. The latter are words inherited from Indic and other Asian languages, including Greek.

Boretzky (1989) is probably one of the most specific analyses of the pattern of treatment of athematic and thematic items in Romani. Here I will follow his description of the system as encountered in a Gurbet dialect in Yugoslavia, a dialect belonging to the Vlax branch of Romani, which is characterized most conspicuously by Rumanian influence. After that I will deal with the treatment of athematic items in some other Romani dialects, in order to show both the generality of the system and the limited number of patterns used for adapting athematic elements.

1.1 Vlax: Gurbet, Yugoslavia

The following formal differences exist between borrowed words and inherited words in this Gurbet dialect of Yugoslavia, as outlined in Boretzky (1989): Inherited nouns have word-final stress, and borrowed words have non-final stress. If a word which has final stress is borrowed, a vowel is added. Some examples are:

(1)   Inherited words: *šoró* 'head', *borí* 'bride', *manúš* 'human, man'
        Borrowed words: *fóro* 'city' (< Greek *fóros*), *amúni* 'anvil' (<Greek *amóni*), *práxo* 'ashes, dust' (<Slavic *prax*), *kitábo* 'book' (<Turkish *kitáb*)

Inherited masculine nouns have plural endings in *-a*, but borrowed masculine nouns usually have plural endings in *-ura* (borrowed from Rumanian). Inherited feminine nouns have a *-ja* plural, whereas borrowed feminine nouns in *-a* have plurals in *-e*.

Nouns have different oblique case endings (or rather: stem markers) for borrowed and inherited words. The case endings are suffixed to the oblique ending *-es* in inherited words, and to the ending *-os* or *-is* in borrowed masculine words, as shown in Figure 1.

	inherited words	borrowed words
Nominative	*rakló* 'boy'	*fóro* 'town'
Dative	*rakl-es-ke*	*for-os-ke*
Ablative	*rakl-es-tar*	*for-os-tar*
Instrumental	*rakl-e(s)-sa*	*for-o(s)-sa*
Locative	*rakl-es-te*	*for-os-te*

Figure 1: Thematic and athematic inflection of masculine nouns in Gurbet Vlax

Most inherited adjectives have masculine forms in *-o* and feminine forms in *-i*[1], both of them bearing stress. In borrowed adjectives there is no formal distinction between masculine and feminine forms. In this Gurbet dialect, both masculine and feminine adjectives end in unstressed *-o*.

(2) a *o   lung-o drom*
      ART-M long   road(M) (*lung* 'long' < Rumanian)
      'The long road'
   b *e   lung-o pori*
      ART-F long   tail(F)
      'The long tail'

Borrowed adjectives sometimes have an *-one* ending in the oblique and plural forms for both genders, e.g. *lungone*.

Inherited and borrowed verbs have a slightly different inflection, as shown in Figure 2. The borrowed verb is derived from the Serbian verb *čitati* 'to read'.

	inherited verbs	borrowed verbs
1 SG	*kam-av* 'want'	*čit-ov* 'read'
2 SG	*kam-es*	*čit-os*
3 SG	*kam-el*	*čit-ol*
1 PL	*kam-as*	*čit-os*
2 PL	*kam-en*	*čit-on*
3 PL	*kam-en*	*čit-on*

Figure 2: Thematic and athematic inflection of verbs

Gurbet also has a much rarer form for borrowed verbs in *-osarel*. Both have parallel forms in other Vlax dialects. Thus we have formal morphological distinctions between borrowed and inherited words for all major categories: nouns have different stress patterns, case endings and plural endings; adjectives have different endings, and athematic adjectives have no gender distinction; verbs have different endings. This dichotomy between borrowed and inherited words is true not only for Vlax dialects, but basically for all Romani dialects - although not always the same patterns are used, or not for all categories, as I will show in the discussion of four other dialects.

1.2 Borrowed items in Welsh Romani

Loanwords from English and Welsh in Welsh Romani (Sampson 1926) are treated differently from inherited items. Welsh Romani shows the following structural features for athematic items: Borrowed nouns have an added vowel or ending -os, e.g. *mēlos* from English *meal*, *brâmla* from English *bramble*, *fōkī* from English *folk*, *kraŋka* from Welsh *cranc* 'crab'. Borrowed masculine and feminine nouns have a plural ending -i: *určos*, plural *určī*, 'hedgehogs' (from an English dialect form *urch*). Only for borrowed nouns is the accusative form identical to the nominative. Inherited words have final stress, borrowed words have pre-final stress.

Borrowed verbs have an added element -as- or -in- between the stem and the endings: θink-*as*-es 'you think' (< English *think*); tiš-*as-om* 'I sneezed' (< Welsh *tisian, tisio* 'to sneeze').

Borrowed adjectives (often derived from verbs) have an ending -*imen*: *dūm-imen* from English *doomed*, *aidlimen* 'idle', *tålk-imen* 'dented, dingy' from Welsh *tolc* 'dinged'.

1.3 Borrowed items in Terzi Mahalla Romani

The data from Terzi Mahalla, a Romani neighbourhood in Prizren, Kosovo were provided by Behjlulj Galjus, a native speaker of this rather deviant dialect of Balkan Romani. This dialect contains loanwords from Turkish, Albanian and Serbian, languages which are all spoken by the Terzi Mahalla Roma. Stress in this dialect is always on the penultimate syllable.

Nouns ending in a consonant have an -i or an -o (less frequent; only after final *k*) added to the noun. Both are always masculine. In the plural they end in -*ija* (with some adjustments). Some examples: *askéri* M 'soldier', PL. *askeríja* < T. *asker*; *basamáko* M 'step (of stairs)' PL. *basamákija* < T. *basamak*.

Most Turkish and Albanian nouns ending in -a are not adjusted (except for a stress shift from the final syllable to the penultimate, which is a feature of this dialect). Feminine nouns in -a have a plural in -e.

(3) *gürümdja* F, PL. *gürümdje* 'sister-in-law, sister of husband' < T. *görümce*
bánka F, PL *bánke* 'bank' < T. *banka*
fošna F, PL *fošne* 'child' < Albanian *foshnje, foshnja*
mahálla F, PL *mahále* 'neighbourhood' < T. *mahala, mahalle*

Some nouns ending in a vowel will have this vowel replaced by *-íja*. They are always masculine and have a plural in *-(ij)e*. Some examples: *kojšíja* M 'neighbour' < Albanian *kojshi* < T. *komşu*; plural *kojšíje* (like in Serbian), *leblebíja* M 'grilled chickpea' (plural *leblebíje*) < T. *leblebi*. This is a more typical Slavic pattern, and these words were probably taken over via Serbian.

Inherited adjectives have gender distinction, but borrowed adjectives end in *-o* both for masculine and feminine nouns, in both singular and plural:

(4) *o prósto Rom* 'the simple man'
e prósto Rómni 'the simple woman'
o prósto Roma 'the simple men'
e prósto Rómna 'the simple women'

1.4 Borrowed items in Roman (Burgenland Romani)

The Burgenland Romani dialect is spoken in Slovenia, Hungary and the Austrian Burgenland. These Roma appear to have settled in the area in the 16th century. The language shows borrowings from Hungarian, Slavic (Serbo-croatian) and the local dialect of German. Data are from Halwachs (1996:9, 16, 41-42, 64-65). In this dialect as spoken in Austria one finds the following features for athematic items:

Borrowed masculine nouns will have an added *-o*, plural *-i*, or an added *-o*, plural *-tscha* (/ča/). The latter is of unclear origin. Examples: *grofo* PL *grofi* 'Duke' from German *Graf*, and *meschteri* PL *mestertscha* 'teacher' from German *Meister*.

Borrowed (feminine) nouns in *-a* remain the same and have a plural ending *-i*, e.g. *baba*, PL *babi* 'grandmother', from Slavic.

Some inanimate borrowings from German show no change in singular, such as *Traktor* 'tractor'. Inflection follows the Romani pattern, but with a *-tscha* plural ending. A few nouns have a plural ending *-ini*, e.g. *pemsl* PL *pemslini* 'brush' from German *Pinsel*.

Borrowed adjectives end in -*i*, with no gender or number distinction. It has for instance *brauni* 'brown' (< German *braun* and *braune*[2]) for both genders and numbers (Halwachs 1996:41-42).

Borrowed verbs will consist of the stem to which the element -*in*- is suffixed, and to which Romani inflection is added. The verbs *pisinav* 'to write' and *roasinav* 'to travel' are borrowed from Slavic *pisat* and German *reisen* respectivally.

1.5 Adaption of Turkish elements in the Sepečides dialect of Izmir, Turkey

In Cech & Heinschink (1997; cf. also this volume) the dialect of the Sepečides Roma of Izmir is described. The following loanword pattern emerges from it: Borrowed nouns have penultimate stress. An element -*i* is added to consonant final nouns (plural -*ja*). The oblique endings are -*is* for masculine loanwords and -*a* for feminine loanwords, but -*es* for masculine inherited words and -*ja* for feminine inherited words. Masculine nouns ending in a vowel will get an -*s* and -*des* in plural added to it (*hodža-s*, PL. *hodžades*) < Turkish *hoca* 'Islamic religious teacher'. Feminine nouns will have -*ja* added (plural -*jes*), e.g. *džadí-ja*, plural *džadí-jes*, from T. *cadı* 'ghost'. Borrowed adjectives of both genders (and numbers??) end in -*i*, and have stress on the penultimate syllable. Verbs are borrowed with the loanword suffix -*din*/-*tin* between the stem and the person inflection.

1.6 Summary

In short, all five of these Romani dialects show a morphological dichotomy between borrowed and inherited words which splits the lexicon formally in two parts. Although the patterns differ slightly, we find similar systems in almost all Romani dialects, even when a dialect shows heavy signs of language contact, e.g. in the loss of the original stress system in the Burgenland and Terzi Mahalla dialects. These dialects belong to all the main branches of Romani dialect groupings (cf. Hancock 1988). Welsh is Northern, Terzi Mahalla and Sepečides are Balkan, Burgenland is Central and Gurbet is Vlax. This means that we can generalize the existence of a thematic-athematic distinction to all Romani dialects.

These are the main points of the distinction generalized and summarized: Borrowed nouns and adjectives have penultimate stress (Gurbet, Welsh, Sepečides), inherited words have final stress. Masculine borrowed nouns ending in a consonant will have an additional syllable of the form -*i*, -*is* (Terzi

Mahalla, Sepečides), -o (Burgenland, Terzi Mahalla after -k, Gurbet) or -os (Welsh). Borrowed nouns that end in a vowel will remain the same, or will have an added -s (Sepečides), or will have the vowel replaced by -ija (Terzi Mahalla, Sepečides). Borrowed adjectives are indeclinable. They end in -i (Burgenland, Sepečides), in -o (Gurbet, Terzi Mahalla) or -imen (Wales). Borrowed verbs have an additional ending before the person inflection. This can be -as (Welsh), -in (Terzi Mahalla, Burgenland, Sepečides, Welsh), -osar (Gurbet). Only in Gurbet the bare stem is commonly used. In some cases the preterit form of the verb is used as the base for borrowing (Sepečides).

This overview shows some variety in the way borrowed elements are adapted into Romani dialects. But although it is variable, there is only a limited number of patterns across dialects. For instance, the elements -isar- (Vlax) and -is-/-iz-(Drindari of Bulgaria, Kenrick 1969) are also found with borrowed verbs in other Romani dialects, but no other verbal loan markers have been described. Boretzky & Igla (1991:35-38) list all the suffixes used for verbal adaptions, and there are only three or four of them in the 26 dialects studied.[3]

In short, there are only a few recurrent patterns across dialects in the way loanwords are adapted, hence this pattern must have been in existence before the major split into dialects some 500 years ago, and must therefore be quite stable and old. In the following section I will show that the adaptions of loanwords are highly reminiscent of the borrowing of foreign elements into Greek.

2. Adaption of foreign elements into Greek

In this section I will describe the way in which foreign words are, or were, adapted into Greek. We will therefore first deal with the adaption of Turkish loanwords in several Greek dialects in Anatolia and Cyprus. The area where Greek underwent the most thorough Turkish influence is Anatolia, in three separate regions. For comparison I also discuss the adaption of loanwords in some other varieties of Greek.

2.1 Turkish borrowings in Silli Greek

Turkish words are borrowed as follows into the Greek dialect of Silli (Dawkins 1916: 43, 45, 48): Turkish nouns which end in a consonant, will have an -i added, e.g. Turkish kismet -> kismeci 'fate' (the palatalization of /t/ to /c/ is a peculiarity of the local Greek dialect). The stress of the borrowed noun is on the penultimate syllable. There are no data on Turkish nouns ending in a vowel.

Adjectives that end in a vowel will have an *-s* added, e.g. Turkish *hasta* ->
Greek *xastás* (M), *xastássa* (F), *xastá* (N) 'ill'. Turkish verbs are borrowed in
their preterit form[4], and the Greek endings follow: Turkish *başlamak* 'to begin',
başla-d-ı 'he began', Greek *bašla-d-o* 'I begin'. The *-d-* is the Turkish preterit
marker. This pattern is common in all Balkan languages.

2.2 Turkish borrowings in Cappadocian Greek

In Cappadocia we can observe similar, but slightly different patterns of
adaption (Dawkins 1916: 67-68, 93, 110, 115, 129, 131, 136): Turkish nouns
ending in a consonant, will have *-is* or *-os* added as the masculine ending, e.g.
Turkish *asker* -> *askéris* 'soldier', Turkish *çoban* -> *čobanos* 'shepherd'. The
stress is on the penultimate syllable.
    Turkish animate nouns ending in a vowel and adapted as masculine will
have an *-s* added to the stem. The stress is on the final syllable.

(5)   Turkish *paşa* -> Greek *bašas*, pl. *bašaδe* (also *bašaja*) 'older brother'

Inanimate nouns ending in *-a* are declined according to *-a* class nouns, e.g.
Turkish *tarla* -> Greek *tarlá* 'field'. They have final stress.
    Adjectives are used only in the neutral singular and plural forms, e.g. *zen-
gin* 'rich', PL. *zenginja*, from Turkish *zengin*[5]. There is no formal gender.
    Turkish verbs show two patterns of adaption. Some have only a *-d-* added
after the borrowed verb stem, others have an element *-diz-* added after the stem.
Some verbs show vowel harmony (*-diz-*, *-dız-*, *-duz-*, *-düz-*), but this is not always observed; the neutral form is *-diz-*. The *-d-* is derived from the Turkish *-d*-
preterit form, the *-iz-* element is from Greek, and used for the adaption of borrowed verbs. Here are examples from both:

(6)   Turkish *düşünmek* -> Greek *düšün-d-üz-o* 'to meditate'
        Turkish *anlamak* -> Greek *anla-d-ız-o* 'to understand'

In the aorist, the verbs have an *-s* or *-ts* marker, e.g. *aratsa* from Turkish *aramak*
'to search', and *angladisa/anlasa* from Turkish *anlamak* 'to understand'.

2.3 Turkish borrowings in Pharása Greek

In Pharása Greek dialects we again see similar adaptions of Turkish borrowings (Dawkins 1916:164, 166-168, 177-182). Turkish nouns ending in a consonant, will have an -i added. The stress is on the penultimate syllable.

(7)   Turkish *izin* -> *izíni* 'permission'

In some cases, following a local dialect rule, the suffix is dropped, leaving a seemingly unadapted item:

(8)   Turkish *hekim* -> *xekím* 'doctor'

To Turkish noun stems ending in a vowel an -s will be added. The stress is on the final syllable.

(9)   T. *komşu* -> Gr. *komšús* 'neighbour'

There are no data on adjectives. Verbs show three patterns of borrowing: the Turkish preterit form with Greek endings, the Turkish preterit form with -*iz*- and Greek endings, and the Turkish preterit form with Greek endings and -*tiez*-:

(10)   Turkish *yašamak* -> *jaša-d-o* 'to live'
        Turkish *dilemek* -> *dile-d-iz-o* 'to request'
        Turkish *ürkmek* -> *urk-t-iez-o* 'to be afraid'

2.4 Turkish loans in Cypriot Greek

Turkish loan nouns in Cypriot Greek show the same endings as the other ones, although the specific endings seem to relate more with the gender than with the shape of the original Turkish words. Pavlou (1994) gives examples like the following:

(11)   Turkish *kuran*, Greek *korani* 'the Koran'
        Turkish *cami*, Greek *tzami* 'mosque'
        Turkish *çanta*, Greek *tsenta* 'bag'
        Turkish *mahalle*, *mahala* Greek *maxallas* 'neighbourhood'
        Turkish *vezir*, Greek *veziris* 'Turkish officer'

We find both *-i*, *(i)s* and a zero ending, but it does not seem to be predictable which ending would be used.

2.5 Greek in the Anglophone diaspora and in Greece

Hatzidaki (1994) studied lexical borrowing in Anglophone immigrant communities. He concluded:

> A comparative study of loanwords from various Greek immigrant communities suggests that, while Greek speakers everywhere employ the same more or less derivational suffixes to "hellenize" foreign items, the outcome depends basically on the community involved (Hatzidaki 1994:367).

We find similar patterns as those mentioned before: words ending in a consonant have an *-i* added, but others show an *-is* or *-ia* ending. This morphological integration may not be true in Greece itself today, about which Mackridge (1985:151) remarked that

> there has been a marked tendency over the past decades for Greek to borrow large numbers of nouns from foreign languages (particularly French and English) without providing them with Greek inflectional suffixes and therefore without their gender being predictable from their endings.

2.6 Adaption of loanwords into the Greek standard language

As a rule, Turkish elements are avoided in the standard language. Those few items given in Mackridge (1985:24, 311) show similar patterns as the borrowings in other Greek dialects, such as addition of *-i* or *-is*, but nothing with words ending in a vowel or *-a*.

(12)   *sóba* 'stove' < T. *soba*
        tzáki 'hearth' < T. *ocak*
        kefi 'mood, high spirits' < T. *keyif*
        batzanákis 'brother-in-law' < T. *bacanak*

There is one example of an adjective:

(13)   *tembélis* (M), *tembéla* (F), *tembéliko* (N) 'lazy' < T. *tembel*

Mackridge gives no examples of borrowed verbs. Recent borrowings from French (e.g. in the domain of fashion) and English are not morphologically integrated (Mackridge 1985: 314-315), as mentioned above.

Apparently old borrowings were integrated by adding an *-i* to a consonant-final word, vowel-final words end in *-a* and adjectives end in *-is*. Recent loanwords do not follow the adaption pattern.

2.7 Adaption of loanwords in the Greek vernacular

Turkish borrowings in the Greek vernacular show the following characteristics: Turkish words ending in a vowel will have an *-s* added, and the plural is in *-des*, e.g. (Thumb 1910: 47):

(14)   *xatzís*, PL *xatzídes* 'pilgrim' (< T. *hacı*)
        arábis, PL *arábides* 'Arab, dark person' (T. *arap*)
        parás, PL *parádja* 'money' (T. *para*)

2.8 Adaption of Turkish nouns in Greek dialects

Boretzky (1981/1982:43-47, 56-57) summarizes the adaption of Turkish nouns in Greek dialects as follows: Almost all Turkish nouns ending in a consonant will have an *-i* added to the stem in Greek and be assigned neutral gender. There are also many Turkish nouns borrowed with the masculine *-as* PL. *-ades* ending, e.g. *xódzas*, PL. *xodzádes* from Turkish *hoca*. Nouns in *-a* become/remain feminine nouns in *-a*, e.g. *káma* 'dagger' < Turkish *kama*. Semantically animate masculine nouns will have an *-s* ending, e.g. Turkish *dana* 'calf' > Greek *danas*. Turkish nouns in *-e* end in *-es* in Greek and are masculine, or end in *-e* and are feminine. The endings in *-es* and *-e* are only used for loanwords. Turkish nouns in *-i* remain formally the same in almost all cases, and have neuter gender. Only masculine persons will end in *-is*.

2.9 Summary: Borrowings into Greek

In all the varieties observed (except for recent loans in standard Greek) we find only a limited set of patterns of adaption of loanwords into Greek. Borrowed nouns ending in a consonant will have an ending *-i*[6] (Silli, Pharasa, Cyprus, standard Greek) or *-is* (Cappadocia, Cyprus). Borrowed nouns ending in a vowel will have an additional *-s* (Cappadocia, Pharasa, Cyprus, Greek vernacular). Borrowed nouns ending in the vowel *-a* will have no ending

(Cappadocia, Cyprus, standard Greek). Borrowed adjectives ending in a vowel will have an added -*(i)s* (Silli, standard).

Verbs will be borrowed in their preterit form. Turkish verbs will have a -*d*-element after which Greek inflection follows (Silli, Cappadocia, Pharasa). In some dialects an element -*iz*- is added as well (Cappadocia, Pharasa).

3. The parallels between borrowings into Greek and Romani

There are a number of striking parallels in the way Greek and Romani treat borrowed words. The differences are minor. These parallels have been observed by others before, notably Boretzky & Igla (1991), whose Romani data and analysis contributed much to the ideas presented in this paper. There are adaption parallels for most of the word classes.

3.1 Nouns

For consonant-final nouns, both languages add an unstressed vowel or syllable to the stem. In both languages, -*os* and -*i(s)* are used for this purpose. In both languages, borrowed nouns ending in a vowel will remain the same (although some Romani dialects add a syllable).

3.2 Adjectives

At least in some varieties of Greek (but not modern Greek), there are no gender differences in borrowed adjectives. This may have to do with the lack of grammatical gender in the source language Turkish. It also happens in other cases of borrowed adjectives, for instance in Turkish adjectives in Serbocroatian and Bulgarian (Boretzky 1981/1982: 22, 23) which do not get Serbocroatian or Bulgarian gender or number inflection.

3.3 Verbs

Borrowed verbs are only integrated with a loan marker between the borrowed verb stem and the inflection. These markers find their source in aorist markers. Anatolian Greek dialects use the Turkish aorist/preterit marker -*d*- as does the Sepečides Romani dialect. Other Anatolian Greek dialects use the -*iz*-

element which is derived from the Greek sigmatic aorist (Boretzky & Igla 1991: 35). This element is also used in several Romani dialects, sometimes followed by the Romani element *-ar-*, notably in Vlax dialects. Other Romani dialects use *-in-*, which is not reported from borrowings into Greek, but which is a common ending in Greek, and of increasing frequency since classical times.

How are the different suffixes distributed over the different dialects? The suffix *-in-* is found in dialects such as Welsh Romani, Terzi Mahalla of Prizren (Kosovo), and Burgenland (Austria). The suffix *-iz-/-is-* is found in some Balkan dialects. The suffix *-isar-* is found in all Vlax dialects and in Catalonia and Spain. Even a cursory search shows that these elements do not coincide with the dialect classifications so far (see the discussion of different proposals for classification in Hancock 1988).

Although some Romani dialects borrow verb stems directly (e.g. the Vlax dialects such as the Gurbet dialect discussed above), most varieties show an element between the stem and the endings. There is some variation in these endings. The most common ones are *-in-*, *-is-/-iz-*, *-(i)sar*, and *-as-* seems limited to Welsh Romani and *-az-* to Bugurdži (Boretzky 1993). As discussed earlier by Boretzky & Igla (1991:35-38) and others, all of these originate in Greek. The suffixes *-as-* and *-is-/-iz-* have their origin in Greek verbs in *-az-o* and *-iz-o* (Sampson 1926:117-118). The suffix *-osar* or *-isar* is the same suffix extended with a derivational suffix *-ar* used in many Romani dialects for causatives and other valency increasing reasons (see Hübschmannová & Bubeník, this volume). The suffix *-in-* is from Greek verbs ending in *-(i)no* (*-ανω*, *-αινω*, *-εινω*, *-ωνω*).

3.4 More on adjectives

There are differences between Greek and Romani with respect to borrowed adjectives. Greek adds *-s* to borrowed adjectives and Romani either unaccented *-i* or *-o* (the inherited adjectives are accented). Welsh Romani is exceptional in that it has the ending *-imen* for borrowed adjectives, but here as well there is a Greek source: there is no doubt that this suffix is taken from the Greek middle passive participle suffix *-μενος* (Sampson 1926: 94; Boretzky & Igla 1991:39). On the other hand, borrowed adjectives are rarely reported upon in the studies of borrowings into Greek. Where do these endings *-o* and *-i* come from? Superficially they are identical to the masculine (*-ó*) and feminine (*-í*) endings of inherited adjectives. But there are arguments in favor of the fact that the Romani endings are from Greek, even though they are identical to the adjectival endings in inherited adjectives. The main argument for this position is that the borrowed adjectives never inflect for gender, in contrast to the thematic adjectives. The endings in borrowed words are unstressed, in inherited words they are stressed. They could be interpreted as generalizations. It has been suggested already by Boretzky & Igla (1991: 39) that the endings go back to Greek neutral endings.

4. Discussion

Even though there is no complete match between the two borrowing patterns, the patterns in Greek and Romani are so strikingly similar that chance has to be excluded. In fact, the formal parallels are even greater when we take into account the borrowed derivational elements in Romani and when we look at the plural endings of borrowed words which are from Greek as well.

First, let us look at derivation. Romani borrowed many Greek derivational suffixes. Some of these have a strictly regional character, but quite a few of them can be found across dialect groupings and are therefore widespread, even though not all dialects use them. These are derivational suffixes like the diminutive suffixes -*ici* (masculine) and -*ica* (feminine) and the denominal suffix -*icko* which indicates geographic origin (cf. Boretzky & Igla 1991 and Boretzky & Igla 1994: 413-415), the -*to* suffix to form ordinal numbers, etc..[7] Most but not all of these are used only with loanwords. The endings -*ici*, -*ica* and -*icko* (and its adverbial equivalent -*icka*) are ultimately of Slavic origin, in both Greek and Romani (V. Friedman, p.c.).

The second fact that points to a Greek origin of the athematic suffixes is the shape of the plural inflection of the borrowed words. Many of these appear to be taken from Greek. The Romani masculine forms in -*is*/-*os* have a plural form in -*ides*/-*odes*, identical to Greek plural forms. It was noted above that Turkish words in Greek also show this same plural ending. Masculine words in -*i* have a plural in -*ija*, just like Greek neuter forms in -*i* have this plural form[8]. Although this -*ija* ending is similar to the plural ending -*ja* for inherited nouns in Romani, it is limited to feminine nouns, whereas for borrowed items it is limited to masculine nouns. Romani nouns in -*a* have a plural ending -*e*, reminiscent of Greek plurals in -*es* for nouns ending in -*a* (for different genders). In fact, feminine Romani forms also have the -*es* ending, exactly as in Greek.

It must further be emphasized that Greek and Romani do not just follow parallel patterns. Both languages are part of the Balkan Sprachbund (cf. Matras 1994, Friedman 1985, 1986), but in a number of points Romani and Greek differ from the other Balkan languages. This can be shown for instance in the adaption of Turkish words. All Balkan languages borrowed from Turkish (Miklosich 1884). The words that Romani borrowed from Turkish are roughly the same as those borrowed into e.g. Serbian (as shown in Friedman 1988). Grammatically, there may be differences in the various Balkan languages. Figure 3 (based on material in Kazazis 1970) shows that Romani and Greek are remarkably similar in their adaption of three Turkish grammatical elements, but they differ from the Balkan Slavic languages (with only the -*li* suffix as an exception).

Turkish source	Greek	Maced.	Bulg.	Serbo-Croat	TM Romani[9]	Sepečides
-*ci*	-*τζης*	-*džija*	-*džija*	-*džija*	-*džis, -dži*	-*čis, -čus*
-*li*	-*λης*	-*lija*	-*lija*	-*lija*	-*lija*	-*lis*
-*lik*	-*λικι*	-*lak*	-*lək*	-*luk*	-*luko,-ləci*	??

Figure 3: Adaption of borrowed suffixes from Turkish in Balkan languages (ignoring vowel harmony)

The grammatical adaption of Turkish words in the Balkan languages (with no mention of Romani) is discussed in a comparative study in Boretzky (1981/1982). This paper deals with Greek, Bulgarian, Serbocroatian, Rumanian, Albanian and Aromunian. Greek appears to stand slightly apart from the other Balkan languages in its adaption patterns. In almost all cases Turkish borrowings get an extra vowel (-*i*) or consonant (-*s*) in Greek, whereas most other languages (except Aromunian) do not adapt the nouns. The only category where Slavic languages extend the Turkish word is in the Turkish words ending in -*i*. Here Bulgarian and Serbocroatian change -*i* into -*ija*. In this respect Romani is like Balkan Slavic rather than Greek.

We have discussed the remarkable parallels between borrowings into Greek and borrowings into Romani, with its athematic component. The striking formal parallels between the Romani adaptive elements and Greek have been remarked several times in the past (Miklosich 1872, Sampson 1926, and more recently Boretzky & Igla 1991). It has not been studied in the context of Greek adaption of foreign elements, however.

It is clear that the form of the morphemes used in athematic words has nothing whatsoever to do with inherited Romani morphology. A suggestion to relate the element -*i*, which is added to nouns, to the Romani adjectival ending -*i* must be firmly rejected for grammatical reasons: the adjectival ending is limited to feminine forms, whereas the nominal element is limited to masculine nouns. Also, the inherited suffixes are always stressed, whereas the borrowed elements never arc. In a similar vein, the verbal adaptive elements have no parallel elsewhere in Romani, but they all appear to be common in Greek.

In short, it cannot be a coincidence that Greek and Romani use almost identical strategies for the adaption of (European) loanwords. They have the same shape, they are used in similar environments, and they differ from patterns in other Balkan languages. In Romani, these Greek endings are limited to the athematic component of the language. There is no doubt that the Romani system is based on the Greek system.

All this points once again to the importance of Greek in the history of the Romani language. The presence of Greek words in all dialects of Romani already led Miklosich (1872) to the conclusion that the ancestors of the Roma must have spent considerable time in a Greek speaking area. This widespread Greek influence shows that it is old, general and widespread, if not universal through all Romani dialects. It is also likely that Greek was the main influence that led to the introduction of Balkan Sprachbund features in Romani. Where Balkan languages differ in their structure, Greek and Romani mostly show the same pattern. For instance, the case/preposition system of Romani bears a striking resemblance with Greek, in both languages the beneficiary is expressed with accusative/oblique rather than the dative case (cf. Kostov 1996), and Greek and Romani are the only Balkan languages with prenominal articles.

In this light it is somewhat amazing that comparatively little is known about Gypsies in Greece and the Byzantine Empire in the late Middle Ages (cf. Soulis 1961, Fraser 1992). One wonders whether this has to do with ignorance or a lack of interest or observance on the part of historians, or with an actual lack of documentation - most likely the latter.

The presence of the ancestors of the Roma in Greek speaking territory in any case had a pervasive influence on the Romani language. The fact that the pattern of adaption of loanwords shows Greek traits in all Romani dialects (though not necessarily exactly the same traits), suggests that the ancestors of the Roma left the Greek speaking areas when still fully competent in Greek.

If these affixes and adaption patterns are indeed borrowed from Greek, it is striking that most of the Greek words in Romani do not show these endings. There are Greek words which behave like inherited words, and others which behave as borrowed words. The Greek word *drom* has a plural form *droma*, whereas Greek *foros* has a borrowed plural form *foruri* in Vlax; the plural ending is from Rumanian. It remains to be studied whether this points to different periods of borrowing of these items or whether other factors play a role.

Almost all Greek words in Romani follow the pattern for inherited words, just as the stems derived from Armenian, Iranian and Indic languages. Boretzky & Igla (1991) already observed this. This led these researchers to suggest that the separate loan paradigms came into use only in the period of Slavic influence. The fact that Slavic words are treated as athematic words suggests that those loans are more recent than the Greek ones. This may point to Asia Minor as the area of Greek influence, as European Byzantium was under influence of Slavic since the 6th/7th centuries (V. Friedman, p.c.).

From Boretzky & Igla's (1991) overview of morphological borrowing in Romani it is clear that the suffixes borrowed from Greek have a different status than those borrowed from other languages. The latter are only locally used, derivational and variable from dialect to dialect, whereas the Greek suffixes are close to pan-dialectal, hardly variable, and both inflectional and derivational. The only borrowed inflections in Romani are from Greek (with the exception of Vlax dialects and some Balkan dialects, e.g. in their Rumanian resp. Slavic plural endings). Furthermore, in probably all cases they are in overwhelming majority limited to athematic words.

Can the actual shape of the athematic paradigm be used for dialect classification, or is it independent of dialect groupings? In other words, are dialects which use -in- as the pattern for verbal loanwords more closely related to one another than to those which use e.g. -is-/-iz-? This does not appear to be the case. The variation in adaption, although clearly inspired by Greek in all cases, does not coincide with dialectal or areal groupings. This suggests that different dialects developed the borrowing patterns independently, just after the Romani speech community split into subgroups. More thorough study of Romani dialects is needed before one can give a definite answer.

There is no language which influenced Romani so pervasively as Greek, especially grammatically. Even though the Vlax dialects are heavily influenced by Rumanian during perhaps five centuries of close contact, the Vlax dialects do not show the same extent of influence from Rumanian. In the Vlax dialects even inflectional morphemes were borrowed from Rumanian, such as the plural marker, and some Balkan dialects borrowed Slavic plural morphemes, in both cases for athematic items only. Some dialects under Slavic influence borrowed aspectual verbal prefixes from Slavic. These are the only exceptions to the observation that Greek was the only source language for borrowed inflectional morphemes in Romani. Even so, Greek is the only source for inflectional morphemes which are used in all branches and all individual dialects of Romani, in contrast to the Rumanian and Slavic examples just mentioned. As with the Greek morphemes in Romani, it is not the most frequent or unmarked plural morpheme that is borrowed from Rumanian, but the suffix used for borrowings into the language (Boretzky & Igla 1991). This, however, needs more thorough study.

Romani borrowed inflectional endings from Greek. The Greek elements in Romani are not used to mark grammatical categories existing in Greek, nor do they have the same function as in Greek. Their sole purpose is the formal marking of the fact that an element is a borrowed word. The morphemes used in Romani for marking borrowed words are those which were used in Greek for borrowings from other languages. It is therefore not morphological borrowing as such, but it is the borrowing of a borrowing pattern. The fact that most Greek words are not treated as borrowed words in Romani shows that the Greek lexical component of Romani belongs to a different stratum than the Greek markers for athematic items.

The differences in the adaption patterns in Romani dialects suggest initial dialectal fragmentation in a Greek speaking environment. All Romani dialects show the Greek patterns, but they differ in the actual suffixes used. Futhermore, these suffixes do not generally follow established dialect classifications.

The thematic/athematic distinction developed when all Romani communities were still in a Greek speaking environment, since all dialect groupings basically share the same system, albeit with variation. This variation is apparently also found in Greek dialects. What is needed is a more detailed study of borrowings into Greek through the ages and in the Greek dialects of the different relevant regions. This could perhaps provide data about where this Greek-speaking area could have been located (the Peloponessos? Attica? Asia Minor?) and the time when the ancestors of the Gypsies left the Greek speaking areas. The historical data are too scarce to give a clue, so that we have to rely on linguistic data for now. The facts referred to above seem to point to Asia Minor rather than Greece.

5. *Conclusion*

The close parallels between Greek and the athematic endings in Romani have been observed before. But it has not been argued, as I did here, that the Romani system of adaption as such has been taken over from Greek. All elements added to borrowed verbs and nouns in Romani are borrowed from Greek, but only rarely applied to Greek elements. These include verbal loan markers, nominal semantically empty suffixes and the nominative plural endings. This is a highly unusual if not unique case of borrowing: a system of adaption of lexical borrowing is borrowed from another language, in this case Greek. The fact that these adaption rules are generally not applied to lexical borrowings from Greek, makes it all the more unusual.

The Greek influence on Romani in general is considerable: lexical, morphological, semantic, grammatical, syntactic and even the system for adapting loanwords. One can summarize the Romani borrowing pattern as follows: It's Greek to me.

Endnotes

I am grateful to the following persons for comments on this paper or parts thereof: Norbert Boretzky, Victor Friedman, Anthony Grant, Yaron Matras, Christos Tzitzilis. None of them bears responsibility for any of my statements. I am also grateful to Behljulj Galjus for his cooperation on the Terzi Mahalla dialect.

1. There are some inherited adjectives which end in a consonant which are not inflected for gender, such as *hor* 'deep'.
2. It is unlikely that the final schwa of *braune* is the source for the Roman adjectival *-i*, even though this form is frequent and also commonly used in German foreigner talk. German schwa becomes /e/ in borrowings into Roman, and never /i/.
3. Boretzky & Igla give the following overview. The suffixes *-is-ar-* and *-os-ar-* are used in Kalderaš, Lovari, Gurbet, Kalpazea and Caló. The suffixes *-is-/-iz-* are used in Bugurdži, Drindari, (Kazanlik), Erli, Arli, Paspati, Methana, East Slovak. The element *-in-* is used in Arli, Erli, Terzi Mahalla, Methana, Bohemia, East Slovak, Kisilevka, Ukraine, Sinti, Caló, Burgenland, Hungary, Cerhari/Lovari, Poland, Czech Republic, Russia. They do not mention the *-din-* suffix of the Sepečides dialect.
4. It is not at all unusual that verbs are borrowed in their preterit or aorist form into other languages. Joseph (1987) describes a dialect of Bulgarian in the Rhodope which borrowed Greek verbs with their aorist stem. He also discusses Turkish verbs which are borrowed into Greek in their preterit forms. This seems to be common in the Balkans (but undoubtedly not only there), see e.g. Friedman (1996).
5. Chr. Tzitzilis (personal communication) mentions the adjective *memnun* borrowed in Pharasa Greek as μεμνουνος.
6. The productivity of the neuter ending *-i* of Greek increased since classical times, especially in the Ottoman period (Boretzky 1975:6, 12). In Middle Greek many Latin nouns were borrowed as neutrals, even though they would fit other classes better on morphological grounds (Boretzky 1975:8).
7. At least this is claimed in Boretzky & Igla (1991:20): "Ordinalzahlen werden im Romani mit dem Suffix *-to* (<griech. -τος) gebildet; ein voreuropäisches Element ist nicht belegt". Sampson (1926:157) points to the Sanskrit ordinal ending *-tha*. Lamani, an Indic language of Ghor nomads in India, has an ordinal suffix with a consonant (s, r, t, w) followed by *-o* or *-i*, e.g. *caat* 'four', *cawt-o/i* 'fourth'. The fact that the Romani ordinal suffix is undeclinable for gender would be an argument for Greek origin.
8. This would be an argument against considering the *-i* ending a truncated form of *-is*, as mentioned as a possibility by Igla (1996:202).
9. The shape of the endings *-lija*, *-luk* and *-ləci* in TM Romani suggests that these are borrowed from Slavic and not directly from Turkish.

References

Boretzky, Norbert. 1969/1970. 'Ein semantischer Turzismus in den Balkansprachen'. *Zeitschrift für Balkanologie* 7:1-2. 16-21.
---- 1975. 'Bildung und Bedeutung der Deminutiva im Griechischen und Makedonischen'. *Zeitschrift für Balkanologie* 11:1. 5-20.
---- 1981/1982. 'Morphologisch-syntaktische Adaptation der Turzismen in den Südosteuropäischen Sprachen'. *Münchener Zeitschrift für Balkankunde* 4. 19-57.

---- 1989. 'Zum Interferenzverhalten des Romani. Verbreitete und ungewöhnliche Phänomene'. *Zeitschrift für Sprachwissenschaft und Kommunikationsforschung* 42:3. 357-374.
---- 1993. *Bugurdži. Deskriptiver und historischer Abriß eines Romani-Dialekts.* Berlin: Harrassowitz.
---- & Birgit Igla. 1991. *Morphologische Entlehnung in den Romani-Dialekten.* (Arbeitspapiere des Projektes 'Prinzipien des Sprachwandels' 4). Essen: Fachbereich Sprach-und Literaturwissenschaften an der Universität Essen.
---- 1994. *Wörterbuch Romani-Deutsch-Englisch für den südosteuropäischen Raum.* Wiesbaden: Harrassowitz.
Cech, Petra & Mozes F. Heinschink. 1997. *Sepečides-Romani.* Munich: Lincom.
Dawkins, R.M. 1916. *Modern Greek in Asia Minor. A study of the dialects of Sílli, Cappadocia and Phárasa with grammar, texts, translations and glossary.* Cambridge: Cambridge University Press.
Fraser, Angus. 1992. *The Gypsies.* Oxford: Blackwell.
Friedman, Victor A. 1985. 'Balkan Romani modality and other Balkan languages'. *Folia Slavica* 7:3. 381-389.
---- 1986. 'Romani *Te* in a Balkan context'. In: Violetta Koseska-Toszewa & Irena Sawicka, eds. *Językowe studia bałkanistyczne*, Vol. 1. Wrocław: Polska Akademia Nauk. 39-48.
---- 1988. 'Turquismes en Romani. A propos de l'établissement d'une langue rom littéraire et des composants lexicaux turcs des différents dialectes'. In: Patrick Williams, ed. *Tsiganes: Identité, évolution.* Paris: Syros Alternatives/ Études Tsiganes. 403-413.
---- 1996. 'The Turkish lexical element in the languages of the Republic of Macedonia from the Ottoman period to independence'. *Zeitschrift für Balkanologie* 32:2. 133-50.
Halwachs, Dieter W. 1996. *Morphologie des Roman. Basisgrammatik der Romani-Variante der Burgenland-Roma.* Oberwart: Verein Roma.
Hancock, Ian F. 1988. 'The development of Romani linguistics'. In: Mohammad Ali Jazayery & Werner Winter, eds. *Languages and cultures. Studies in honor of Edgar C. Polomé.* Berlin: Mouton de Gruyter. 183-223.
---- 1995. *A handbook of Vlax Romani.* Columbus: Slavica.
Hatzidaki, Aspassia G. 1994. 'Lexical borrowing in immigrant varieties of Greek'. In: I. Philipakki-Warburton, Katerina Nicolaidis & Maria Sifianou, eds. *Themes in Greek Linguistics.* Amsterdam: Benjamins. 365-372.
Igla, Birgit. 1996. *Das Romani von Ajia Varvara: Descriptive und historisch-vergleichende Darstellung eines Zigeunerdialektes.* Wiesbaden: Harrasowitz.
Joseph, Brian D. 1987. 'A Bulgarian Mischsprache from the Rhodope?' In: Brian D. Joseph & Arnold M. Zwick, eds. *A Festschrift for Ilse Lehiste.* (Ohio State University Working Papers in Linguistics 35). 117-123.
Kazazis, K. 1970. 'The status of Turkisms in the present-day Balkan languages'. In: H. Birnbaum, & S. Vryonis, eds. *Aspects of the Balkans. Continuity and change.* The Hague: Mouton. 87-116.
Kenrick, Donald. 1969. *Morphology and lexicon of the Romany dialect of Kotel (Bulgaria).* Ph.D. dissertation, School of Oriental and African Studies.
Kostov, Kiril. 1996. 'Neugriechischer syntaktischer Einfluß auf das Balkanzigeunerische: Zum Ersatz des Dativs durch den Akkusativ'. *Zeitschrift für Balkanologie* 32:2. 167-173.
Mackridge, Peter. 1985. *The Modern Greek Language. A descriptive analysis of standard Modern Greek.* Oxford: Clarendon.

Matras, Yaron. 1994. 'Structural balkanisms in Romani'. In: Norbert Reiter, Uwe Hinrichs, & Jiřina van Leeuwen-Turnovcová, eds. *Sprachlicher Standard und Substandard in Südosteuropa und Osteuropa.* Wiesbaden: Harrasowitz. 195-210.

Miklosich, Franz. 1872. *Über die Mundarten und die Wanderungen der Zigeuner Europas* III. Wien: Karl Gerold's Sohn.

---- 1884. 'Die turkischen Elemente in den südost- und osteuropäischen Sprachen'. *Denkschriften der Kaiserlichen Akademie der Wissenschaften in Wien, Phil.-Hist. Kl.*, 34, 35, 38.

Paspati, Alexandre G. 1870 [1973]. Études sur les Tchinghianés ou Bohémiens de l'Empire Ottoman. Constantinople: Koroméla. [Osnabrück: Biblio].

Pavlou, Pavlos. 1994. 'The semantic adaptation of Turkish loan-words in the Greek Cypriot dialect'. In: Irene Philipakki-Warburton, Katerina Nicolaidis & Maria Sifianou, eds. *Themes in Greek linguistics.* Amsterdam: Benjamins. 443-448.

Pott, Augustus F. 1844-1845 [1964]. *Die Zigeuner in Europa und Asien. Ethnographisch-linguistische Untersuchung vornehmlich ihrer Herkunft und Sprache.* Halle: Heynemann. [Leipzig: Edition Leipzig].

Sampson, John. 1926 [1968]). *The Dialect of the Gypsies of Wales.* Oxford: Clarendon Press.

Soulis, George C. 1961. 'The Gypsies in the Byzantine empire and the Balkans in the late Middle Ages'. *Dumbarton Oak Papers* 15. 141-165.

Thumb, Albert. 1910 [1974]. *Handbuch der neugriechischen Volkssprache. Grammatik. Texte. Glossar.* Strassburg: Karl. J. Trübner. [Berlin: de Gruyter]

TOWARDS A MORPHOLOGY-BASED
TYPOLOGY OF ROMANI

VIKTOR ELŠIK
Charles-University, Prague

0. Introduction

The present paper aims at setting out an elementary typological description of Romani. The object language is the Slovak-and-Czech variety of Romani (SCR); analysis of data from other varieties of Romani is, for the sake of basic comparison, only briefly outlined. The Prague School typology (PST) is my theoretical point of departure and conceptual framework, and the morphological domain of typology is the main object of the paper.

1. Prague School typology

PST can be briefly introduced as a 'major' grammatically-based construct-oriented typology. It was created by Vladimír Skalička (1909–1991), a pre-war member of the Prague Linguistic Circle, and has been further developed particularly by Petr Sgall (1926–). For a detailed introduction to PST see Sgall (1979, 1993) and mainly Skalička & Sgall (1994).

The notion of type in the approach of PST (Skalička 1966, 1977, Sgall 1971) is not a concept classifying languages, but rather a construct of an extreme cluster of logically independent but empirically favourable linguistic properties which is not realizable in the actual languages. A label of a type ascribed to an actual language only indicates its proximity to a given extreme: features of the extreme prevail in the language. The properties of languages can be organized according to several dimensions; only in some of them are the endpoints of the dimensions realizable (Skalička 1966). The interrelations among individual properties are of probabilistic nature, being conditioned, for example, by the economy of language systems (Skalička & Sgall 1994:341). A 'major' typology should have a major predictive power, i.e. it should comprise a wide range of language properties. The most relevant basis for such a typology is the domain where the arbitrariness of the language structure leaves enough room for cross-linguistic variation and for clustering of various properties, i.e. the domain of morphology and surface-syntactic features such as word order, agreement etc. (Sgall 1971, Skalička & Sgall 1994, forming already in Skalička 1958a).

The fact that two different extremes may have a common language property necessitates that some properties differentiating these extremes be favourable to the common property rather than the converse (Sgall 1971). The asymmetry of the relation of favourability of logically independent features (Skalička insisted that it is the mutual favourability of individual features which constitutes an extreme, however) renders possible a consideration of some of the properties more essential to the specification of a type than others. Sgall sees the basic property as being the relationship between phonemic means that convey lexemic meaning and those that convey grammatical function. There are only a few possibilities: grammatical function is implemented a) by the order of lexemic units – in poly-semicity, b) by non-lexemic units similar to the lexemic ones in their shape – in analyticity, c) by non-lexemic units differing from the lexemic ones in their shape and their combinatorical properties – in agglutination, and d) by modifications of the lexemic units – in introflection and inflectivity (the term modification includes both concatenative and non-concatenative devices and it does justice to the fact that in the inflective type there is at most one grammatical affix in a word). Enumeration of the other individual properties constituing the Prague School types, the interconnections which hold between them, and an explanation of their clustering will be given in the course of Sections 3 to 10 only if they are relevant to the typological analysis of Romani.

Different types can be realized (i.e. features of different types can prevail) to differing degrees in actual languages. In connection with that, some combinations of different types in a language are more likely to appear than others (cf. Popela 1985). Elementary limits of an extreme spring from the contradiction between some of its dimensions, and result in *inevitable* combinations with other types. (The problem of maintaining the particular five PST types vis-à-vis the existence of inevitable and empirically more convenient combinations is not dealt with here.) Highly plausible or inevitable combinations will be termed, for example, the inflective-analytic combination, while instances of the less plausible or contingent combinations, for example, a combination of inflectivity and ana-lyticity. Both sorts, however, need to be specified in terms of the particular properties combined.

The typological terms 'inflectivity / inflective' will be distinguished here from the morphological terms 'inflection / inflectional'. A most confusing point in PST terminology is the term 'polysynthesis' which is used in a manner different from its common use (cf. Mithun 1988). Skalička (1968a) characterizes so-called polysynthesis as a type where autosemantic and synsemantic elements are only slightly, if at all, differentiated and where autosemantic elements are joined without means of other morphemes. Both incorporating languages and languages employing non-incorporative juxtaposition (e.g. Vietnamese or Yoruba) may be labelled polysynthetic according to his approach (cf. Skalička 1946, 1955). In typical incorporating languages (polysynthetic in the common sense), the unquestionable postulation of incorporation is, according to Skalička (1958a), due to the important role played by agglutination in these languages; in the agglutinative type, word is a perspicuous unit. On the other hand, not all incorporating languages would be labelled polysynthetic by Skalička (1946), since in many of them extensive use is made of non-lexemic elements. Here, to avoid misunderstanding, the more appropriate term 'polysemicity' is used for PST 'polysynthesis'.

2. The typology of Romani

PST has been applied, in particular, to Finno-Ugric (and Turkic) languages (Skalička 1935, 1965), Slavic languages (Skalička 1941, 1951, 1958a, Sgall 1960 and others), Balkan languages – with no overt mention of Balkan Romani (Skalička 1968b, 1972, 1974), Bantu languages (Skalička 1945), Chinese and other polysemic languages (Skalička 1946, 1955 and others), Germanic languages (Čermák 1978) etc.. A diachronical perspective has been employed in a typological description of Czech declension (Skalička 1941), seeing the inflectivity peak in fourteenth century Czech, and in a work on typological development of Indo-European (IE) languages (Sgall 1958a, 1958b).

So far, PST has not been applied to Romani or, indeed, to any New Indo-Aryan (NIA) language. In Sanskrit, a high portion of inflectivity has been determined (mainly Sgall 1958a). Only a few remarks have been made about the general development in the Indo-Iranian languages away from inflectivity towards agglutination (Skalička 1958b, Sgall 1958b), about the prevalence of agglutination in Hindi (Skalička 1984), and about the certain extent of polysemicity in the languages of the Indian subcontinent (Skalička 1946 and 1955). A brief remark about a more developed cumulation and grammatical synonymy in Romani, in contrast to the other NIA languages, has been made by Sgall (1958b:16).

Outside PST, Romani has often been said to be an agglutinative language. However, the meaning of the term agglutinative in these typological statements

only partially agrees with its meaning in PST: it usually concerns word structure, namely the fact that there are several affixes in a declinable word.
According to Boretzky (1989:358) Romani is an agglutinative language, having
mostly suffixes, which rarely fuse with the stem, the two-degree case system in
nouns, and the combined tense-number-person inflection in verbs. Boretzky &
Igla (1994:393) regard the Romani verbal as well as the nominal system as having both inflective and agglutinative features; in verbs, periphrastic expression
can be found as well. The agglutinative character of case markers is advocated
by Friedman (1991:98). Romani is assumed to have undergone a move from
'postposed analyticity' to agglutination, but the tendency toward analyticity in
Balkan nominal structure is also taken into consideration. Case inflection is
termed agglutinative by Matras (1996:65 and this volume) as well, analyticity of
the nominal system being regarded as a tendency common to all Romani
dialects. Ventcel' (1964:96, 1980:135, and 1966:648) describes the North
Russian dialect of Romani as an inflective language with inflection of an
agglutinative character, where synthetic means of syntax are being replaced by
analytic means. This progression towards analyticity is exemplified by the
replacement of noun case-endings by prepositional constructions, the reduction
of attributive agreement, and the reduction of morphological oppositions in
verbs. The agglutinative character of inflection is explicated by the uniform
shape of the final suffixes in nouns and verbs. The term inflective as used by
Ventzel seems to include agglutination (cf. Ventzel 1983:91).

    In the present paper, I claim that Romani is a language with prevailing ag-
glutination, complemented to a high degree by inflectivity, to a lesser but still
significant degree by analyticity, and in the domain of lexicon by polysemicity.
Introflection is almost completely absent.

    The object language is SCR, a partially standardized variety of Romani,
based on dialects formerly spoken in Eastern Slovakia, and, since the period
immediately after the World War II also in the Czech Republic (Hübschmannová
et al. 1991, Lípa 1963). The elementary typological description of SCR according to the main areas of the character of word, word structure, paradigm relations and word classification, morphonology and phonology, word-formation,
and syntax is given in Sections 3 to 10.

3. The word

    The existence of polymorphemic words, i.e. the presence of 'synthetic'
forms, is a feature common to all 'synthetic' types, i.e. agglutination, inflectivity, and introflection. The existence of monomorphemic words only, on the

other hand, is peculiar to analyticity, while polysemicity remains indifferent in this respect (though radical in combinations: extremely high synthetism in combination with the agglutinative type, and low synthetism in combination with the analytic type). Another classification of words is the one distinguishing autosemantic from function words: that is to say, a function word may be morphologically complex and an autosemantic word may be monomorphemic. Autosemantic words, of course, exist in all languages and all language types. Function words, on the other hand, are peculiar only to analyticity and the inflective-analytic combination, while polysemic and agglutinative extremes have no function words whatsoever.

The word in Romani is generally a perspicuous unit. It is often polymorphemic, and there are also function words, which classes Romani among languages exhibiting a considerable portion of some of the 'synthetic' types, and, at the same time, a considerable extent of analyticity or the inflective-analytic combination. Before further specification of the 'synthetism' in Romani in Sections 4 to 6, a typological explanation of function words is carried out.

Pronouns, prepositions, conjunctions, syntactic particles, and articles of definiteness are the function words in Romani. None of them is necessary in agglutination: subject and object markers in verbs may have the function of personal pronouns, while possessive pronouns may be replaced by possessive affixes of nouns; prepositions or postpositions may be replaced by extensive case inflection; conjunctions may be substituted for special affixes; verbal forms may replace syntactic particles; and, finally, separate articles may be replaced by affixal markers of definiteness. Of course, no actual language can be consistent in this agglutinative strategy. But the fact that Romani does not possess either special 'conjunctional' forms of verbs or nouns (e.g. Latin -que 'and'), or possessive affixes (e.g. Finnish -ni 'my'), or affixes of definiteness (e.g. Basque singular definite -a), shows clearly that it is not a strongly agglutinative language.

On the other hand, the existence of subject agreement, the non-obligatory personal pronouns in the function of subject, and the existence of both prepositions and a rather developed case system, reveals that function words in Romani have a strong non-analytic counterpart. Some of the function words, namely pronouns, prepositions, and conjunctions, are very common even in crystallized inflective languages, and can therefore be ascribed to the inflective-analytic combination. Articles and syntactic particles, on the other hand, manifest an exclusively analytic feature. The fact that pronouns and particularly articles are inflectible, and that prepositions tend towards a sort of inflection (in a non-rigid sense), due to regular, syntactically conditioned phonological processes (andre jekh kher 'in/to a house' vs. andr-o kher 'in/to the house'), also denies a pronounced character of the analytic component in Romani. The main argument,

however, in favour of the statement that Romani is basically a 'synthetic' language only supplemented by analyticity, is the elaborate and differentiated
Romani morphology.

4. Word structure and its analysis

In the 'synthetic' types, grammatical meanings are formally expressed in the
frame of a polymorphemic word unit together with a lexical meaning. The basic
difference between agglutination, on the one hand, and inflectivity and introflection, on the other, is that the former expresses each grammatical meaning separately (each of the grammatical meanings has its own segmentable counterpart in
the phonological form of the word), i.e. glutinatively, while the latter cumulate
more grammatical meanings in a morphological element. To say that there is a
(maximum) cumulation of grammatical meanings, is equivalent to saying that in
a word-form, there is only one morphological element expressing grammatical
meanings. So the word structure in the inflective and introflective types is a stem
+ an affix or a non-concatenative modification (which is the morphological formant), while the structure of an agglutinative word is a stem + a *chain* of affixes,
all of which together form the morphological formant. The syntagmatically
combinatorical character of agglutinative word structure contributes to the high
valuation of constructional diagrammaticity in agglutination. It is much less val-
ued in inflectivity (Dressler 1985:66), which is instead optimal in indexicality,
through grammatical elements being close to lexical elements and closely bound
to them, thus signalizing word units (Dressler 1985:53) and their syntactic function (Sgall 1988:464).

The morphological devices in Romani are stem-external affixes (prevalently
suffixes). Introflective features are not present to any significant extent in
Romani, since there are no stem-internal affixes, and stem alternations are rare
and only attendant to suffixes (see Section 8). In Romani as well as in many
other languages, there are forms with an apparent cumulation of grammatical
meanings (e.g. nominative singular *rikon-o* 'dog' vs. nominative plural *rikon-e*
'dogs') and forms with an apparent glutinative expression of grammatical
meanings (e.g. oblique feminine singular of the possessive singular form of the
masculine noun *rikono* 'dog' in Figure 1). The example in Figure 1 also shows
that both word structure principles are present not only in one and the same language, but even in one and the same form. Both ideal cases, whether the expression of grammatical meanings is extremely glutinative or extremely cumulative, are easy to analyse: grammatical meanings are either expressed by respective segments, or by one segment which is not further analysable. Romani,

however, as well as most actual languages close to the agglutinative or inflective type, exhibits a much more complicated picture. Thus, the general principles of determining a relation between agglutinative and inflective features in the structure of polymorphemic words have to be briefly discussed.

rikon	-e	-s	-ker	-a
'dog'	(Class)	Masc.Sg	Poss	Obl.Fem.Sg

Figure 1: Segmentation of the noun

4.1 Analysis

The opposing word structure principles of cumulation and glutination are crucial for determining the typological character of a 'synthetic' language. It seems clear to me that the particular morphological analysis employed is relevant for typological interpretation. Some morphological analyses may even be a source of incorrect typological conclusions (I am indebted for this idea to Zavadil 1995:8-9, cf. also Comrie 1981:45). The effort to find which particular grammatical meaning is expressed by which particular segment (string of phonemes) may ultimately lead to the Word and Paradigm model of morphology (cf. Matthews 1974). For our present purposes, however, some segmentation is necessary, since typologically relevant concepts of cumulation and glutination are determined by the recognition of segments.

Positing a 'zero morph' (as an extreme case of the concept of morphological segment) in a word-form may, in some instances, distort the typological image of the analysed language: positing a 'zero' segment for the sake of word structure parallelism of forms is an outright *a priori* imposition of an agglutinative word structure upon the actual one (e.g. the segmentation of the nominative singular of *rikono* 'dog' as *rikon-o-Ø* or *rikon-Ø-o* making it conformable to accusative singular *rikon-e-s*; or even as *rikon-o-Ø-Ø* etc. conformable to dative singular *rikon-e-s-ke*). A 'zero' symbol will be employed in our analysis in the following sections only in case it is necessary to make explicit the absence of a positive segment as the *only* device of morphological opposition (e.g. accusative singular segmented as *rikon-e-s-Ø* in opposition to dative singular *rikon-e-s-ke* etc.).

The concept of cumulation can be employed on differing levels of abstraction. Cumulation of meanings in a word-form can be sought for in the linearity of phonological material, or in the linearity of more abstract segments (acquired through distributional criteria). The former approach is based on the search for immediate one-to-one correspondence between lexico-grammatical meaning and phonological form (if no constant segment is present, then the meaning is expressed cumulatively with another meaning or other meanings), while the latter interposes a mediating level between them: cumulation is then detected on the more abstract level of variants of morphological segments. Distribution of an allomorph would be treated as cumulation by the 'immediate' analysis: if distribution of a segment is restricted, then the meanings of the possible environments are co-designated (i.e. cumulated) by the segment. E.g. the Romani segments *-v-* in *kerav* 'I do' and *-om-* in *kerd'om* 'I did' cannot be disclosed by the 'immediate' analysis as the 1st person singular markers, unless cumulation with tense, aspect and mood meanings in the two 'person-number' affixes is recognized.

Matthews (1974:147-149) recommends that fused exponence, overlapping exponence, and cumulative exponence proper, which all would be treated alike by the 'immediate' segmentational analysis, be distinguished from each other. Here, similarly, cumulation is considered a property of segments of the phonotactical level of abstraction. Phonotactically conditioned surface segments are not necessarily cumulative: e.g. *-tar* in *romestar* 'from the husband', and *-dar* in *romendar* 'from the husbands' mark the ablative case (in the 'immediate' analysis the segment *-ar* would be found to express the meaning). Although both cumulation as a principle of the morphological structure of a word-form, and phonotactically conditioned variation manifest inflectivity, the degree of typological significance of the former is higher.

5. Verbal inflection

Agglutinative languages, having the possibility of linear concatenation of non-lexemic morphemes in a word, can express a greater potential of semantics in verbs derivationally and/or inflectionally. On the other hand, in the inflective extreme, all possible combinations of verbal meanings would have to be expressed cumulatively in distinct single segments; this is less likely to occur. Actual inflective languages, therefore, combine inflective devices with non-inflective (mostly analytic and agglutinative) ones.

According to Bybee (1985), the degree of semantic 'relevance' of an element to a lexical element and the degree of generality and predictability of this semantic relationship correlates with the degree of closeness of connection of the two elements in form. Bybee's (1985:12) expression types are organized according to this diagrammatic principle: lexical (the most 'relevant', the least general and predictable) – derivational – inflectional – free grammatical –

syntactic. Free grammatical and syntactic expression is central in analyticity, while derivational expression is important in agglutination. In inflective languages, devices of analyticity are therefore used in the domain of less 'relevant', more general, and more predictable semantic relationships, and devices of agglutination in the domain of more 'relevant', more specific, and less predictable semantic relationships.

5.1 Analytic expression

There is a number of analytic features in Romani verb inflection. The subjunctive mood in SCR is, apart from one exception, expressed only by means of a modal particle (*te, mi, šaj, našti* etc.), without having any specialized synthetic forms (contrary to some other Romani varieties; see Section 11); this is a strongly analytic feature. The exception, which confirms the existence of the subjunctive as a morphological category, is the formation of the subjunctive of the verb 'to be' from a particle and suppletive forms: *som* 'I am' vs. *šaj avav* 'I can be', *hiňi* 'she is' vs. *šaj jel* '(s)he can be', *salas* 'thou were' vs. *našti uľal* 'thou could not be' etc. (see discussion in Boretzky, this volume). The conditional present is in a similar way confirmed to be a specific formal categorical value, not merely a function of the indicative imperfect: *salas* 'thou were' vs. *avehas* 'thou would be' etc.. The almost general homonymy of the conditional present with the indicative imperfect forms, is nevertheless an analytic feature (see Section 7). In SCR and some Romani varieties strongly influenced by Slavic languages (Boretzky & Igla 1994:402), this homonymy is facultatively precluded, but, again, by means of an analytic particle (SCR *asavas* 'I was laughing / I would laugh' vs. *bi asavas* 'I would laugh').

Predicative negation in Romani is not expressed by crystallized agglutinative means in contrast to more agglutinative languages such as Turkish (*yazıyorum* 'I write' vs. *yaz-mı-yorum* 'I do not write'), although the analytic character of the negative morphemes is not without doubt, which is reflected by arguments as to whether to write the morphemes as separate graphic words or not. Passive voice in SCR is expressed either analytically or synthetically. Synthetic 'passives' (expressing not only passive, but also stative and inchoative meanings) are not inflectional, since they are not lexically general and their meaning is not generally predictable. The position of the analytic passive of the type *te jen mardo* 'to be (being) beaten' in SCR (Lípa 1963:103) is not clear as to whether it is general (for transitive verbs) or not; the construction of the auxiliary verb + the passive participle is much more common in Romani dialects of Western Slovakia: *andre amaro gav hi terďi khangeri* 'in our village a church is

standing' (Hübschmannová 1995:35). The status of the passive expressed analytically by means of a reflexive pronoun (Lípa 1963:103) from the point of
view of its lexical generality is also obscure.

A typological interpretation of analytic features in Romani is somewhat
problematic. In terms of combinations of properties of the individual *extremes*,
the analytic features, of course, exhibit the analytic type. However, in the light
of what has been said about the plausible combination of inflective and analytic
means in verb inflection, the analytic features in Romani verbs may be regarded
as a deviation *from* agglutination, rather than specifying the type they exhibit.

5.2 Synthetic expression

The number of positive inflectional suffixes in SCR verb forms ranges from
zero to four (*sikhl'-uv-a-v-a* 'I learn'), the average being two or three. The fact
that there are forms with more than one suffix is clearly agglutinative. With most
verbs, the imperative form of the 2nd person singular has no positive inflectional
formant; the imperative is the unmarked member of mood oppositions in a third
of the languages of the world (Bybee 1985:53-54). The fact that base form verb
inflection prevails in Romani, i.e. that with most verbs there is a form equal to
the stem, manifests the high valuation of diagrammaticity, which is typical for
agglutination. Some verbs, however, possess stem inflection (the imperative being, for example, *chut'-i* 'jump', *chud-e* 'get, catch', *sikhl'-uv* 'learn'). Both
'zero' and positive imperative forms exhibit an inflective word structure, having
a unimorphemic formant.

The interpretation of the formants in *asa*(-Ø) 'laugh' or *chut'-i* 'jump' as
being unimorphemic is determined by the analysis accepted in Section 4.
Positing a second segment (*chut'-i-Ø* and *asa-Ø-Ø*) would inadequately im-
pose parallelism: both the *-i* in *chut'i* and the 'zero' segment in *asa* sufficiently
differentiate the forms from any other form of the respective verbs (e.g. *asa*
from *asav* 'I laugh' even though the latter has a bimorphemic formant itself; cf.
below). On the other hand, the single 'zero' segment in *asa* must be posited,
since it is the *only* means differentiating the form from some other ones.
Although there are many forms with one positive affix only (*asa-v* 'I laugh' *asa-l*
'(s)he laughs' etc.), the only means of differentiating them from some other
forms (*asa-v-a* 'I will laugh', *asa-l-a* '(s)he will laugh' etc.) is the absence of a
positive expression. The stating of an agglutinative bimorphemic formant is
therefore necessary.

The only inflectional non-finite form is the passive participle, which contains agglutinatively expressed classificatory suffix ('participle marker') and the

adjectival cumulative suffix (see Section 6): e.g. *ker-d-o* of *kerel* 'do, make'. Unlike some other dialects, there are no participle-like forms of the 3rd person singular preterite in SCR (see Section 11). Regular finite forms have a cumulative morphemic segment of person and number, which also expresses a complex of tense, aspect and mood meanings, there thus being two sets of person-number segments (Figure 2), which is an inflective feature (see Section 7). Some of the segments of the second set (β-forms) show certain agglutinative features: the 1st singular *-om-* and the 1st plural *-am-* could be interpreted as bimorphemic, *-m-* being the exponent of the 1st person. However, this pattern is not regular (cf. a different situation in other dialects, in Section 11).

'laugh'	1st Sg	2nd Sg	3rd Sg	1st Pl	2nd Pl	3rd Pl
α	-V-	-S / -H-	-L-	-S/-H-	-N-	-N-
Ind Pres	asa-v	asa-s	asa-l	asa-s	asa-n	asa-n
Ind Fut	asa-v-a	asa-h-a	asa-l-a	asa-h-a	asa-n-a	asa-n-a
Ind Impf	asa-v-as	asa-h-as	asa-l-as	asa-h-as	asa-n-as	asa-n-as
= Cond Pres						
β	-OM-	-AL-	-A(S)/-AH-	-AM-	-AN-	-E/-EH-
Ind Pret	asa-ň-om	asa-ň-al	asa-ň-a(s)	asa-ň-am	asa-ň-an	asa-n-e
Cond Pt	asa-ň-om-as	asa-ň-al-as	asa-ň-ah-as	asa-ň-am-as	asa-ň-an-as	asa-n-eh-as

Figure 2: Regular finite forms

Inflectional meanings of tense, aspect and mood are expressed by agglutinative devices, namely by a chain of affixes. The difference between preterite (perfect, aorist) and imperfect is partly an aspectual one; the inflectional aspect opposition restricted to the past tense must be distinguished from the derivational aspect, which is expressed by means of employing prefixes of Slavic origin in SCR as well as in some other Romani varieties, and which is in the process of formation (Boretzky 1989:368). The traditional non-compound terms (imperfect for past imperfective etc.) do justice to the fact that the temporal and aspectual meanings are not expressed separately.

Two different structures of tense, aspect and mood morphology can be considered: the semantic (or more widely functional) structure and the formal structure. The ideal agglutinative solution would be a matching / isomorphism of both structures: any combination of the categorical values of tense, aspect and mood would be expressed by concatenation of the respective markers. The universal / common semantic restrictions on combinations, e.g. the imperative being usually indifferent as far as tense is concerned, and language-specific cumulations of meanings and neutralizations of certain meaning oppositions (e.g. indicative imperfect vs. conditional present in Romani), reduce the degree of isomorphism. The determining of isomorphism of the semantic and formal structures is analysis-dependent: the way a paradigm is constructed may influence the resulting typological statement. Again (cf. Section 4), an *a priori* accepted analysis may distort the typological image of the analysed language; an example of this may be an *a priori* assumption about the existence of an *invariant* meaning of grammatical units (cf. Novák 1959). Nevertheless, the perfect matching of both structures seems to be far less common than perfectly agglutinative word structure.

Is there any semantic correlate to the formal differentiation between α-forms and β-forms? Does the same semantic relation hold true between the forms *asav* and *asav-as* as does between *asaňom* and *asaňom-as*? According to the traditional labels of the categorical values, there is no perfect analogy between the formal and the semantic structures: although *-as-* could be considered to be the marker of the conditional mood, it may also mark the imperfect; *-ň- / -n-* (etc.) could be considered to be the markers of 'perfectness' (i.e. of one of the meanings of the preterite and one of the pluperfect), if they did not also mark the conditional past – moreover, the pluperfect meaning has not been recorded in SCR. Matras (1994a:69-114) has suggested an interpretation of the Romani verbal system based on a functional analysis in terms of the semantic and pragmatic properties of the verb forms as well as their communicative properties concerning mental processing of the linguistic events by the hearer. The imperfect and conditional (and pluperfect) *-as-*, for example, is then interpreted as a 'mental caesura' (Matras 1994a:73, 82, 99) between the actual knowledge of the hearer and the information about an event presented by the verb stem; the difference between the tense-aspect-mood complexes α and β is understood as being that between progressive and resultative aspect forms (Matras 1994a:71, 96, 99). The interpretation of the 'participle markers' as aspect markers is justified by their adherence to Bybee's (1985:33-35) diagrammatical principle of morpheme order with respect to a stem: aspect is predicted to be expressed closely to the stem. The only violation of the principle in Romani is that markers of agreement precede tense-mood markers. However, this particular ordering has been explained by Matras (1994a:69-114) in terms of his analysis.

Most verbs have a positive thematic / classificatory segment, which cumulatively co-designates grammatical meanings of tense, aspect, and mood (complexes α vs. β) as well as person and number: e.g. *as*-A-*l* '(s)he laughs' vs. *ker*-E-*l* '(s)he does' vs. *sikhľ*-O-*l* '(s)he learns'; *asa*-Ň-*om* 'I laughed' vs. *ker*-D'-*om* 'I did' vs. *kam*-Ľ-*om* 'I loved' vs. *sikhľ*-IĽ-*om* 'I learned' etc. (the thematic affix in β equals to the 'participle marker' of the same verb). The classificatory segment can be unimorphemic or bimorphemic, the first person being marked in length and/or shape of the segment (*-a-* vs. *-e-*, *-uv-a-* vs. *-o-*).

5.3 Variants

Contracted forms of the 1st person singular in the indicative future (*asá* 'I will laugh' or *kerá* 'I will do') and in the indicative imperfect / conditional present (*asás* 'I was laughing' etc. or *kerás* 'I was doing' etc.), which are more common than uncontracted forms (*asavas* etc. do not even exist in the SCR dialects decribed by Lípa 1963:105), represent a local tendency towards the inflective character of word structure. Whatever the morphological analysis, the forms lose their original formal transparency. Moreover, an introflective feature is exhibited by the opposition of the contracted *asá* [as'a] and the imperative *asa* ['asa]. Elision of *-e-* in forms of the 3rd person in the indicative future (*kerla* '(s)he will do', *kerna* 'they will do') and in the indicative imperfect / conditional present (*kerlas* '(s)he was doing', *kernas* 'they were doing') is also an inflective feature. Although it is a classificatory segment which is elided, the subclassification of verbs (see Section 7) remains intact in its totality, and, moreover, parallelism of positive suffixes in different forms is lost.

6. Nominal inflection

The number of positive inflectional suffixes in Romani noun forms ranges from zero to four, the average being two or three; exactly the same numbers have been found in verbal forms. The fact that there are forms with more than one suffix is clearly agglutinative. The form with no positive inflectional formant is the nominative singular of some original nouns, both masculine and feminine. There are many noun subclasses with a positive suffix in the nominative singular, i.e. stem inflection is common (e.g. *rakl-o* 'boy', *rakl'-i* 'girl', *grof-o-s* 'count', *rokl'-a* 'skirt'), which brings Romani near to inflectivity in this respect. On the other hand, in languages which are more inflective, there can even be a non-nominative form equal to the stem, i.e. a counter-diagrammatic instance (e.g. Czech *žen-a* 'woman': genitive plural *žen*).

In the nominative and vocative of most noun subclasses, the case meaning is cumulated together with number and gender in a 'zero' expression or in a positive formant containing one suffix. The inflective character of those cases which have a purely syntactic function is also known from other languages where agglutinative features prevail, for example from Finnish (plural in most cases *-i-* / *-j-* vs. cumulative nominative plural *-t*). The remaining case markers are, following Friedman (1991), considered here to be suffixes, i.e. not postpositions, and, consequently, interpreted as genuinely agglutinative (see Section 10; cf. also Matras, this volume). In the noun forms with more than one suffix

(Figure 3), it is necessary to take into consideration the interplay of glutination and cumulation in the principally agglutinative structure. The forms of accusative of animate nouns, dative, locative, ablative, and (somewhat irregularly) instrumental and possessive have a parallel structure, the form of the accusative animate having no positive expression for case.

	M Sg (-s-)					F Sg (-a-)	Pl (-en-)
	phral- 'brother'	grof- 'count'	lavutar- 'fiddler'	pap- 'grandfather'	chart'- 'smith'		
AccAn	-E-s	-O-s	-I-s	-U-s	-A-s	-a	-en
Dat	-E-s-ke	-O-s-ke	-I-s-ke	-U-s-ke	-A-s-ke	-a-ke	-en-ge
Loc	-E-s-te	-O-s-te	-I-s-te	-U-s-te	-A-s-te	-a-te	-en-de
Abl	-E-s-tar	-O-s-tar	-I-s-tar	-U-s-tar	-A-s-tar	-a-tar	-en-dar
Instr	-E-ha	-O-ha	-I-ha	-U-ha	-A-ha	-a-ha	-en-ca
Poss	-E-s-ker-	-O-s-ker-	-I-s-ker-	-U-s-ker-	-A-s-ker-	-a-ker-	-en-ger-

Figure 3: Nominal inflection

The segment preceding the case marker expresses gender and number cumulatively. The forms of the plural and of the feminine singular of these cases have a bimorphemic inflectional formant, while masculine singular formants are trimorphemic. The segment closest to the stem of masculine singular noun forms is a thematic / classificatory suffix: it is a means of masculine nouns' subclassification (see Section 7). The different position of different means of classification is worth noting: the thematic suffix stands closer to the stem than the marker of gender (and number).

6.1 Instrumental

A slight deviation from the regular agglutinative pattern can be seen in the instrumental of masculine singular. Its formant consists of two *positive* segments only; however, how this fact is interpreted typologically depends on the morphematic analysis employed. The formant requires either a bimorphemic interpretation (which results in a consideration of the form as more cumulative, i.e. inflective in its structure) or the determination of a 'zero' allomorph of the masculine singular morpheme (which results in considering the form more glutinative, i.e. agglutinative in its structure). Nevertheless, the allomorphy assumed in the latter analysis is an inflective feature by itself (see Section 8).

6.2 Possessive

The forms of the possessive case are considered here to be a part of the paradigm of a noun: 12 (8 non-homophonous) forms per noun (Figure 4). Since they are lexically general and fully predictable in their meaning, they must be considered inflectional, not derivational (cf. Friedman 1991:94-96). However, the possessive forms do represent a special instance: they form a subparadigm analogous to that of an adjective, making the whole inflectional paradigm of a noun asymmetrical; they behave syntactically much like adjectives, thus also possessing the possibility of further formal substantivization. The specific paradigmatic and syntactic character of the possessive forms corresponds to their specific word structure. The trimorphemic or quadromorphemic formants exhibit strong agglutination, although the last suffix is highly cumulative. Combination of more case markers in a word-form is common in some agglutinative languages, e.g. Basque: This can occur in Romani possessive forms (Friedman 1991:90) when substantivized (e.g. possessive + dative *phral-e-s*-KER-*en*-GE 'to those of the brother').

phral- 'brother'	Sg M		F		Pl M/F	
	Nom	Obl	Nom	Obl	Nom	Obl
Possessor: Sg	*-e-s-ker-o*	*-e-s-ker-e*	*-e-s-ker-i*	*-e-s-ker-a*	*-e-s-ker-e*	*-e-s-ker-e*
Possessor: Pl	*-en-ger-o*	*-en-ger-e*	*-en-ger-i*	*-en-ger-a*	*-en-ger-e*	*-en-ger-e*

Figure 4: Possessive forms

6.3 Adjectives

Adjectives (and the passive participles), if not substantivized, have only one suffix for their inflectional morphology, expressing cumulatively case (nominative vs. oblique), number, and gender; this is clearly an inflective feature. The suffix may have no positive expression. Substantivized adjectives (as well as the possessive case of nouns) have the same forms of the so-called oblique cases as nouns. Adjectives marked for non-originality contain a classificatory segment in the oblique case: e.g. nominative singular *šarg-o* 'yellow' (like *bar-o* 'big'), but oblique plural *šarg*-ON-*e* (vs. *bar-e*). Comparison of adjectives, a morphological category on the border between inflection and derivation, is in SCR implemented by a non-cumulative suffix (*-eder-*) in the comparative, and by this suffix + a non-cumulative prefix (*jekh-* etc.) in the superlative; comparison is clearly agglutinative. Also the formation of deadjectival 'passive' and causative verbs is very regular (cf. Hübschmannová & Bubeník, this volume) and this strengthens the agglutinative character of Romani.

6.4 Diminutives

The nominal and adverbial derivational category of diminutives is almost lexically general and contributes to the agglutinative component of Romani. At the same time, its morphological peculiarities increase noun subclassification of original nouns: e.g. *phralor-o* 'little brother' is declined as *rikon-o* 'dog', but it retains the nominative plural suffix of its non-diminutive basis (*phralor-a* 'little brothers' as *phral-a* 'brothers', but unlike *rikon-e* 'dogs'). The diminutive suffixes also serve as one of the means of differentiation between original and non-original nouns (*-or-* vs. *-ic-* and *-c-*). Diminutives justify the bimorphemic analysis of nominative singular formants of non-original masculine nouns in SCR: *lavutar(-i-s)* 'musician', *chart'(-a-s)* 'smith', *pap(-u-s)* 'grandfather', and diminutives *lavutar-i-c(-i-s)*, *chart'-a-c(-i-s)*, *pap-u-c(-i-s)*.

7. The structure of paradigms and word classification

In an inflectional paradigm, some forms may be homophonous. In this case, mostly, neutralizations of categorical oppositions occur, which is an analytic feature: a growth of word-form homophony would lead, ultimately, to the loss of morphological oppositions, i.e. to analyticity. Non-neutralizing homophony, i.e. instances where a categorical opposition is not immediately affected, is quite common in inflective languages (e.g. Czech *muž-i* both dative singular and nominative plural of *muž* 'man').

If there is a homophony of semantically differing affixes in *different* paradigms ('grammatical homophony'), then the whole word-forms are distinct. The meaning of the affix form is then dependent on the meaning of the stem or a wider morphological construction it is attached to (e.g. the final suffix *-a* marks plural in *phrala* 'brothers', but future in *asala* '(s)he will laugh'), and vice versa (e.g. the stem *čor-* means 'steal' in *čorel* etc., but 'orphan, poor' in *čoro* etc.). The presence of such interparadigmatic homophony of affixes and, at the same time, the absence of the intraparadigmatic homophony imply a phenomenon termed 'synonymy of affixes' in PST: the same grammatical meaning is expressed by various segments, depending on the meaning of the other segments present in the word. Different sets of grammatically synonymous segments are mostly selected by the stem (e.g. the nominative plural markers in *phral-a* 'brothers' vs. *rakl-e* 'non-Romani boys' vs. *grof-i* 'counts'), but they are sometimes conditioned by grammatical meanings as well (e.g. the 1st person singular markers *-v* and *-om* in *asav* 'I laugh' vs. *asaňom* 'I laughed'). Different stems are suppletive, if they are not mutually segmentable and, at the same time, if they are selected by the grammatical meanings (which is the mirror phenomenon to grammatical synonymy).

The ambiguity of grammatical segments (i.e. grammatical homophony) as well as grammatical synonymy is peculiar to inflectivity, and properties of the inflective type are more susceptible to suppletion than those of the agglutinative type. The agglutinative extreme is optimal on the iconic parameter of semantic transparency (Dressler 1985:55), i.e. agglutinative affixes are typically non-ambiguous. Any complex meaning can be expressed by concatenation of the non-cumulative segments, which makes them independent of their morphological environment. Semantic independence and transparency of agglutinative segments do not favour grammatical synonymy. There is only one set of grammatical affixes and only one morphological class of lexemes in the agglutinative extreme, while the cumulative / idiosyncratic character of a word in inflectivity contributes to the immense morphological classification. This general notion entails such phenomena as a sharp differentiation between parts of speech, the presence of classificatory categories such as noun gender, and the abundance of morphological subclasses and 'irregularities' in a given word class.

In SCR, neutralizations affect only noun syntactic cases (nominative vs. accusative with inanimate nouns etc.), a few forms in verbs and, mainly, adjective forms. The analytic features of adjectival inflection, however, can be interpreted as a manifestation of agglutination in syntax (see Section 10). Non-neutralizing homophony in the frame of a paradigm as well as grammatical homophony is very rare in Romani.

Romani has only a few lexemes with suppletive forms, namely the verb 'to be' (*s-, hin-* / *hiň-, u-, av-, j-, nane*) and a few other verbs, some adjectives in their comparison (e.g. *lačho* 'good' vs. *feder* 'better'), personal pronouns of the third person (*jo-, l-*), the definite article (*o, e, l-*), and some others. In this respect, Romani occupies an intermediate position between crystallized agglutination and crystallized inflectivity: a delimitation of Romani in relation to strongly inflective languages can be advanced by instances where Romani, unlike most inflective languages, does not exhibit suppletion.

Verbs and nominals are sharply differentiated in Romani. Only one verbonominal (verboadjectival) form is inflectional, namely the passive participle. The so-called adverbial participle (e.g. *ker-indos* of *kerel* 'do, make'), being derivational and unproductive, does not represent a regular verbonominal form, and is therefore of little typological significance. The infinitive, which does exist in SCR, represents a syntactic construction (cf. Section 10) rather than an autonomous morphological form, and its typological relevance in the domain of morphological word classification is equal to zero. A striking agglutinative feature is the facultative gender and number inflection in SCR of the copula in the present tense by means of adjectival affixes (masculine singular *hin-o*, feminine singular *hiň-i*, plural *hin-e*). The word structure of nouns and other nominals which have primarily a non-attributive rather than attributive function (so-called substantivals), such as personal and some interrogative pronouns, is in principle identical, although the particular inflectional devices are materially different. The weaker differentiation between some noun and adjective patterns (e.g. *raklo* 'non-Romani boy' as masculine *kalo* 'black', *rakl'i* 'non-Romani girl' as feminine *kal'i*; but *rakl'(ij)a* 'non-Romani girls' vs. plural *kale*) contributes to the wide-ranging potential for substantivization of adjectives (cf. Section 10) and their conversion into nouns.

Romani verbs are mainly subclassified by classificatory segments in α-forms (cf. Section 5; this subclassification tends to have a syntactic correlate in the category of transitivity), by various 'participle markers', and by imperative forms. The number of conjugational patterns is low. Romani nouns are not strongly differentiated into subclasses having more than a dozen (in SCR) of central and a few peripheral (*Del* 'God': accusative singular *Devl-es* etc.) patterns. The regular classificatory criteria are the classificatory categories of gender and animacy, the markedness of non-originality, and the nominative singular formant (equal to the stem, having an adjectival shape etc.). The category of animacy manifests itself in the different homonymical structures of paradigms, while the categories of gender and markedness of non-originality are manifested materially. The variety of different classificatory morphemes, the different nominative forms, and the different diminutive formations differentiate nouns according to the markedness of non-originality. Neither adjectives (with two original and one non-original pattern), nor adjectivals in general (demonstratives, declinable article etc.), are strongly morphologically subclassified: similarities prevail in the different inflections. However, the subclass of non-original adjectives has a positive material classificatory marker.

To summarize the typological position of Romani with respect to word classification, the sharp differentiation between verbs and nouns, the existence of general classificatory categories such as gender, and the existence of materialized classificatory devices, are clear manifestations of inflectivity. On the other hand, the relatively low rate of subclassification of individual parts of speech, the less clear-cut differentiation in nominals, and also the fact that the category of gender has only two values, contribute to a relative balance between the two types prevailing in Romani.

8. Morphonology and phonology

In the agglutinative extreme, any morphological meaning has a uniform realization. The predominantly syntagmatic character of word structure in agglutination provides an explanation for the autonomy of the shape of agglutinative affixes. From a diachronic point of view, the tendency for uniformity maintenance (phonological changes being slower and less effective than in inflective languages) contributes to the self-maintaining power of agglutinative languages (Sgall 1958b:16). The uniformity of form is much smaller and the boundaries of the morphological segments are less clear-cut in inflectivity.

Two prototypical cases of variation in the phonological form of morphological segments (i.e. allomorphs determined through distributional criteria) can be distinguished: first, the formal variation is convertible into phonological alternations more or less common in other parts of the language structure, i.e. the segments are phonologically related (morphonological relationships); second, the segments are not phonologically related. The latter is often a case of grammatical synonymy. Prototypically, morphological variation can be conditioned either semantically (grammatically in most instances), or phonotactically. The semantically cumulative / idiosyncratic character of a word is a clear symptom of inflectivity, while the typological interpretation of the latter alternative is less obvious: vowel harmony, a phonotactically conditioned phenomenon, is typical for crystallized actual agglutinative languages.

Grammatical segments in the agglutinative type are formally autonomous through their phonological structure being similar to that of lexical morphemes, i.e. through being autosyllabic and including consonants. In contrast, the shorter inflective grammatical segments only form a syllable together with part of the stem, i.e. they mostly have the structure of -C, -V, or -VC. The important role of consonants in agglutinative grammatical segments renders vowels not to be more than carriers of syllabicity that are not loaded with an expression of grammatical meanings. Thus, vowel harmony in grammatical affixes is favoured by agglutination, the principle of uniformity being outweighed by the principles of the phonological structure of a word in actual languages.

Morphonological alternations may be the only means of expressing grammatical meanings in the word, which is an introflective feature: SCR has no such alternations (but variantly, cf. Section 5). Only alternations attendant to concatenative expressions of grammatical meanings are present in Romani. Phonotactically conditioned alternations in SCR appear mostly in nominal inflection: *t ~ d, k ~ g,* and *h ~ c* in case suffixes (cf. locative *mande*, dative *mange*, instrumental *manca* of 'I'); the word-final neutralization of the opposition of voiced vs. voiceless and aspirated vs. unaspirated, and, in some SCR dialects, also neutralizations such as *n ~ ň* (*phen* 'sister' vs. *pheň-a* 'sisters'), *n ~ nd* (*skamin* 'table' vs. *skamind-a* 'tables'), *s ~ st* (*vas* 'hand' vs. *vast-a* 'hands') etc.. SCR possesses no vowel harmony.

There are a few grammatically conditioned alternations: *s ~ h* in verbal inflection (e.g. *asa-s* 'thou / we laugh' vs. *asa-h-a* 'thou / we will laugh'); Ø *~ h* in segments *-e* / *-eh-* and *-a* / *-ah-* in verbal inflection (e.g. *asa-n-e* 'they laughed' vs. *asa-n-eh-as* 'they would have laughed'); *d ~ d', t ~ t', n ~ ň, l ~ l'* in adjectival (e.g. masculine *cikn-o* 'small' vs. feminine *cikň-i*, but also the diminutives *cikn-or-o* vs. *cikň-or-i*) and verbal inflection (e.g. *ker-d'-om* 'I did' vs. *ker-d-e* 'they did') as well as derivation (e.g. *rakl-o* 'non-Romani boy' vs. *rakl'-i* 'non-Romani girl'); *v ~* Ø in verbal inflection (e.g. *tav-e-l* 'cook' vs. *ta-d'-om* 'I cooked'), and so forth. The form of the 'participle marker' is determined both grammatically and phonotactically. In fact, the choice between *-n-* vs. *-ň-* is dertermined grammatically, and the choice between *-n-* / *-ň-* vs. *-d-* / *-d'-* is determined phonotactically. The use of morphophonemic ('alternating') phonemes in the marker stresses the inflective character of verb alternations. Verb inflection is generally less agglutinative than noun inflection in the domain of morphonology.

Romani autosyllabic affixes appear only in the case inflection of nouns (*-ke* / *-ge*, *-te* / *-de*, *-tar* / *-dar*, *-ha* / *-ca*, *-ker-* / *-ger-*) and in derivation. The verbal affixes are mostly consonantal (*-v-*, *-s-* / *-h-*, *-l-*, *-n-* etc.) or vocalic-consonantal (*-as-*, *-om-*, *-al-*, *-a(s)* / *-ah-*, *-an-*, *-e* / *-eh-*). Segments expressing inflective properties such as word classification (*-e-*, *-o-*, *-i-*, *-u-*, *-a-* and *-n-* / *-ň-*, *-d-* / *-d-*, *-t-* / *-t'-*) or attributive agreement (*-o, -i, -e, -a*), and cumulative segments mostly have a phonological structure typical for inflectivity. On the other hand, non-cumulative affixes exhibit an agglutinative phonological structure. Thus, it seems, inflective, resp. agglutinative features of different levels or dimensions tend to cluster together. Romani appears to have a relatively inflective phonological structure of grammatical segments: noun inflection, again, is more agglutinative than verb inflection.

9. *Word-formation*

Word-formation by specific affixes is favoured by agglutination. Suffixal derivation is by far the most common in Romani. The regular morphological expression of a high number of meanings and functions is something typical for agglutinative languages: diminutives, iterative, causative, factitive, and 'passive' (stative, inchoative) verbs in Romani, are regular formations on the border between word-formation and inflection.

Composition and juxtaposition of lexemic elements (the word-formational strategies peculiar to polysemicity) exist in a limited, but significant number of instances in Romani (Hübschmannová et al. 1991:637-641): *ternechar* 'youngster' (*tern-o* 'young' and *char* 'donkey'), *adadives* 'today' (*ada* 'that' and *d'ives* 'day'), *lačhejileskero* 'genial, warm-hearted' (*lačh-o* 'good' and *jil-o* 'heart'), *koromaťol* 'drink dead' (*kor-o* 'blind', *mat-o* 'drunk') etc.; *phrala pheňa* 'siblings' (literally 'brothers sisters'), *svetos vilagos* 'wide world' (literally 'world world'), *koro mato* 'drunk as a lord' (literally 'blind drunk'), *chal čaľol* 'eat enough' (literally 'eat satiate') etc.. The formation of the iterative / intensive verbs (suffix *-ker-*) is a feature on the border between polysemicity and agglutination (cf. the verb *ker-el* 'do, make'); a relatively strong polysemic character is obvious in such iterative derivational sequences as *phirel* 'walk', *phirkerel* 'walk, stroll', *phirkerkerel* 'stroll, rove, wander'. Compared to some clearly polysemic compounds of the verb *del* 'give' (e.g. *čhuridel* 'have a stitch', cf. *čhur-i* 'knife'), there are only traces of polysemicity, which has progressed to agglutination, in verbs such as *randel* 'scrape, rub' (**ran-*).

Inflectivity favours word-formation by means of inflections, without any specific derivational affixes (e.g. *-o* in *bar-o* 'big' and *-ol* in *bar-ol* 'grow' are the inflectional formants as well as the only means of word-formation). This way of lexical enrichment is common only with 'passive' verbs (the example above) and some nouns in Romani (e.g. *rikon-o* 'dog' vs. *rikoň-i* 'bitch'). In general, agglutinative word-formation is very common in inflective languages, since non-cumulative symbolization of categories is mostly required in derivational morphology; its decay is tolerated only in inflectional morphology, as the categories are also expressed by syntactic means (Wurzel 1996:276).

In the analytic type, the lexicon has a weak formal organization, since autosemantic words, being monomorphemic, are not mutually derivable or segmentable. Semantically related words thus remain formally isolated (cf. English *calf* vs. *veal*). The main source of formally isolated words are borrowings from other languages (Skalička 1975); the favourability of the analytic type for loanwords is of interest for contact linguistics. Also periphrastic expression of some meanings, in contrast to their morphological expression in the 'synthetic' types, is preferred in analyticity. There are some instances of periphrasis in Romani in comparison with, for example, Czech: e.g. *kerel buťi* 'to work' ('to do' + the noun 'work') vs. Czech *pracovat* (derived from the noun *práce* 'work').

Words borrowed by Romani are integrated into 'synthetic' inflection without being left undeclinable, but there are distinct inflectional noun, adjective, and participle subclasses and the distinct derivational affixes, specialized for most

European (so-called athematic) loan-words (cf. Boretzky 1989; Bakker, this volume), which are thus marked for non-originality. This strategy for integrating loan-words has increased morphological word classification and may be therefore considered inflective.

10. Syntax

10.1 Agreement

Contrary to Zograf's (1976) consideration of both attributive and verb agreement to be of an inflective character, here subject verb agreement is considered to be common in both inflectivity and agglutination, while object agreement to be typical only of agglutinative languages. Since adjectivals and nouns are not morphologically differentiated in agglutination, it is highly uneconomical for the inflectional formants to occur more than once in an agglutinative nominal phrase. Phonological shortness of the inflective formants, on the other hand, and the existence of synonymous affixes, render possible a rather economical adjectival agreement in inflectivity. The lack of function words in the agglutinative extreme and the general tendency of agglutinative verbs to express morphologically as many meanings as possible implies marking of (the 1st and the 2nd) person (of subject, direct object, and indirect object) on the verb. To speak of person *agreement* does make sense in actual agglutinative languages, as personal pronouns exist, and are used at least emphatically. The verb agreement with a noun is morphologically unmarked in agglutination, while, due to cumulation with number, it is positively expressed in inflectivity. Verb agreement in gender or class is expected to be present in languages having a significant extent of both inflectivity (for classificatory categories to exist) and agglutination (as nominal meanings expressed by the verb signal blurring of differences between parts of speech).

Attributive case agreement in Romani is restricted to a binary opposition: nominative vs. non-nominative; some presence of agreement signals a certain portion of inflectivity. In SCR, in the stylistically marked postposition of an adjective, full agreement, the adjective having noun forms, is present. The lack of or the considerable reduction of adjectival inflection in 'normal' syntactic circumstances can be interpreted either as an analytic or as an agglutinative feature. The above-mentioned facts favour an agglutinative interpretation in Romani: it is the syntactic function, not the adjectival stem itself, which determines full or reduced inflection. The existence of subject agreement and the non-existence of object agreement determines a 'synthetic', but not strongly agglutinative character of Romani in this respect. The gender agreement in the 3rd person singular preterite, which has not been recorded in SCR, adds another morphological category expressed by the verb, namely evidentiality in a wide sense (Matras 1995a).

10.2 Word order

PST has not elaborated on word order typology and has not sought systematically for any connections between its own results and those of the Greenbergian school of thought. A grammatically 'fixed' word order is plausible in languages with a small number of morphological markers of grammatical relations, i.e. in analyticity and polysemicity. Inflective and introflective languages, on the other hand, having nominal cases and attributive and verb agreement, are likely to have a grammatically 'flexible' word order. Agglutination with no attributive agreement lies somewhere in between, although Skalička (e.g. 1965:259) assumes a grammatically 'fixed' word order. Word order in Romani is, in principle, grammatically 'flexible' and it can express discourse pragmatic functions (Matras 1995b). A typological interpretation of this feature is problematic, but it would not distance Romani from the area of inflectivity and/or agglutination.

Skalička (1951) distinguished two different agglutinative strategies of expressing case and spatio-temporal relations in a nominal phrase. The first one, more consistent as far as the extreme is concerned, is morphological noun cases without any function words, i.e. without prepositions and postpositions. The other strategy employs postpositions which are not sharply differentiated from nouns, being sometimes declinable. Since postpositions are favoured by SOV word order, and since the SOV languages mostly have an elaborate verb morphology (Bybee 1985:46-47), SOV word order is indirectly drawn into the PST connections of favourability as a feature preferred in the agglutinative type.

Prepositions, on the other hand, are typical for the analytic type. Inflective languages, again, are liable to combine with the analytic type in this respect, the difference being that an inflective preposition governs the noun case, while the analytic one is connected with a non-declined noun. Inflective prepositional constructions are peripheral in Romani, being obligatory with pronouns and only under special circumstances with nouns; analytic prepositional constructions are the most common and progressive.

10.3 Numeral constructions

The fact that the opposition of the category of number in Romani constructions with numerals (*jekh phral* 'one brother' vs. *duj phrala* 'two brothers') is
not neutralized is an inflective feature, not one of agglutination (cf. Hungarian
egy fivér 'one brother' like *két fivér* 'two brothers' vs. *fivérek* 'brothers'), although in some more inflective languages, there are even more morphosyntactic
peculiarities in numeral constructions (cf. Czech *jeden bratr* 'one brother' vs.
dva bratři 'two brothers' vs. *pět bratrů* 'five brothers').

10.4 Clauses

The low number of verbonominal forms in the inflective type makes condensation of more predications less common, and requires subordinate clauses
with verbal predicates. Agglutination, on the other hand, prefers condensation
through participles, gerunds, infinitives etc.. Romani exhibits clear inflectivity in
this respect. The existence of a syntactic infinitive, formed analytically from the
particle *te* and a finite verbal form either of the 3rd person singular (*kamav te
phenel* 'I want to say') in some SCR dialects (Hübschmannová et al. 1991:628)
or the 3rd and 2nd person plural (*kamav te phenen* 'I want to say') in others
(Lípa 1963:112), is difficult to interpret (Skalička 1942 offers no direct solution): It cannot be considered an agglutinative feature, since the SCR infinitive is
not an autonomous form. On the other hand, it is a means of condensation,
which is not typical for inflectivity (although actual inflective languages usually
have even a morphological infinitive). Finally, the analytic type would require a
non-inflected verbal form. It appears reasonable to consider the SCR infinitive a
typologically mixed construction, perhaps lying closest to the analytic strategy.
   The existence of nominal sentences as well as the existence of ergative constructions is a manifestation of clause structure diversity, which is considered to
be typical for the agglutinative type (Skalička 1984:62). Nevertheless, most agglutinative languages have no ergativity, which leads Skalička in one of his later
works (1984:62-63) to acknowledge a separate ergative type. The existence of
nominal sentences is connected to the low differentiation of word classes
(Skalička 1942, 1979:176): the structure of clauses with a nominal or with an
intransitive verb as the predicate is identical. The lack of a lexeme for predicative
possession, i.e. of the verb 'to have', is explained (Skalička 1958a:84) as an
asymmetry between the syntactic and the semantic structure of the clause. I do
not find these connections, which are given only in a form of abstract statements

and lack explicit lines of deductive explanation (in the probabilistic sense of favourability), sufficiently substantiated.

Evidence from actual languages, however, supports Skalička's conclusions: nominal sentences, predicative possession expressed through the help of the verb 'to be', and ergative constructions are mostly present in languages with a significant amount of agglutination. Ergativity does not exist in Romani, but nominal sentences are common in SCR: e.g. *joj lači* 'she (is) good', *oda o baro kher* 'this (is) the big house'. Also the absence of the verb 'to have' manifests agglutination: e.g. *man hin phral* (accusative of 'I' + is + nominative of 'brother') 'I have a brother'.

11. Comparison: Varieties of Romani

The basic typological character of the conservative (in Boretzky's 1989 sense) dialects of European(-American-Australian) Romani is more or less the same. Various Romani varieties differ due to inherited dialectal differences and later internal changes, but mainly due to the interference of different contact languages. Skalička (1968b:39-40) only outlined a typological characterization of a language league ('Sprachbund'): the common structures of the league are a combination of different types, the combination not being necessarily plausible in terms of favourability; any language of a given league is active in adopting only those features which are in accord with its own tendencies of development. Interference is a regular way of typological development.

A limitation of the comparison is the narrow selection I have made of descriptions, which are, moreover, of different method and detail. Data from the North Russian dialect (Ventcel' 1964 / Wentzel 1980 / Ventzel 1983, Ventcel' 1966), the Lovari dialect of Poland (Pobożniak 1964), Bugurdži (Boretzky 1993), and the Romani dialects spoken in Bosnia and Yugoslavia (Boretzky & Igla 1994; 'Yugoslav' for short) have been used. The comparison does not claim to be more than a mere sketch: only major and striking differences will be mentioned here.

11.1 Analyticity

The manifestations of analyticity in which Romani varieties actually differ, are the grammaticalized periphrastic constructions corresponding to synthetic forms in other varieties, and intraparadigmatic neutralizations or non-existence of certain categorical values.

An important analytic feature is exhibited by those Yugoslav varieties which possess uninflected particles for the formation of the future tense. The North Russian dialect has two imperfective future constructions: one congruent in person and number, i.e. more inflective, and one with reduced person congruence, both of which are, nevertheless, also formed periphrastically. Polish Lovari as well as SCR, show agglutination in the formation of the future. A syntactic infinitive as a more or less analytic feature exists, beside SCR, in the South Russian dialect of Romani (Wentzel 1980:93-94). In the North Russian dialect as well as in the Yugoslav varieties and Polish Lovari, a congruent construction, which has a more inflective than analytic character, is used instead (cf. a pragmatic explanation given in Matras 1994b:201). In Polish Lovari as well as in SCR, a periphrastic passive voice is in the process of grammaticalization, which is a striking analytic tendency. The conditional mood is either expressed analytically, using the subjunctive, the future or a special conditional particle (*te*, *ka*, and *bi* etc. respectively), or, as in SCR, Polish Lovari, and in the North Russian dialect, it is a function of the indicative forms of the imperfect and the pluperfect.

Prepositional constructions with a non-declined noun, common in SCR as well as in Yugoslav varieties, manifest a strongly analytic feature. Analyticity is even stronger in Lovari and Bosnian Gurbet, since pronouns in prepositional constructions are restricted in case as well. On the other hand, the North Russian dialect is less analytical in this respect, since nominative prepositional constructions occur, except for a few prepositions, only with inanimate nouns. Non-original nouns in many Yugoslav varieties are rarely declined (Boretzky & Igla 1994:380), being replaced by prepositional constructions; locative is rare in Polish Lovari, and neutralized with inanimate nouns in the North Russian variety; both locative and ablative are rare in Yugoslav dialects, etc.. The fact that some prepositional constructions may substitute a nominal case form, and that there are neutralizations of case is clearly analytic (see discussion in Matras, this volume).

In Polish Lovari and in Kalderaš, which are more analytic than other varieties in this respect, the category of number is affected by neutralization in the nominative of a number of nouns. In most dialects, unlike SCR, Lovari and the Prizren dialect, there is a neutralization of number and gender in the oblique case of adjectivals (Boretzky & Igla 1994:381-382). This morphologically analytic feature contributes to a reduction of attributive agreement, which is a syntactically agglutinative feature. In Polish Lovari, the preterite as well as the verb 'to be' have, in contrast to other dialects, number neutralization in the 2nd person. In the North Russian dialect, the 2nd and 3rd person plural are also neutralized in the preterite. The number of tense and mood forms is also typologically relevant: the pluperfect form (only the past conditional function being recorded in SCR) is absent from the North Russian dialect, and some Yugoslav varieties, in addition, lack also the imperfect form. A more pronounced analytic feature than a neutralization of categorical values is their consecutive periphrastic expression; this is the case of Arli imperfect and pluperfect. Varieties with present indicative *a*-forms show less analyticity in this respect than the varieties (Vlax as well as SCR) where the only difference between the present indicative and the subjunctive is the subjunctive particle.

A typological interpretation of the comparative and superlative in Vlax dialects as well as in Arli and Bugurdži depends on the morphological interpretation of the segments *maj, po, naj, em* etc.. Boretzky & Igla (1994:383) speak of analytic formation by means of borrowed particles of comparison, in the case of *maj-*, however, the term 'prefix' is used as well. Boretzky (1989:366) uses the term 'marker' for a graphically separate segment. The terminological vacillation may (but need not) signalize the transitional analytic-agglutinative character of the segments. The fact that in Vlax varieties the comparative and superlative are morphologically identical is, nevertheless, a manifestation of analyticity.

11.2 Agglutination

The emphatic imperative suffixes (*-ta, -ba*) in the Yugoslav varieties and in Polish Lovari, the facultative suffix of the 2nd plural imperative (*-t'e*) and the reflexive suffix (*-pe*) in the North Russian dialect, as well as the emphatic suffix with some verbs of motion (*-tar*) in Vlax dialects, clearly manifest the agglutinative word structure. Also prefixes of Slavic origin, extensive particularly in SCR, Polish Lovari, and the North Russian dialect, exhibit agglutination.

More problematic and partially analysis-dependent is the interpretation of thematic suffixes in nouns. In Bugurdži, for example, the productive class of non-original nouns has a thematic suffix even in plural oblique forms: Bugurdži *májstoros* / SCR *majstros* 'master' with the dative plural *majstor-o-j-én-ge* vs. *majstr-en-ge*. The Bugurdži word structure of nouns is therefore more agglutinative than that of SCR, even if one interprets the *-j-* segment as a non-morphological / postmorphological phenomenon ('antihiatus' consonant). A possible argument against this conclusion seems to be the fact that the suffix *-o-* has the higly inflective function of noun subclassification. The noun, however, is sufficiently classified by its singular forms even in SCR: the only difference is that Bugurdži is more consistent in maintaining parallelism in the word structure of singular and plural noun forms, which is an agglutinative feature. Moreover, the aforementioned *-j-* segment does have a morphological function in oppositions such as *bakr-en-ge* (dative plural of 'ram, sheep') vs. *bakr-j-en-ge* (dative plural of 'ewe'), or *džuv-en-ge* (dative plural of 'louse') vs. *phuv-j-en-ge* (dative plural of 'earth'); in SCR only forms *bakr-en-ge*, *džuv-en-ge*, and *phuv-en-ge* are possible.

In most dialects, the verbal person-number suffixes of the preterite and the past conditional (as well as of the present of the copula) have a more agglutinative character than those in SCR and Sinti: not only *-m-* may be regarded as the exponent of the 1st person (singular *-om*, *-um* or *-em* vs. plural *-am*), but also *-n-* as the exponent of the 2nd person (singular *-an* vs. plural *-en*).

Dialects with a higher number of derivative verbal meanings are more agglutinative than others: e.g. causatives are abundant in SCR and Hungarian dialects (cf. Hübschmannová & Bubeník, this volume), but rare in Yugoslav varieties. The iterative / intensive transitivizing suffix is productive in SCR, Arli (*-ker-*), and in the North Russian dialect (*-k'ir-*). The developing aspectual system, which is becoming generalized in varieties under the influence of West and East Slavic languages (Boretzky 1989:368), is also an agglutinative progression. In SCR and Arli, the iterative / intensive suffix is a feature on the border between polysemicity and agglutination (cf. Section 9), while in the North Russian variety, it has already become rather agglutinative (derivational *-k'ir-* vs. lexical *-ker-*). Similarly, there is more agglutination in varieties where the inflection of verbs which are historically compounds of *dav(a)* 'I give', partly differs from that of the verb *dav(a)* itself: e.g. Arli preterite *dengjum* 'I gave' vs. *rodingjum* 'I looked for' (Boretzky & Igla 1994:399).

The weaker agglutinative differentiation between verbal and nominal forms can be observed in the 3rd singular preterite participle-like forms of some verbs, e.g. *gel-o* 'he went' and *gel-i* 'she went' (Boretzky & Igla 1994:396): they express the nominal category of gender and have an adjectival / participial shape. As has been shown by Matras (1995a), in some Romani varieties these forms perform a different function than the non-participial forms of 3rd singular preterite, e.g. *gel-as* '(s)he went'. This functional opposition increases the number of meanings expressed by a verb, which is an agglutinative feature. In some dialects, however, the different forms are conditioned by the lexical semantics of particular verbs (Boretzky & Igla 1994:396, Matras 1995a:119-120), which is a manifestation of grammatical synonymy, itself something typical of inflectivity. In SCR and the North Russian dialect, the agglutinative participle-like forms are not used. Predicative 3rd person nominal forms of the copula are very extensive in SCR (cf. Section 7), and there are copulas expressing gender and number of the 3rd person in some Yugoslav dialects as well (Boretzky & Igla 1994:404-406). The Vlax predicative form of adjectives (Pobožniak 1964:55) of the type *phuroj* '(s)he is old' is also a manifestation of the agglutinative lack of a clear differentiation between verbs and nominal parts of speech.

Uniformity of word structure as well as phonological uniformity of morphological segments is another agglutinative feature. The former may be exemplified by the nominative singular formant of non-original masculine nouns *-o* (etc.) as opposed to *-os* (etc.): the *-s-* segment is reserved for expressing masculine singular in oblique cases as it is with original masculine nouns in most Yugoslav dialects and in the North Russian dialect, e.g. nominative *sok-o* 'juice' vs. accusative *sok-o-s* as nominative *rakl-o* 'non-Romani boy' vs. accusative *rakl-e-s* (Boretzky & Igla 1994). In Kalderaš and Gurbet, a uniform classificatory suffix is present in the oblique forms of both numbers: dative singular *sok-o-s-ke* vs. dative plural *sok-o-n-ge* (Boretzky & Igla 1994:377); phonological uniformity goes hand in hand with constructional uniformity here. The absence of alternations in the formation of the preterite in some Vlax dialects and in the Prilep dialect (Pobożniak 1964:52-54, Boretzky & Igla 1994:396-401) contributes to a phonological uniformity of affixes. Vowel harmony, a morphonological phenomenon favoured by agglutination, can be found in the possessive forms ending in *-kor-o*, *-kir-i*, *-ker-e* in Arli and Bugurdži, while the shorter forms ending in *-k-o*, *-k-i*, *-k-e* present in Vlax dialects (Boretzky & Igla 1994:372) exhibit more inflectivity. On the other hand, the longer forms of instrumental *-sar* and vocative plural *-alen* are more agglutinative than their shorter counterparts.

11.3 Inflectivity

A typologically important feature is the number and stability of inflectional patterns. The more stable subclasses there are in a variety, the more inflective it is. Nevertheless, comparable descriptions are necessary for this domain, more than for any other: Pobożniak (1964), for example, pays much less attention to subclassification than Wentzel (1980) does. I would conjecture that SCR inflection is one of the least subclassified (weak subclassification of feminine nouns, complete inflectional integration of non-original verbs etc.). Differences in the weight of various classificatory criteria may also be typologically significant: in the North Russian dialect, for example, the noun animacy opposition seems to be having an increasing importance (different prepositional constructions, diverse homonymical structures of paradigms). Another example is that the gender opposition is lost in the plural in SCR.

One of the most striking inflective features is the optionally full attributive agreement of adjectives in the North Russian dialect; it is quite rarely used, however (Wentzel 1980:80). A few remarks about inflectivity in the syntax of Romani varieties, have been made in the paragraphs on analyticity in this section.

Contracted verb forms, present in SCR and Polish Lovari, are clearly inflective. In Polish Lovari, the conditional and the imperfect indicative may be distinguished by contraction (Pobożniak 1964:51), thus avoiding a complete neutralization of these categories. Also the differentiation between the preterite inflection and the copula forms (1st singular -em vs. sim) is a local inflective tendency. If it could be considered to be a reliable piece of evidence (Pobożniak 1964:44), a most striking inflective feature of Polish Lovari would be the grammatically conditioned allomorphy of -an- vs. -en- suffixes with feminine nouns. As plural forms of romñi 'wife' the following are given: possessive romñ-an-g-o and dative romñ-an-ge, but instrumental romñ-en-ca and ablative romñ-en-dar.

Morphonological alternations generally cause a lack of phonological uniformity of stems and of affixes. The Gurbet and Arli dialects seem to be the most inflective in this respect. In some of them, stem-internal alternations even occur (e.g. bori 'bride' vs. bojra 'brides'); since they must be accompanied by affixes, it is a combined introflective-inflective feature. The fact that some word forms are distinguished only by a different accent position (e.g. North Russian Romani 'wife' in singular: nominative romní vs. vocative rómni; Bugurdži 'uncle, mother's brother' in singular: nominative dájos vs. accusative dajós) is introflective. Phonological shortness of affixes as a property of inflectivity has been mentioned in the final paragraph on agglutination in this section.

Problems of typological interpretation and comparison may arise if a dialect exhibits different local tendencies to different types, or if two dialects tend towards the same type in different respects, which is often the case of Romani varieties compared. Some more definite conclusions are given in Section 13.

12. Comparison: Indo-Aryan languages

A brief and basic examination of the typological position of Romani among New Indo-Aryan (NIA) languages is carried out in the next paragraphs.

12.1 Verbs

Verb inflection is elaborate in the subcontinental NIA languages, being carried out by 'synthetic' as well as periphrastic means. Finite forms, unlike in Romani, commonly have a tense-mood auxiliary, which may be inflected for subject agreement categories. Verb agreement is often expressed by adjectival number-gender suffixes, which shows an agglutinative weak classification; an adjectival verb agreement does not exist, however, in the Eastern NIA languages: here, though, this is due to the more agglutinative feature of the lack of gender. Most of the 'synthetic' parts of the verb forms possess an agglutinative structure, expressing non-cumulatively aspect and agreement; there are only few verb forms with an inflective word structure. Non-finite forms are incomparably less developed in Romani than in the subcontinental NIA languages, particularly in Marathi and Punjabi, which are strongly agglutinative in this respect. Non-finite forms are less common in the Eastern languages, and this weakens their otherwise clear agglutinative character. The most extensive inflectional systems of verbs have developed in Marathi and Nepali (Masica 1991:305, 314).

Derivational verbal morphology is rich and tends towards regularity; this agglutinative feature is present in Romani as well as in the subcontinental languages. Marathi and Kashmiri, for example, have a kind of an object agreement, which strengthens their agglutination. Passive voice is expressed agglutinatively or analytically according to individual languages: analytic expression is less common in Romani. A striking polysemic-analytic phenomenon are the Indian 'compound' verbs: the polysemic character is being converted towards analyticity by gradual formalization of the elements of 'specification'; Romani verbs of the type *čhuridel* or *phirkerel* (cf. Section 9), which nonetheless manifest a transition towards agglutination, are by far not so common.

Regular subclassification of verbs exists, in comparison to Romani, only to a small degree in the subcontinental NIA languages (Zograf 1976): e.g. according to transitivity mainly in Marathi and Sindhi (Masica 1991:261). A high number of irregularities is present in Sindhi, Punjabi, or Gujarati, while Hindi, in this respect, is the most agglutinative (Masica 1991:296, 300). Nevertheless, grammatical synonymy is common (different agreement suffixes in forms of differing aspect, tense, and mood), which is an inflective feature. Generally, the subcontinental NIA languages are more analytic in their verbal systems than Romani. Although they exhibit a comparable portion of agglutination in the verbal word structure, they are more agglutinative with respect to verb subclassification and to the differentiation between verbs and nominal parts of speech.

12.1 Nouns

Marathi, Gujarati and Konkani exhibit clear inflectivity in having three values of the classificatory category of gender. The Eastern NIA languages, having no gender, are clearly agglutinative. Romani as well as the remaining NIA languages (including Sinhalese with its primary category of animacy) occupies an intermediate position, being still inflective in this respect. The reduction of gender the farther east one goes is connected with the profound reduction of adjectival agreement. Also, number agreement is lost in the Eastern languages. If there are overt markers of noun gender, then they are materially identical with adjectival gender agreement markers, an agglutinative feature shared by most NIA languages. Materialized markers of definiteness, an agglutinative feature, are present in the Eastern languages and in Sinhalese. Inflective word structure, i.e. the cumulative expression of nominal categories, is absent from the Eastern languages, while agglutinative word structure of a few word-forms (there are at maximum seven agglutinative case markers) complemented by analytic postpositions is common to all subcontinental languages. Although the boundary between agglutinative and analytic expression is not clear, the postpositional analyticity itself may be interpreted in favour of agglutination (cf. Section 10).

From the point of view of subclassification, the most inflective languages are Shina and Marathi, while the most agglutinative are, again, the Eastern NIA languages. Romani occupies an intermediate position in this respect. Morphonological alternations are common in the more inflective Marathi, Kashmiri (though here vowel harmony also exists), Shina, and in Sinhalese. The prepositional character of Romani seems to be more analytic than the postpositional character of the other NIA languages. On the other hand, there are instances of less analyticity in Romani (e.g. the possessive forms), and there is no doubt about the strong agglutinative nature of its word structure in nouns.

12.3 Adjectives

The inflection of adjectives is partly or totally reduced in the NIA languages; this leads to a reduction of attributive agreement, which is an agglutinative feature. Eastern NIA languages and Sinhalese are, in this respect, the most agglutinative, since they lack any adjective inflection whatsoever. Sindhi, Konkani, and Marathi, on the other hand, show the least agglutination, having the least number of neutralizations of inflectible adjectives (8, 7, and 6 non-homonymous forms, respectively). Also Punjabi, Gujarati, and Landha are less agglutinative than Romani in this respect. Romani, with its 3 to 4 non-homonymous forms ('big': *baro, bari, bare*, and in some dialects *bara*), occupies an intermediate position between the Eastern and the Western languages, being roughly on a par with the remaining NIA languages. There is a tendency, to differing degrees, towards a complete loss of adjective inflection in all NIA languages, manifested by the expanding class of non-inflectible adjectives and by multiplying neutralizations. Regular substantivization of adjectives is an agglutinative feature shared by Romani, while the agglutinative comparison of adjectives, preserved or newly constructed (cf. the discussion in Section 11) in some Romani dialects, has been replaced by analytic devices in other NIA languages.

12.4 Syntax

The subcontinental NIA languages are, except for Kashmiri, verb-final and postpositional, which may be regarded as an agglutinative feature (cf. Section 10). Nominal sentences without a copula are peculiar to the agglutinative Eastern NIA languages as well as to Sinhalese. Ergativity exists in the Central languages, but not typically in the other NIA languages (cf. Matras 1995a:96-99); a typological interpretation of this difference according to PST is problematic (cf. Section 10). Although subordinate clauses are commonly used, the vast employment of non-finite verbal forms is a striking agglutinative feature.

13. Conclusion

The Slovak-and-Czech variety of Romani as well as the other varieties compared contain features of nearly all Prague School types. Polysemicity is present to a significant extent only in word-formation, while features of introflection are almost entirely absent. Agglutination, inflectivity, and analyticity, in this order of significance and in a complex interplay, constitute the typological image of Romani.

A typological interpretation of some phenomena is aggravated by the following facts. Firstly, some properties are common to more than one type. Secondly, some properties peculiar to an extreme may also be peculiar to a highly plausible combination of the extreme with another type. Thirdly, one and the same phenomenon may be interpreted in a different way according to a different viewpoint. In Romani, the second point is represented by some analytic features, which, with regard to the important inflective component in the language, may also be considered a manifestation of the plausible inflective-analytic combination. The third point mainly concerns the relation between agglutination and inflectivity in the structure of word-forms and paradigms, and may be exemplified by the inflective function but agglutinative realization of the classificatory morphological segments.

An explicit hierarchy of the typological significance of different properties has not been attempted in this paper. However, the flow of exposition does reflect the flow of probabilistic connections between various features, and it assumes a certain emphasis on morphology. The lines of explanation, less distinct especially in the domain of syntax, need further deductive examination and further evidence.

Agglutination in Romani manifests itself principally in the structure of word-forms, both in nominal and verbal ones. The other agglutinative features are: the rare grammatical homonymy of affixes, the less sharp differentiation between nominal parts of speech and a low rate of subclassification, the pronounced shape of nominal and derivational affixes, rich derivational morphology, restricted attributive agreement, and the nominal clauses. Nominal inflection is more agglutinative than verbal inflection in a few respects. The main inflective features in Romani are: extensive cumulation in the principally agglutinative word structure, a few inflective word-forms, grammatical classificatory categories, the materialized devices of subclassification, the sharp differentiation between verbs and nominals (possessing only one inflectional verbonominal form), the 'flexible' word order, the specific character of numeral constructions, and subordinate clauses.

Some properties of Romani clearly show its intermediate, agglutinative-inflective character: the interplay of both types in the word structure, the medium extent of word classification and suppletion, the character of morphonological alternations, and subject verb agreement. Some of the analytic features in Romani, namely the existence of pronouns, conjunctions, and prepositions, form a part of the inflective-analytic component. On the other hand, the existence of articles and syntactic particles, a number of analytic verb forms (including the syntactic infinitive in some dialects), and specific prepositional constructions exhibit a strong proper analytic component in Romani.

Zograf (1976:300-322) characterizes Romani as the most inflective and the least analytic of the New Indo-Aryan languages. The latter is decidedly true in the verbal system, less obviously in the nominal system. The more inflective character of Romani is clear in many respects, while there are also many typological features which place Romani rather *between* the Eastern and the Western languages. Nevertheless, Romani is typologically closer to the less agglutinative Western and Central Indo-Aryan languages.

Agglutination in Romani seems to be very stable and even increasing in some developments. However, dialects tending towards agglutination more than others cannot be clearly determined: I have found a specific agglutinative feature in every variety compared. Inflectivity is also stable, but the new inflective features, increasing especially due to phonetic changes, are mainly of a local character in the language systems: the self-maintaining power of agglutination precludes any radical change towards inflectivity. The analytic component of the typological image of Romani seems to be the most progressive: it is in analytical constructions that Romani varieties differ most strikingly. Analyticity seems to be a little more profound in Vlax and Balkan dialects than elsewhere. The position of SCR is not among the less agglutinative and decidedly not among the more analytic dialects.

References

Boretzky, Norbert. 1989. 'Zum Interferenzverhalten des Romani (Verbreitete und ungewöhnliche Phänomene)'. *Zeitschrift für Phonetik, Sprachwissenschaft und Kommunikationsforschung* 42:3. 357-374.
---- 1993. *Bugurdži. Deskriptiver und historischer Abriß eines Romani-Dialekts.* Berlin: Harrassowitz.
---- & Birgit Igla. 1994. *Wörterbuch Romani-Deutsch-Englisch für den südosteuropäischen Raum: mit einer Grammatik der Dialektvarianten.* Wiesbaden: Harrassowitz.
Bybee, Joan L. 1985. *Morphology. A study of the relation between meaning and form.* Amsterdam & Philadelphia: John Benjamins.
Čermák, František. 1978. 'Typology of the Germanic languages with special reference to Dutch'. *Folia Linguistica* 12. 65-106.
Comrie, Bernard. 1981. *Language universals and linguistic typology. Syntax and morphology.* Chicago: University of Chicago Press.
Dressler, Wolfgang U. 1985. 'Typological aspects of natural morphology'. *Acta Linguistica Academiae Scientiarum Hungaricae* 35:1-2. 51-70.
Friedman, Victor A. 1991. 'Case in Romani: old grammar in new affixes'. *Journal of the Gypsy Lore Society* 5:1-2. 85-102.
Hübschmannová, Milena. 1995. 'Pojem 'učit se' v romštině'. *Romano džaniben* 2:3. 35-40.
---- Hana Šebková, & Anna Žigová. 1991. *Romsko-český a česko-romský kapesní slovník.* Prague: Státní pedagogické nakladatelství.
Lípa, Jiří. 1963. *Příručka cikánštiny.* Prague: Státní pedagogické nakladatelství.
Masica, Colin P. 1991. *The Indo-Aryan languages.* Cambridge: Cambridge University Press.
Matras, Yaron. 1994a. *Untersuchungen zu Grammatik und Diskurs der Romanes. Dialekt der Kelderaša / Lovara.* Wiesbaden: Harrassowitz.
---- 1994b. 'Structural balkanisms in Romani'. In: Norbert Reiter, Uwe Hinrichs & Jiřina van Leeuwen-Turnovcová, eds. *Sprachlicher Standard und Substandard in Südeuropa und Osteuropa.* Berlin: Harrassowitz. 195-210.
---- 1995a. 'Verb evidentials and their discourse function in Vlach Romani narratives'. In: Yaron Matras, ed. *Romani in contact. The history, structure and sociology of a language.* Amsterdam & Philadelphia: John Benjamins. 95-123.
---- 1995b. 'Connective (VS) word order in Romani'. *Sprachtypologie und Universalienforschung* 48:1-2. 189-203.
---- 1996. 'Prozedurale Fusion: Grammatische Interferenzschichten im Romanes'. *Sprachtypologie und Universalienforschung* 49:1. 60-78.
Matthews, Peter H. 1974. *Morphology. An introduction to the theory of word-structure.* Cambridge: Cambridge University Press.

Mithun, Marianne. 1988. 'System-defining structural properties in polysynthetic languages'. *Zeitschrift für Phonetik, Sprachwissenschaft und Kommunikationsforschung* 41:4. 442-452.
Novák, Pavel. 1959. 'K otázce obecného vyznamu gramatickych jednotek'. *Slovo a slovesnost* 20. 81-87.
Pobożniak, Tadeusz. 1964. *Grammar of the Lovari dialect*. Kraków: Państwowe wydawnictwo naukowe.
Popela, Jaroslav. 1985. 'K otázce kombinace typologickych vlastností v jazycích'. *Bulletin ruského jazyka a literatury* 26. 37-67.
Sgall, Petr. 1958a. *Vyvoj flexe v indoevropskych jazycích*. Praha: Academia.
---- 1958b. 'Synonymie koncovek v indoevropskych jazycích'. In: *Sborník slavistickych prací věnovanych IV. meziárodnímu sjezdu slavistů v Moskvě*. Praha: Státní pedagogické nakladatelství. 11-17.
---- 1960. 'Soustava pádovych koncovek v češtině'. *Slavica Pragensia* 2. 65-84.
---- 1971. 'On the notion "type of language"'. *Travaux linguistiques de Prague* 4. 75-87. Reprinted in Petr Sgall, ed. 1984. *Contributions to functional syntax, semantics, and language comprehension*. Prague: Academia. 19-37.
---- 1979. 'Die Sprachtypologie V. Skaličkas'. In: Vladimir Skalička, ed. *Typologische Studien*. Braunschweig & Wiesbaden: Viewegh. 1-20.
---- 1988. 'Natürlichkeit, Syntax und Typologie'. *Zeitschrift für Phonetik, Sprachwissenschaft und Kommunikationsforschung* 41:4. 463-470.
---- 1993. 'Skaličkas Sprachtypologie und ihre Fortsetzungen'. *Sprachtypologie und Universalienforschung* 46. 318-329.
Skalička, Vladimír. 1935. 'Zur ungarischen Grammatik'. Reprinted in: Vladimir Skalička, ed. 1979. *Typologische Studien*. Braunschweig & Wiesbaden: Viewegh. 59-125.
---- 1941. *Vyvoj české deklinace*. Praha: Jednota češkych matematiků a fyziků.
---- 1942. 'Problém druhého slovesa'. *Česky časopis filologicky* 1. 9-14.
---- 1945. 'Über die Typologie der Bantusprachen'. *Archiv orientální* 15, 93-127.
---- 1946. 'Sur la typologie de la langue chinoise parlée'. *Archiv orientální* 15. 386-412.
---- 1951. *Typ češtiny*. Praha: Státní pedagogické nakladatelství.
---- 1955. 'Sur les langues polysynthétiques'. *Archiv orientální* 23. 10-28.
---- 1958a. 'Typologie slovanskych jazyků, zvláště ruštiny'. *Československá rusistika* 3. 73-84.
---- 1958b. 'Kakovy osnovnyje zadači i problemy tipologii slavjanskix jazykov?' In: *Sbornik otvetov na voprosy po jazykoznaniju k IV. meždunarodnomu s'ezdu slavistov*. Moskva: Nauka. 9-10.
---- 1965. 'Über die Typologie der finnisch-ugrischen Sprachen'. In: *Congressus secundus internationalis fenno-ugristarum* I. Helsinki. 494-498. Reprinted in: Vladimir Skalička, ed. 1979. *Typologische Studien*. Braunschweig & Wiesbaden: Viewegh. 258-262.
---- 1966. 'Ein "typologisches Konstrukt"'. *Travaux linguistiques de Prague* 2. 157-164.
---- 1968a. 'Die Inkorporation und ihre Rolle in der Typologie'. *Travaux linguistiques de Prague* 3. 275-279.
---- 1968b. 'Über die Typologie der Balkansprachen'. *Les Études balkaniques tchécoslovaques* 3. 37-44.
---- 1972. 'Über die typologische Eingliederung der Balkansprachen'. *Les Études balkaniques tchécoslovaques* 4. 27-33.

---- 1974. 'Typologischer Vergleich der Balkansprachen'. *Les Études balkaniques tchécoslovaques* 5. 5-14.
---- 1975. 'Lehnwörter und Typologie'. *Revue roumaine de linguistique* 20:4. 409-412.
---- 1977. 'Konstrukt-orientierte Typologie'. *Acta Universitatis Carolinae, Philologica 5, Linguistica generalia* 1.17-23.
---- ed. 1979. *Typologische Studien*. Braunschweig & Wiesbaden: Viewegh.
---- 1984. 'Die Ergativität und die Typologie'. *Acta Universitatis Carolinae, Philologica 1, Linguistica generalia* 3. 59-63.
---- & Petr Sgall. 1994. 'Praguian typology of languages'. In: Philip A. Luelsdorff, ed. *Prague School of structural and functional linguistics: a short introduction*. Amsterdam: John Benjamins. 333-357.
Ventcel', Tat'jana V. 1964. *Cyganskij jazyk (severnorusskij dialekt)*. Moskva: Nauka.
--- 1966. 'Cyganskij jazyk'. In: *Jazyki narodov SSSR. Tom pervyj. Indoevropejskie jazyki*. Moskva: Nauka. 630-651.
--- [Wentzel] 1980 *Die Zigeunersprache (Nordrussischer Dialekt)*. Leipzig: Enzyklopädie.
--- [Ventzel] 1983. *The Gypsy language*. Moskva: Nauka.
Wurzel, Wolfgang U. 1996. 'On the similarities and differences between inflectional and derivational morphology'. *Sprachtypologie und Universalienforschung* 49:3. 267-279.
Zavadil, Bohumil. 1995. *Současny španělsky jazyk II. Základní slovní druhy: slovesa*. Praha: Karolinum.
Zograf, Georgij A. 1976. *Morfologičeskij stroj novyx indoarijskix jazykov (opyt strukturno-tipologičeskogo analiza)*. Moskva: Nauka.

THE TYPOLOGY OF CASE RELATIONS AND CASE LAYER DISTRIBUTION IN ROMANI

YARON MATRAS
University of Manchester

0. Introduction

Case (in the broader sense of the term) is represented in Romani by a mixed system of three different structural layers, showing inflectional (Layer I), agglutinative (Layer II), and analytic (Layer III) features respectively. While the layered case system in itself is characteristic of Indo-Aryan (cf. Masica 1991: 231 ff.), or even to an extent of Indo-Iranian, Romani differs from many of its genealogical relations in its treatment of Layer II elements, which in Romani are agglutinated into case suffixes (see discussion in Friedman 1991). It also differs from Modern Indo-Aryan in the analytic component (Layer III), which in Romani is prepositional, and not postpositional. Since Older and Middle Indo-Aryan, like most of their modern descendants, are postpositional, prepositions in Romani may be considered to be quite young, and can be taken to represent the outcome of a process of typological shift which affected the overall syntactic structure of the language after it came into contact with the European, especially Balkan languages (cf. Matras 1994; Bubeník 1995 and this volume).

The mixed system of inflectional, agglutinative and analytic case representation in Romani is currently still at a stage of transition, with case endings generally declining and prepositions gaining ground. At this stage, the distribution of the respective markers varies according to the case role itself, the object of reference, as well as the dialect under consideration.

In this paper I attempt to provide a general account of the way case is represented in Romani. In the first part, the system of case layers is introduced, and some parallels and differences are drawn between Romani and related languages. Special attention is given to the analytic or adpositional component (Layer III), to the sources from which it recruits its forms, and to a basic semantic distinction which it contains - that between 'incorporative' and 'non-incorporative' local relations.

The second part deals with the distribution of synthetic case endings (Layers I-II). Here I discuss the Distribution Hierarchy, an implicational hierarchy which helps explain the fact that while some potential carriers of nominal inflection allow synthetic case endings, others do not, or only do so in a restricted manner. My claim is that the structural distribution of case endings, which makes them obligatory with pronouns, but not with nouns, and their semantic distribution with nouns along the Animacy Hierarchy recently pointed to by Boretzky (1993:22) and Holzinger (1993:30 ff.), in fact constitute a single distributional hierarchy. Carriers of case markers are arranged on this hierarchy according to prominence of reference or the degree of retrievability of the referent in discourse. The Distribution Hierarchy is therefore, essentially, one of pragmatic features, rather than a structural or semantic one.

Part three is devoted to the Stability Hierarchy of Layer I-II synthetic case markers. I discuss the stability of the Genitive, Instrumental, and Dative, which show no general tendency toward replacement by prepositions, as opposed to the lower positions on the hierarchy, occupied by the Ablative and Locative, which are more common candidates for such replacement. The Stability Hierarchy is a generalization about the extent to which case relations are expressed by case suffixes of Layer I-II, especially on the lower positions of the Distribution Hierarchy. But it also invites an interpretation in terms of diachronic depth, its lower positions being those local relations which were presumably affected earlier, and therefore more extensively, by the drift toward analytic, preposed case marking.

In part four I refer to Dialect Variation as a third dimension in the pattern of Layer I-II synthetic case retention. Dialect differences apply in particular to the actual distribution of Layer II markers along the Stability Hierarchy, the more conservative dialects showing a greater distribution of case suffixes on the lower positions, i.e. among elements that are less likely to be retained.

The three tracks followed below may be combined into a three-dimensional illustration of synthetic case retention in Romani. By tracing the position of a given nominal element, or other potential carrier of case, on each of the scales, it should be possible to explain, or predict, its actual behavior with respect to case marking.

The analysis is based on a comparative investigation of material representing five of the main dialect groups of Romani. Data on the Central dialect were taken from written sources published in Czechoslovakia between 1991-1992 (see list of sources at the end); I also consulted Hübschmannová et al. (1991). Data on Sinti were taken from a published Bible translation, and from Holzinger

(1993). For the non-Vlach dialects of the Balkans I consulted Boretzky's (1993) grammar and text collection of Bugurdži. My own tape-recorded data of spoken Lovari, along with informants' replies to a questionnaire, represent the Vlach group. Informants' replies to a set of questionnaires are also the basis for data on the Lešaki dialect of central Poland, representing the Northern or Polish-North Russian-Baltic group. Additional data were provided by an oral Romani translation into three different dialects (Lovari, Lešaki, and Gurbet) of a series of twelve childrens' booklets, transcribed and published by Verlag Pädagogischer Medien (VPM) in Hamburg, Germany.

1. Case layers: the overt marking of case relations

1.1 Layer I

Masica (1991:230 ff.) applies the term 'layers' to the components of a system of three basic paradigms used to mark case relations in the Indo-Aryan languages. Layer I consists of inflectional material inherited from Old and Middle Indo-Aryan. It is characterized by declensional differences, gender differences, and a singular/plural distinction. The declensional nature of Layer I affixes, their etymology, which makes them the oldest case markers in the current system, their synthetic nature, and the fact that they are attached directly to the (nominal or pronominal) base, all justify their working characterization as 'primary' case affixes (see Masica 1991:231).

Romani distinguishes three cases at the Layer I level: Nominative, Vocative, and Accusative. Nominative (NOM) is either represented by zero-marking, as in *manuš* 'man' (Accusative *manuš-es*), or by a nominative vowel ending, as in *rakl-o* 'boy' (Accusative *rakl-es*). The Vocative typically shows a vowel ending in the singular (*manuš-a*), and *-ale* in the plural (*manuš-ale*). As expected from its semantic function, it only appears with human animates. However, in many dialects, human referents which are not typically addressed in Romani may not take the Vocative either. Thus, the Vocative for *roma*, 'people' or 'men' of Romani descent, is *rom-ale*; but the word *gadže*, which is reserved for non-Romani 'people' or 'men', has no Vocative **gadž-ale*. Due to the clear restrictions on the distribution of the Vocative, it is excluded from this investigation and from the discussion below.

The Accusative (ACC) is marked by *-s* in the masculine singular and appears, according to declension class, as *-s*, *-es*, *-os*, or *-is* (in some dialects, *-s* is either aspirated, or it disappears completely, and ACC is only marked by change of stress). The Accusative marker for the feminine singular is *-a*, and for the plural *-n*, which appears as *-n*, *-en*, *-on* (masculine), or *-n*, *-en*, *-an* (feminine). The Accusative provides the extended base for the formation of the other synthetic cases, which are formed by attaching Layer II suffixes, and so in a sense it serves as a general Oblique, much like in the subcontinental Indic languages. However, it is necessary to distinguish between ACC, which is an independent case role with nouns and pronouns, and the Oblique marking on adjectives, possessive adjectives, and demonstratives, as well as numerals and definite and indefinite articles. The latter is part of a twofold inflectional paradigm in which only nominative and non-nominative are differentiated:

(1)   *mur-i   dej*
       my-NOM mother.NOM
       'my mother'
       dikhlem mur-a   da
       I.saw   my-OBL mother.ACC
       'I saw my mother'
       phendem mur-a   da-ke
       I.said   my-OBL mother-DAT
       'I said to my mother'

Consequently, I use the designation Oblique (OBL) only for adjectives, demonstratives, articles etc., while the Accusative for nouns is marked 'ACC', and the general oblique as the base for forming the agglutinated cases (*d-a-ke*) is taken for granted, and is therefore not glossed.

1.2 Layer II

Layer II elements in Romani are agglutinated suffixes which are attached to the base through Layer I affixes. While they are basically identical for all persons and declensions, the initial stop of the suffixes is voiced following *-n*, thus resulting in a split within the pronominal system (*man-ge* 'to me', *tu-ke* 'to you'), but also in a general difference between singular and plural (*rakl-es-ke* 'to the boy', *rakl-en-ge* 'to the boys'). Similarly, the *-sa* of the Instrumental is in some dialects affricated to *-ca* following *-n*. Masica (1991:233) characterizes Layer II elements in subcontinental Indo-Aryan as "reduced (typically one syllable or less) and unrecognizable forms of once independent words", a description which applies to the Romani forms as well.

At this level, five forms are distinguished: Dative (DAT), Ablative (ABL), Locative (LOC), Genitive (GEN), and Instrumental/Sociative (INSTR). (I use the abbreviations henceforth to denote the actual case affixes of Romani, while terms like 'genitive' and 'ablative' refer to universal semantic case roles). Figure 1 summarizes the synthetic formation of Layer I-II case marking in Romani, disregarding the Nominative and Vocative. Forms in brackets represent dialectal variations included in this study (the Genitive also varies according to the gender and number of the object of possession):

	sg. fem/masc		plural	
	Layer I	Layer II	Layer I	Layer II
ACC	-a/-s		-n	
DAT	"	-ke	"	-ge
ABL	"	-tar (-ter,-tyr)	"	-dar (-der,-dyr)
LOC	"	-te	"	-de
GEN	"	-ko (-kero,-kro)	"	-go (-gero, -gro)
INSTR	"	-sa (-ha)	"	-sa (-ca)

Figure 1: (Non-nominative) Layer I-II case markers in Romani

1.3 Layer III

Layer III elements are generally longer than one syllable, show a direct connection to another independent word, and are semantically more specific. Masica (p. 234) carefully defines them as case elements which are "potentially mediated" by Layer II suffixes. This holds for Romani with even more restrictions than for subcontinental Indo-Aryan: First, Layer III elements in Romani are preposed. They are structurally separated from Layer II case suffixes, and therefore cannot be 'mediated' by the latter in the strict structural sense. Second, of all Layer III elements, only *bi* 'without', always governs a Layer II suffix, namely GEN (*bi le rakl-esko* 'without the boy'). Other Layer III elements govern the LOC with top positions on the Distribution Hierarchy, i.e. with pronouns, and occasionally with human animates, but usually not with other nouns. In some dialects, borrowed prepositions which join Layer III take ABL, INSTR, or DAT suffixes.

1.4 The position of Romani case layers in Indo-Iranian

The layer system exists, at least historically, not just in Indo-Aryan, but in Iranian as well. Iranian provides an interesting comparison with Romani, since here too Layer III elements have shifted from postpositions to prepositions, and a general weakening of the suffix pattern has affected the system. Figure 2 pre-

sents a small sample of related languages in order to give a general impression of
the position of the Romani case marking system in Indo-Iranian:

	Layer III	Layer I	Layer II	Layer III
Romani	pala, ka, and-, paš-, etc.	sg. -s, -a pl. -n	-ke/-ge,-tar/-dar, -te/-de, -sa, -ko/-go	
Hindi		sg. -e pl. -ō	kā, ko, ne, se, mē, par	pās, sāth, sāmne, liye, etc
Kashmiri		sg. -is, -as pl. -an	hund	kyut, sı̄ı̄t, niš, etc.
Kurdish/ Kurmanji	bi, ji, li, di, etc.	sg. -ê pl. -an	ra, da, va	
Persian	az, bā, be, dar, etc.		rā	

Figure 2: The position of Romani case layers in Indo-Iranian

Layer I markers derive from the Old Indo-Aryan genitives *yāh* (sg.f.), *ānam*
(pl.), and *asya* (sg.m.), which in Old Iranian is aspirated to *ahya*, eventually
giving rise to a long front vowel in Kurmanji (cf. Bloch 1970:190; Sampson
1926:132-133). Apart from Romani, the consonant-final forms are preserved
among the Indic languages only in Kashmiri. Hindi shows the typical reduction
of Layer I markers to vowels. In West-Iranian, the Kurmanji or northern variety
of Kurdish is unique in preserving case distinction at this level, while Persian
has lost Layer I case suffixes entirely.

Layer II markers typically derive from late Middle Indo-Aryan or Middle
Iranian postpositions or postposed nominal elements, such as *kēra* indicating the
possessive, *anta* indicating the locative, *sahu* for the sociative, etc. (cf. Singh
1980:99 ff.). They have been integrated into the modern system in a general or
abstract meaning, compensating for the reduction of the case suffixes of the Old
system. The inventory of Layer II elements is restricted in all modern Indo-
Iranian languages, and while Romani and Hindi have several, Kurmanji has
only three *ra, da,* and *va,* and Persian just one, *rā,* denoting the accusative. Only
Romani shows a partial phonological assimilation to the final consonant of the
preceding nominal stem, an indication of the agglutinative integration of Layer II
markers into the nominal inflection paradigm.

Layer III elements are the most productive in all languages under consideration. They derive from postposed nominal and adverbial relational expressions,
and they often co-exist with their adverbial counterparts. While the pre-positioning of Layer III elements in Iranian is not at all obvious given their verb-final

configuration, in Romani the shift to preposed Layer III markers corresponds to the shift to a theme-verb-rheme configuration and so to the overall change in syntactic structuring (cf. Matras 1994:115 ff.).

Given the general productivity of Layer III elements, whereas the set of Layer II elements is always restricted, and Layer I elements have been in constant decay since Old-Indo-Iranian times, Romani is clearly, unlike Hindi or other subcontinental Indic languages, a pre-positioning language. Moreover, owing to the process of phonological integration of Layer II elements and the emergence of phonologically conditioned allomorphs, the argument in favor of viewing Layer II markers as unbound postpositions (see e.g. Hancock 1995:66; Cortiade 1990, cited in Friedman 1991) is even weaker for Romani than it is for any of the other languages represented in the figure (cf. discussion in Friedman 1991; Boretzky 1994:31-32).

1.5 Types of grammaticalization patterns in Layer III

In its formation of Layer III elements, Romani draws on essentially three different patterns of grammaticalization (cf. Boretzky 1993, 38ff.): 1) Old adverbial expressions, such as *ande-* 'in', *opr-* 'above', *pal-* 'behind; after', *paš-* 'beside', *avr-* 'outside', *tel-* 'beneath', etc.; 2) old adpositional forms, such as *ka* 'at', *pa* 'about', *pe* 'on', *ži* 'until', *katar* 'from'; and 3) dialect-specific borrowings from the respective contemporary or historical contact language, such as *de* 'since' (Romanian), *prečiv* 'against', and *posle* 'after' (Slavic), or *mit* 'with', and *von* 'from' (German).

As regard the second group, the old adpositional expressions, Boretzky (1993:38 ff.) suggests that they are connected directly to the case suffixes (see also Sampson 1908). If so, it is possible that we are dealing with Layer II markers which have been copied into Layer III. There is no direct evidence for this, and such cases of de-grammaticalization are generally thought to be quite rare (cf. Hopper & Traugott 1993:94 ff.). However, given the diachronic weakening of Layer II elements as regard the precision of expression (i.e. their development into abstract markers accompanying relational notions, rather than establishing them), and given the change in the linear position of Layer III elements (i.e. their shift into pre-nominal position and so their separation from postposed Layer II markers), a need to reduplicate the effect created by Layer II elements is conceivable. A similar process takes place in Kurmanji, where Layer III locative *di* duplicates Layer II locative *da*, and so constructions emerge such as *di malê da*, 'in the house'.

Prepositions may not be the most favorite candidates for grammatical borrowing, but it is indeed common for languages with an entirely oral tradition to borrow those relational markers that are more typical of planned and pre-structured discourse from a contact language which serves for written and institutional purposes. Examples are Arabic elements in Turkish and Persian, Persian elements in Hindi, or Hebrew prepositions in Yiddish. The preposition *prečiv* in Lovari may be such a case: 'against' expresses a relation which, unlike spatial or temporal relations, presupposes a well-organized analysis of interests and intentions, and is therefore to be expected in discourse forms such as argumentation.

The preposition *posle* 'after' in Bugurdži and Gurbet, as well as Turkish *sonra* 'after' in other Balkan dialects, could have entered the language as a discourse marker, structuring a chain of speech actions, rather than in its temporal meaning. There is evidence that so-called discourse markers are indeed one of the first grammatical categories affected by interference and borrowing; an indication is the diversity of discourse markers among Romani dialects, in agreement with the respective contact language (see Matras 1996). Having been established in a pragmatic function, its usage in Romani may have expanded to include the semantic meaning covered by the expression in the source language as well.

I will return to *mit* 'with' later on; at this stage it is sufficient to note that the Instrumental, being high on the Stability Hierarchy for Layer I-II elements, is one of the last relational notions to enter Layer III. Apparently, its infiltration into Layer III occurs after the grammaticalization process of inherited material to Layer III markers has aready been completed, or else at a stage or a situation in which the native system of the Romani dialect in question is too weak in order to carry out its own, language-internal grammaticalization process.

1.6 Incorporation: a semantic opposition in Layer III

To conclude part 1, a further argument might be considered in support of the productivity of Layer III. While Layer I-II markers assume only very general relational meanings, Layer III elements are semantically differentiated. A central feature involves the distinction between incorporative and non-incorporative relations. Incorporative prepositions classify the following noun as one which incorporates a predicate argument. Incorporation is found with locative and ablative relations. The locative incorporative preposition is *and-* (Lovari), *an-* (Bugurdži), or *andr-* (Lešaki; Central); consider these examples from Lovari:

(2) *Bešasas and-e Beči*
we.lived in-DEF Vienna
'We lived in Vienna'

(3) *mur-i mami garádžulas and-e veša*
my-NOM grandmother hid in-DEF woods.NOM
'My grandmother hid in the woods'

(4) *e Rom phirenas inke and-e romane gada*
DEF.NOM Rom they.walked still in-DEF Romani clothes.NOM
'The Roms still dressed in Romani clothes'

(5) *bišaldas la avri and-o šil*
sent her out in-DEF cold.NOM
'He sent her out into the cold'

(6) *avilam parpale and-o Njamco*
we-came back in-DEF Germany.NOM
'We came back to Germany'

Note that locative relations in Romani express both stative location and motion. Non-incorporative locative relations are expressed by *ka* or *ki* (which in combination with the definite article render *ko/ke* and *kijo/kije*). They categorize the head noun as a point of location which sets the limit to, or serves as a point of reference for an action or state:

(7) *žav khere ka mur-i dej*
I.go home to my-NOM mother.NOM
'I'm going home to my mother'

(8) *šudkerde maškar jekh them k-o kaver them*
thrown.PL between one land to-DEF other land.NOM
'Expelled from one land to another'

(9) *simas adžes k-o ministerstvo*
I.was today at-DEF ministry.NOM
'I was at the ministry today'

(10) *ka-l deš u duj*
at-DEF ten and two
'At twelve o'clock'

With ablatives, the incorporative preposition in Lovari is *anda*:

(11) *šudas la avri anda kher*
threw her out from house.NOM
'He threw her out of the house'

(12)   *leski dej   si anda Rusija*
        his mother is from Russia
        'His mother is from Russia'
(13)   *si vi anda Njamcura   kaj si čore*
        is too from Germans.NOM who are poor.PL
        'There are poor people among the Germans too'

While (11) and (12) are obvious examples of physical incorporation, in (13) the incorporative preposition *anda* categorizes the noun *Njamcura* as an integrated group, highlighting the fact that single members are included in it. Compare this with (14), where a similar noun is classified by the non-incorporative counterpart of *anda*, the ablative preposition *katar*:

(14)   *mangen katar e   Gaže*
        they.ask from DEF.NOM non-Roms.NOM
        ·'They ask/demand/beg the non-Roms'

Non-incorporative *katar* classifies the noun as a target or point of reference which sets a limit to the duration, the direction, or the initiation of an action. While the non-incorporative locative *ka* sets either a terminal limit to motion away from the speaker, or else it limits the scope of a stative location, ablative *katar* demarcates the source or point of initial reference of an action:

(15)   *Astaras   katar o   mur-o   dad:*
        we.begin from DEF.NOM my-NOM father.NOM
        'Let us begin with my father:'
(16)   *šel   kilometri maj dur katar o   Stockholm*
        hundred kilometers more far from DEF.NOM
        'One hundred kilometers past Stockholm'
(17)   *Voj márdžolas but katar pesko   rom*
        she was.beaten alot from REFL.GEN husband.NOM
        'She was often beaten by her husband'

Both non-incorporative elements, *ka* and *katar*, are what might be assumed to be secondary derivations mirroring synthetic Layer II markers. Apparently, the need to differentiate semantic functions triggers a process by which material capable of expressing local relations is recruited into Layer III.

    An indication of the fairly recent emergence of the incorporation distinction is the distribution of incorporative and non-incorporative prepositions in various dialects. While all dialects seem to show the distinction with locative prepositions, using *an-/and-/andr-* for the incorporative and *ka/ki* (Sinti *paš*) for the non-incorporative, with ablative relations the picture is somewhat more complex. Lešaki has no ablative prepositions at all, and uses synthetic ABL to mark all ablative relations. The Central dialect, which makes more extensive use of ABL than Lovari, uses ABL to classify the head noun 1) as a source, if physical texture (in Lovari *anda*) is expressed, or 2) as an initiation point, if physical demarcation (Lovari *katar*) is involved:

(18) *o   pindre les-te   ehas sar kaštes-tar*
      DEF.NOM legs   he-LOC were like wood-ABL
      'His legs felt like they were made of wood'

(19) *amen   thode   te   bešel dur le   gaves-tar*
      us.ACC they.put COMP sit   far DEF.OBL village-ABL
      'They made us settle far from the village'

The incorporation distinction exists in the Central dialect nonetheless with prepositions. However, while incorporative *andal* is different in distribution, but similar in function, to Lovari *anda*, non-incorporative *khatar* is less strictly an ablative relation, but assumes a more 'praeterlative' meaning, classifying the head noun as a demarcated point of reference for a continuing action in progress, rather than a source or point of initiation of an action:

(20) *man   čhide   avri andal o   kher*
      me.ACC they.threw out from DEF.NOM house.NOM
      'They threw me out of the house'

(21) *...kana mate   džan   andal e   karčma*
      when drunkards they.go from DEF.NOM bar.NOM
      '...when drunkards come out of the bar'

(22) *me džavas   khatar le   čhibales-kero   kher,*
      I   I.was.going from DEF.OBL president-GEN house.NOM
      so   dikhav...
      what I.see
      'I was walking past the president's house, what do I see...'

(23) *denašavas, kaj   so jekhsigeder te   našl'uvav*
      I.escaped COMP what faster   COMP I.sneak
      khatar kodi   karčma
      from that.NOM bar.NOM
      'I escaped in order to sneak as fast as possible past that bar'

In Sinti, there is a tendency, especially with animates, to 'double' ablative prepositions with synthetic ABL. Sinti has an incorporative ablative preposition *dran*:

(24)   *und te wen   jon dran o   foro...*
       and if they.come they from DEF.NOM town.NOM
       'And if they came out of the town...'

(25)   *dscha wi dran kol mensches-ter, tu   dschunglo geisto!*
       go   out from this man-ABL   you ugly   spirit
       'Leave this man, you evil spirit!'

(26)   *hoi   dran kol mensch-ester wi wela,   ko hi,*
       what from this man-ABL   out will.come that is
       hoi   kol mensch-en   tschiklo krela
       what this man-ACC(GERM) dirty   will.make
       'It is what comes out of a person that makes him unclean'

The non-incorporative ablative, however, appears to be a more recent relation, as it is expressed by the preposition *von*, borrowed from German:

(27)   *und von ko   diwes an   fastaren jon*
       and from that day   onwards they.fast they
       'And since that day they are fasting'

(28)   *phutschan les-ter, ob   darfte scheiderel pes*
       they.asked he-ABL whether may   divorce   REFL.ACC
       i   morsch von peskri   romia-ter
       DEF.NOM man   from REFL.GEN wife-ABL
       'They asked him, whether a man is allowed to divorce his wife'

(29)   *tu ˙ hal   kowa kai weh   von o   dewles-ter*
       you you.are that   who you.come from DEF.NOM God-ABL
       'You are the one who comes from God'

The position of the incorporation distinction with ablatives therefore suggests that ablatives are affected later than locatives by the process of semantic and structural innovation in Layer III.

2. *The Distribution Hierarchy*

A striking feature of the Romani case system is the uneven distribution of synthetic case suffixes among potential carriers of nominal inflection:

(30) *dikhav l-es*
      I.see he-ACC
      'I see him'
      dikhav le   rakl-es
      I.see   DEF.OBL boy-ACC
      'I see the boy'
      dikhav o   kher
      I.see   DEF.NOM house.NOM
      'I see the house'
(31) *karing   les-te*
      opposite he-LOC
      'Opposite him'
      karing   o   rakl-o
      opposite DEF.NOM boy-NOM
      'Opposite the boy'
      karing   o   kher
      opposite DEF.NOM house.NOM
      'Opposite the house'

The problem addressed by the postulation of the Distribution Hierarchy in this section is therefore the following: *How is synthetic case marking distributed among the potential carriers of case?*

Grammars of Romani usually attribute the distribution of Layer I-II markers to an animate/inanimate distinction (cf. Wentzel 1988:63 ff.; Boretzky 1993:22; Hancock 1995:60-61; Holzinger 1993:30 ff.). While animates allow all synthetic case forms, it is often claimed that inanimates do not take ACC, and according to Wentzel (1988:65) and Holzinger (1993:30) inanimates do not allow LOC either. Pronouns, as in the above examples, might be incorporated into the animacy restriction as, given no contextual domain of reference, they tend to be interpreted as referring to persons. But in fact the appearence of synthetic case marking with pronouns is obligatory, regardless of the animate/inanimate character of the entity to which they refer. We are thus left seemingly with two conditions: the first semantic (animacy), the second structural (pronouns> nouns).

Holzinger (1993:30) argues in favor of a semantic hierarchy of animacy, rather than a strict division between animate and inanimate. However, he admits that even lexical entities with a high-ranking position on the animacy hierarchy, such as 'grandfather', will occasionally 'drop' synthetic case marking "if the meaning is made clear through word order or a preposition". Thus, it appears

that the animacy hierarchy is in fact a scale on which nominal entities are arranged according to their semantic and pragmatic saliency and the predictability
of their semantic case roles. Holzinger merely provides a hint to this extent,
mentioning that topicality might be involved.

But there are instances of synthetic ACC-marking with inanimates as well.
Boretzky (1994:102) mentions the following example from the Kelderaš dialect:

(32)   *phandel vo (e)   gon-es*
        closes   he DEF.OBL sack-ACC
        'So he ties the sack'

Boretzky suggests that the case assignment in (32) might occur as a result of
"transfer of animacy", since a person had been put in the sack. Consider the following from Lovari:

(33)   *Antenne si kodo-le   Marsmenschin-os   sar kodo, E.T.*
        antenna is this-OBL mars.man(German)-ACC like this
        'This Alien has an antenna, like that E.T.'

The possessive construction in Romani employs the verb 'to be', placing the
possessor in ACC and the object of possession in NOM. While the 'Alien' in
this context is clearly treated as a human animate, for literary rather than for
grammatical reasons, as regards the productivity of Layer I it is nevertheless
significant that German *Marsmensch(en)*, an athematic element (cf. Bakker, this
volume), is assigned synthetic case marking.

Other instances of ACC marking of the possessor show Layer I case assignment to nouns which are more obviously inanimate as well as athematic;
here further examples from Lovari:

(34)   *aj kodo-le provizoričn-e   prezidijum-os si l-es*
        and this-OBL provisional-OBL presidium-ACC is it-ACC
        numa trin   legitimacija
        only three authorization
        'And this provisional presidium has only three tasks'
(35)   *amare problemuri sas le   Njamc-os   bi*
        our.PL problems were DEF.OBL Germany-ACC without
        bučja-ko   pala marimo
        work-GEN after war
        'A post-war, unemployed Germany was confronted with our problems'

One might argue that, here too, it is the possessor role of the ACC-carriers which triggers an analogy to human or animate actors. At any rate, we are dealing with the assignment of synthetic case markers to non-animate entities which, as important institutions, assume a prominent role as central, topical participants in discourse.

Translations show that there are dialectal, and perhaps idiolectal differences in assigning ACC-marking to non-human referents. Consider the Lešaki and Lovari versions of the following:

(36) Lešaki: *Saturn-os sy jekh rota*
            Saturn-ACC is INDEF ring
     Lovari: *O   Saturn si l-es   jekh   angrušti*
            DEF.NOM Saturn is it-ACC INDEF ring
            'Saturn has a ring'

Lešaki treats the noun 'Saturn' as already topical or contextually retrievable, while in the Lovari version topicality is first established through extraposition, and case is then assigned to the resumptive pronoun.

With human animates, a distinction is commonly made between close members of the family and other persons. Consider (37)-(38) from Sinti, (39)-(40) from Lovari, and (41) from the Central dialect:

(37) *und joi dschajas wi und putschas peskri   da-ter*
     and she went   out and asked   REFL.GEN mother-ABL
     'And she went out and asked her mother'
(38) *und ap ko drom phutschas job von peskre   mala:*
     and on that way asked   he from REFL.GEN friends
     'And on the way he asked his friends:'
(39) *mur-e dades-tar   manglas*
     my-OBL father-ABL he.asked
     'He asked my father'
(40) *šundem katar mur-o   amal*
     I.heard from my-NOM friend
     'I heard from my friend'
(41) *aver   čord'a o   saksofonos peskere   dades-tar,*
     another stole DEF.NOM saxophone REF.GEN father-ABL
     o   Jančku and'a e   bugova khatar
     DEF.NOM   brought DEF.NOM bass   from
     o   phur-o Bugošis
     DEF.NOM old-NOM basist

'Another one stole the saxophone from his father, Jančdu brought the bass
from the old bassist'

Ambiguity often arises with non-referential animates, and dialects tend to
adopt different solutions:

(42)   Lovari: *Me lav   man-ge rom*
                       I   I.take me-DAT man.NOM
       Lešaki: *Me lav   rom-es*
                       I   I.take man-ACC
                       'I am getting married' (no specification to whom)
       Lovari: *Me dikhav biš   grast*
                       I   I.see   twenty horse
       Lešaki: *Me dikhav biš   graj-en*
                       I   I.see   twenty horse-ACC.PL
                       'I see twenty horses'

On the other hand, there is little ambiguity with animates that are clearly topical,
referential, or contextually retrievable, and they almost always take synthetic
case endings; consider these examples from Lovari (43), Central (44) and Sinti
(45):

(43)   *či   astarde   e   šimijak-os*
       not they.caught DEF.OBL mouse-ACC
       'They didn't catch the mouse'
(44)   *na bikenehas man-ge   tir-e   rikon-es?*
       not you.sell   me-DAT your-OBL dog-ACC
       'Won't you sell me your dog?'
(45)   *hoi   kren   tumer koi, hoske pandawen tumer*
       what you.do you   there why   you.tie   you
       kol esel-es   los?
       this donkey-ACC free
       'What are you doing there, why are you letting this donkey loose?'

Parts of the body might be considered to rank relatively high on the animacy
hierarchy (cf. Igla, this volume, section 3.2); but examples show that this is
generally restricted to stereotype expressions, especially to those in which parts
of the body assume the semantic case role of manner, and are assigned ABL:

(46) *cirdle   man   kanes-tar*
      they.pulled me.ACC ear-ABL
      'They pulled me by the ear'
(47) *lelas la balen-dar ando muj marelas la*
      took her hair-ABL in   face beat   her
      'He used to grab her by the hair and beat her in the face'

Note that in (47), *muj* 'face' receives a prepositional locative, rather than a synthetic one. There are two possible explanations: First, LOC is lower on the
Stability Hierarchy and so generally less likely to appear than ABL. Second, the
indirect object is placed in a pre-verbal, thematic or 'establishing' position (cf.
Matras 1995), highlighting the fact that the victim was beaten in her face (rather
than somewhere else).

    With ablative relations too, prepositions tend to appear when the indirect
object expresses source rather than manner, when it is highlighted, or when it is
less expected to assume its particular semantic case role; here examples from the
Central dialect (48) and Lovari (49):

(48) *andral o   jakha   leske o   apsa peren*
      from DEF.NOM eyes.NOM he.DAT DEF.NOM tears they.fall
      'Tears are dropping from his eyes'
(49) *cikne barore čišaj anda jekh   cikno vast*
      small grains sand from INDEF small hand.NOM
      'Small grains of sand from [falling out of] a small hand'

    The evidence concerning the distribution of Layer I-II markers among po-
tential carriers of case inflection may be summarized in (50) in a series of single
hierarchical statements:

(50) a deictic and anaphoric reference (=pronouns) > other potential carriers of
      nominal inflection
   b important institutions > other inanimates
   c well established (topical) actors > other participants
   d close members of the family > other humans
   e referential animates > non-referential animates
   f parts of the body in stereotype roles > parts of the body in other roles

    To round up the discussion on the Distribution Hierarchy, the question of a
common denominator for the single hierarchical relations summarized in (50)
arises. Much of what is said in (50) connects to the broad idea of 'topicality', to

which reference in this section was occasionally made. Given the ambiguity of
the term 'topicality' in functional literature, I prefer, however, at the end of this
section to stick to a more general notion of pragmatic prominence, that of
'retrievability'. By 'retrievability' I mean the ability of the hearer to identify the
referent spoken of as a unique and unambiguous entity (compare Givón's
(1990:900 ff.) 'topicality' and 'referential accessibility'). In an implicational order, the Distribution Hierarchy might thus be displayed as follows:

(51)   *The Distribution Hierarchy*
        HIGH RETRIEVABILITY deixis and anaphora > well established ani-
        mate actors > important institutions > close family relations > parts of the
        body in stereotype roles > non-referential animates LOW
        RETRIEVABILITY

The animacy/inanimacy opposition, while shown not to function necessarily
as a strict semantic condition on synthetic case-marking, is compatible with the
retrievability feature, animates being more likely to assume central roles in discourse. For close members of the family, retrievability is an expression of intimate relations. Institutions, well established animates, and stereotype roles (and
in some dialects stereotype expressions, such as *račate* 'at night', *lažavestar* 'out
of shame') are highly familiar to the hearer, whereas non-referential animates,
although they may assume Layer I-II synthetic case marking, rank low on famil-
iarity and therefore occupy the lowest position on the scale.

        High retrievability - contextual or situational - is also a pre-condition for the
use of deictic and anaphoric expressions (personal pronouns, demonstratives). It
is on these grounds that what is claimed to be a structural condition on the distribution of Layer I-II synthetic case markers, namely pronouns>nouns, in fact fits
nicely into the pragmatic-based retrievability hierarchy.

3. The Stability Hierarchy

        The problem addressed by the Stability Hierarchy is: *How is the appearance
of Layer I-II synthetic markers affected by the choice of a specific case?* The
Stability Hierarchy too is in principle implicational, as it is expected that if Layer
I-II case suffixes will appear for a lower-ranking category, then they will appear
for higher-ranking categories as well. However, the distribution of Layer I-II
markers is also connected to semantic case roles, and so to the occurrence of certain nouns as objects of specific verbs, or 'case occurrence' (Fillmore 1968).
Place names, for example, take ABL in the more conservative dialects if they are

the source of motion. But since they are seldom beneficiaries of human action, they are less likely to appear in DAT. Nevertheless, DAT is higher on the Stability Hierarchy, since genuine dative objects are more likely to be marked by synthetic DAT than by a preposition, while this does not generally hold for ablative objects.

Furthermore, the Stability Hierarchy is intended to grasp the general pattern typical of the language as a whole. Thus, the fact that Lešaki has no preposition expressing an ablative relation, but that Sinti and some other dialects have (borrowed) prepositions for instrumental/sociative, does not justify a hierarchical arrangement ABL>INSTR, since on the basis of dialect comparison an earlier and more thorough replacement of ABL by Layer III elements can be reconstructed for the language as a whole.

Bearing this in mind, let us now turn to the first position on the hierarchy, GEN. There seems to be no Romani dialect which has not preserved GEN as a productive case. Moreover, the position of GEN at the top of the hierarchy is justified by the fact that the preposition (or rather prefix) *bi* 'without' always governs GEN, regardless of the position of the case-carrier on the Distribution Hierarchy. Having said this, let us look at some examples for an analytic expression of genitive relations. There is no analytic genitive in Romani which is used exclusively as such. GEN may be substituted occasionally by a non-incorporative ablative preposition, but such substitutions usually occur alongside synthetic GEN. In Lovari, possession may be expressed by GEN or *katar*:

(52) *vov si e   šaves-ko   dad*
      he   is DEF.OBL boy-GEN   father.NOM
      'He is the boy's father'
(53) *vov si o   dad   katar mur-o   amal*
      he   is DEF.NOM father from my-NOM friend.NOM
      'He is my friend's father'

But Lešaki, which does not have prepositional ablative expressions, will always show GEN:

(54) *jov sy dad   dal-e   čhaves-kro*
      he is   father this-OBL boy-GEN
      'He is this boy's father'
(55) *jov sy dad   mir-e   males-kro*
      he is   father my-OBL   friend-GEN
      'He is my friend's father'

In Sinti, we find occasional substitution by an ablative preposition, with 'doubling' through ABL occurring with human animates. Note, however, that GEN is productive here too:

(56)   o   baro pani von Galiläa
       DEF.NOM big water of   Galilee
       'The big sea of Galilee'
(57)   i   romni von o   Herodes-kro prales-ter
       DEF.NOM wife of   DEF.NOM Herod-GEN brother-ABL
       'The wife of Herod's brother'

The distribution of GEN vs. ablative possession could be connected to the intensity or intimacy of the relationship between the two nouns in the possessive construction. A more intimate or closer relationship is expresed by GEN, relationships in which each of the participant is regarded as a discrete entity are expressed by an ablative preposition. Synthetic vs. analytic procedures thus mirror iconically what is known as 'semantic integrality' (Tobin 1992).

In addition to possessive constructions, we find variation in the use of GEN in partitive constructions:

(58)   Lovari: jekh   pahosko kher kaj bušol Iglu
                  INDEF ice-GEN house that is.called
       Gurbet: ćer   katar o   ledo kaj bučel   les-e   Iglu
                  house from DEF.NOM ice   that is.called it-DAT
                  'A house made of ice that is called Iglu'

But while the Lovari version shows partitive GEN, Gurbet simply re-interprets the relation as pertaining to physical texture and therefore source, resulting in the choice of an ablative preposition.

To summarize the position of GEN, we can conclude, 1) that it is the only case which may be governed by a preposition regularly with all referents, 2) that its substitution in possessive constructions is not complete, but occurs in complementary distribution alongside synthetic GEN, and finally 3) that its substitution both in possessive and in partitive constructions is dialect-specific, and not general.

GEN is followed closely on the Stability Hierarchy by INSTR, which also occurs with virtually all potential carriers of nominal inflection. Although an instrumental relation may often be paraphrased (cf. Boretzky 1994:109), there is no native Romani element which serves as an instrumental or sociative preposition; Borrow's *sar* is shown by Sampson (1907) to be a ghost-word (cf.

Hancock, this volume). But there are cases of replacement of synthetic INSTR through borrowed prepositions. These are most frequent in Sinti:

(59)   *job rakeras mit bar-i   sor*
        he spoke with big-NOM power.NOM
        'He spoke with much power'
(60)   *und jon dikan   o   Elia   mit o   Mose*
        and they they.saw DEF.NOM Elias with DEF.NOM Moses
        'And they saw: [there was] Elias with Moses'

Foreign instrumental/sociative prepositions also occur in other dialects. (61) is reported by Bernal (1994) for the dialect of the Grekuri in Argentina, and shows Spanish *con*. Example (62) was recorded by myself from a speaker of Erli from Thessaloniki, and has Greek *me*:

(61)   *me zhav te   kerav buki kon mur-o   phral*
        I   I.go COMP I.do   work [with] my-NOM brother
        'I am going to work with my brother'
(62)   *e   rakli me   to   parno gad*
        DEF.NOM girl [with the] white shirt
        'The girl with the white shirt'

A remarkable feature of (62) is the occurrence not only of the Greek preposition *me* 'with', but also of the Greek definite article *to*. It seems that we are dealing not with a genuine process of grammatical borrowing of single elements into Romani, but rather with structural mixing at the clause level. A switch into the second language occurs at the beginning of the noun phrase, while within the noun phrase itself the Romani adjectival inflection is retained.

Evidence for such structural mixing at the clause level is found in our data of Lovari as well. Consider the following examples of Romani-German mixing, recorded from a speaker who is the first generation in her family to have been raised in Germany:

(63)   *muri   dej sas phari   mit die Marika*
        my-NOM mother was pregnant [with the]
        'My mother was pregnant with Marika'
(64)   *vorta sar dam   mit die Scheinwerfer/ o   auto/*
        direct as we.gave [with the headlights]   DEF.NOM car
        našel avri jekh   lisica
        runs out INDEF fox

'Just as we turned on the headlights/ the car/ a fox jumps out'

In (64) *mit* 'with' accompanies a lexical code-switch (*Scheinwerfer* 'headlights'), in (63) it precedes a name, but the expression might be calqued on German (*schwanger sein mit...*). There are several comparable cases in the corpus. In both Lovari examples we find German definite articles following the preposition, much like the Thessaloniki example.

Romani usually does not borrow definite articles, and the presence of definite articles from the contact languages accompanying the prepositions in (63)-(64) means that the speakers, rather than borrow a foreign preposition into Romani, switch into a second luuage in order to express instrumentality/ sociativity through an analytic construction. The lack of German case-agreement in *die* in (63)-(64) is not an argument against the switch-hypothesis, since case-reduction is typical of the variety of German spoken by the Roma.

While the tendency to switch languages at the clause level in order to express the instrumental/sociative relation is an indication of language-internal pressure to replace INSTR by analytic constructions, it also illustrates that in the dialects in question there is yet no established analytic expression for the instrumental/sociative. In this respect Lovari or Greek Erli differ from Sinti, which has actually borrowed the preposition *mit* from German and which applies it within the Romani clause, without inserting German articles.

Following INSTR, DAT appears to be the most widely distributed Layer I-II case marking. There is no genuine dative preposition in Romani, and in our corpus occurrences of borrowed dative prepositions, as in (65), where *für* is doubled by DAT, are restricted to Sinti:

(65)   *muken*   *l-es*   *für o*   *dades-ke*   *oder für*
        they.leave he-ACC for DEF.NOM father-DAT   or   for
        i   *da-ke*
        DEF.NOM mother-DAT
        'They leave him to his father or to his mother'

However, there is a tendency toward substitution of DAT by an analytic locative expression. Motion toward an object is conceived of in Romani as a locative relation, and is expressed by *and-/an-/andr-* or by *ka/ki*. In addition, there are also occurrences of a locative-prepositional substitution of DAT, for certain verbs, with human beneficiaries or recipients; consider (66) from Lovari and (67) from Lešaki:

(66)   *de l-es   ko Marko!*
        give it-ACC to
        'Give it to Marko!'

(67)   *Janko phendža ki pes-kry   phen*
               said   to REFL-GEN sister
        'Janko said to his sister'

In Lovari, there is one preposition, *prečiv* 'against', borrowed from Slavic, which, combined with *ka*, actually governs DAT with prominent referents:

(68)   *politika prečiv ke Romen-ge*
        polics against to Roms-DAT
        'Anti-Romani politics'

On the whole, despite occurrences like (66)-(67), DAT is most common as a case marking for dative relations with human or animate beneficiaries or recipients, and non-agent human topics:

(69)   *me pekav jekh   bokoli mur-a   deja-ke*
        I   I.bake INDEF cake   my-OBL mother-DAT
        'I'm baking a cake for my mother'

(70)   *pomožind'a le   gres-ke   te   cirdel o   verdan*
        helped   DEF.OBL horse-DAT COMP pull   DEF.NOM wagon
        'He helped the horse pull the wagon'

(71)   *la   terňa-ke   džanas o   apsa tele*
        DEF.OBL young.F-DAT they.went DEF.NOM tears down
        le   čhamen-ca
        DEF.OBL cheeks-INSTR
        'The young girl had tears running down her cheeks'

While the position of DAT on the Stability Hierarchy beside INSTR is justified by the fact that neither case relation can be expressed by a genuine preposition (except in Sinti), the hierarchical arrangement INSTR>DAT is based on the impression that there are no structural restrictions on the appearance of INSTR, but there are semantic restrictions with regard to the distribution of DAT. It is therefore likely that every carrier of DAT might also appear in INSTR, but not vice versa. Furthermore, INSTR is, in most dialects, only occasionally replaced by a switch into a second language. DAT, on the other hand, can be substituted by an analytic locative relation.

The position of ACC on the Stability Hierarchy is ambiguous, for a number of reasons. First, all synthetic case formations, with the exception of the Vocative, are based on the Layer I ACC. In ranking ACC we are thus concerned not with its plain structural distribution, but with its function as a marker of the semantic role of an accusative patient (and possessor, see section 2). Second, Romani has no adpositional element expressing an accusative relation. The criterion for the stability of ACC is therefore not the degree of its replacement by Layer III elements, but its mere presence or absence, that is, its admittance by potential carriers of nominal inflection.

We have seen above that there are instances of analytic substitution of GEN and INSTR; nevertheless, the appearance of Layer II GEN and INSTR is hardly affected by the Distribution Hierarchy (expect, perhaps, to the extent that 'semantic integrality' might be considered as a case for pragmatic retrievability). The appearance of ACC, on the other hand, is congruent with the conditions of the Distribution Hierarchy discussed in section 2. The position of ACC on the Stability Hierarchy will therefore be lower than that of GEN or INSTR.

DAT and ACC share, to a certain extent, a dependency on the Distribution Hierarchy, the dative usually being the case of animate beneficiaries and recipients. But they differ in that the accusative direct object is, in universal terms, less dependent on overt marking, since its role is more easily predictable from the semantics of the verb (cf. Givón 1984:183). Thus, objects that are low on the Distribution Hierarchy will not admit ACC. But if they happen to occur in a genuine dative role, that is, as recipients or beneficiaries, they may admit DAT, since there is no genuine analytic replacement for synthetic DAT. This is illustrated by the following example from Bugurdži (Boretzky 1993:180), as well as by (73) from Lovari:

(72)   *me ka   pazizav o   kher,   ma sikirizen*
       I   FUT I.find DEF.NOM house.NOM not   you.worry
       ništa   kheres-ke!
       nothing house-DAT
       'I'll find the house, don't you worry about the house!'

(73)   *kada-le   kheres-ke   phenas 'Bieberhaus'*
       this-OBL house-DAT we.say
       'We call this house 'Bieberhaus''

In (72), the direct object *kher* appears in NOM, while the dative object is marked by DAT. (72)-(73), and comparable examples from the corpus, thus provide us with evidence for an arrangement DAT>ACC (cf. also Igla, this volume, Figure 5).

Of all synthetic Layer II markers, ABL is most strongly affected by dialect variation. On the extreme edge of its retention scale we find Lešaki, which has developed no ablative prepositions and which consistently shows ABL with all ablative relations. In Sinti, ABL, like other synthetic markers, often occurs in 'doubled' constructions, i.e. in combination with prepositions. But unlike genitive, instrumental/sociative, and dative relations, for which Sinti shows borrowed prepositions, there is an Indic (or 'native' Romani) ablative preposition *dran*, which appears alongside (non-incorporative) borrowed *von* (see section 1.6). Thus, although from a distributional point of view ABL in Sinti may be comparable with the other synthetic markers in the dialect, the language-internal grammaticalization process shown by *dran* is an indication of an earlier shift to Layer III marking in the ablative domain.

All other dialects have semantically differentiated, native ablative prepositions (cf. section 1.6). In general, the appearance of ABL is connected to the Distribution Hierarchy. In the Central dialect, ABL is productive with place names, sources, texture, as well as with all higher-ranking (animate) referents. With other objects, its distribution is connected to specific semantic case-roles:

(74) *khatar o   phike   man-ge pat'arde   čhingerd-o gad*
      from   DEF.NOM shoulders me-DAT they.covered torn.NOM shirt
      'They covered me down from the shoulders with a torn shirt'
(75) *chudenas   le   čhavor-en   phiken-dar*
      they.grabbed DEF.OBL children-ACC shoulders-ABL
      'They grabbed the children by the shoulders'

For the same noun, *phike* 'shoulders', the ablative of spatial demarcation in (74) is expressed by a preposition, whereas the ablative of manner in (75) is marked by ABL.

For Bugurdži, Boretzky (1993:27) mentions texture as one of the functions expressed by ABL with full nouns:

(76) *sine les   o   kher lones-tar*
      was he.ACC DEF.NOM house salt-ABL
      'His house was made of salt'

While ablative motion is generally expressed by prepositions, there are single examples of ABL marking the ablative of local demarcation (Boretzky 1993:203):

(77) *dur kakale   thanes-tar*
      far this-OBL place-ABL
      'Far from this place'

In Lovari, source, texture, spatial demarcation, and the point of departure for motion are all expressed by prepositions. Productive ABL appears only with the most prominent referents, that is with pronouns and selected human animates. But even with prominent nouns it is subject to competition with ablative prepositions. Compare the following two examples:

(78) *but   amar-e   manušen-dar garádžonas*
      many our-OBL people-ABL they.hid
      'Many of our people were hiding'
(79) *lav   man-ge   manro katar   mur-i   dej*
      I.take me-DAT bread   from my-NOM mother
      'I'm getting some bread from my mother'

Apart from such cases, ABL in Lovari is found only in stereotype expressions:

(80) *me lažaves-tar   či   kerav kodo*
      I   shame-ABL not I.do   that
      'I'm ashamed to do that'

Finally, LOC can be said to occupy the lowest position on the Stability Hierarchy for Layer I-II case markers. The Romani LOC is often referred to as a 'prepositional case' (see Sampson 1926:179-180), as it is governed by prepositions expressing spatial relations. However, in most dialects, this function of LOC is absolutely restricted to the highest positions on the Distribution Hierarchy, that is, to deictic and anaphoric expressions (cf. example 31). Widespread LOC marking on nouns in locative relations is found only in Sinti, where it fits the general pattern of case 'doubling' (example from Holzinger 1993:321):

(81) *dšajas paš miro kamlo dades-te*
      went   near my late   father-LOC
      'He came to my late father'

Apart from Sinti, LOC on lower-ranking nouns is found occasionally in Bugurdži, alongside locative prepositions. Compare the following (from Boretzky 1993:180-181):

(82)   ... te   džal pes-ke   kol-e   bijaves-te
        COMP go   REFL-DAT that-OBL wedding-LOC
        '... in order to go to that wedding'
(83)   gele   on   ko bijav   pale
        they.went they to wedding back
        'So they went back to the wedding'

There are also single occurrences of LOC in the Central dialect:

(84)   o   jakha les-te   sar guruves-te
        DEF.NOM eyes   he-LOC like ox-LOC
        'His eyes were like those of an ox'

But here too, it is evident that locative relations are more likely to be expressed by prepositions, than are ablative relations:

(85)   dodžavas Terňa-tar   dži kijo Perješis
        I.go   Terni-ABL till in Prešova
        'I will go from Terni to Prešova'
(86) a o   luftos kal'il'a   le   thuves-tar
        DEF.NOM air   darkened DEF.OBL smoke-ABL
        'The air darkened with smoke'   •
     b khasalas, tašl'olas   andro thuv
        coughed suffocated in   smoke
        'He coughed and suffocated in smoke'

In Lovari, the appearance of LOC, except with pronouns, is restricted to stereotype expressions of the type račate 'at night', ivende 'in the winter'. In Lešaki, LOC has disappeared completely. Instead, local prepositions govern ABL with pronouns:

(87)   varykon   džal ki man-dyr
        somebody goes to me-ABL
        'Somebody is approaching me'
(88)   Janko phenel ki la-tyr:
              says   to her-ABL

'Janko says to her:'

Beside the restricted distribution of LOC, the fact that all dialects show native prepositions for spatial locative relations serves as an indication of the strong tendency to replace LOC by analytic Layer III expressions at an early stage. The reason for the early replacement of the synthetic locative by analytic markers might be found in the universal primacy of spatial relations, especially those expressing stative location. For LOC is essentially the case of spatial stative location, and by analogy of temporal location, or of spatial displacement, i.e. of motion in space.

There are also language-internal structural factors facilitating an early replacement of synthetic locative marking: The availability of a differentiated inventory of local and spatial adverbial expressions in Indo-Aryan allows Romani to recruit material for analytic prepositions once the dynamics of a gradual shift to preposed analytic formation are set in motion. Location adverbs of the type *andr-* 'inside' express essentially the same relation as does the LOC synthetic case-marker, and may easily be employed to duplicate its semantic function.

The generalization of LOC as a 'prepositional case' is probably connected to the historical rise of prepositions from adverbial specifiers of expressions of stative location, of a type somewhat similar to that found, for example, in contemporary Turkish, where the specifying adverb in stative expressions takes a Locative case-ending (*ev-in iç-in-de*, literally 'in the inside of the house'). But it might also be explained by the semantics-pragmatics of the locative case role. LOC is most consistently the patient-case, and so most rarely the agent-case. It is least likely to occur with human actors and is therefore one of the lowest cases, even in universal terms, on the topicality scale (cf. Givón 1984:139, 142). Romani has an Ablative-agent in passive constructions, a Genitive-possessor, an Accusative-possessor, an Instrumental co-agent, and a Dative-topic. At the same time the semantics-pragmatics of the Locative, combined with the rise in prominence of alternative analytic locative expressions, lead to the gradual reduction of LOC to a stereotype, frozen case-marker; it loses its semantic function and ultimately only occurs in combination with specifying prepositions, or in fixed expressions. Thus, the generalization of LOC is not at all contradictory, but in fact complementary to its decay as a productive semantic case marker.

To conclude, the Stability Hierarchy for Layer I-II markers may be summarized as follows:

(89)   *The Stability Hierarchy for Layer I-II case markers*:
        (NOM) > GEN > INSTR > DAT > ACC > ABL > LOC

4. Dialect variation

There are a number of specific dialect features, some of which appear to be in conflict with the generalizations of the Stability Hierarchy in (89). First, Sinti shows a productive retention of most Layer I-II synthetic case-markers, and does not seem to have strong hierarchical conditions on their appearance. But at the same time, Sinti is also the most far-reaching dialect with regard to the adoption of analytic case-markers (prepositions), applying them regularly even for instrumental/sociative and for dative relations. This 'doubling' strategy is a result of a combination of conservative traits with heavy interference from the contact-language, German. It puts Sinti on the highest position on the scale for synthetic case-retention among the Romani dialects considered in this study, but it also places it in an ambiguous position outside, or beyond this scale.

Lešaki, representing the Northern group of dialects, is found to be the most consistent in applying Layer I-II synthetic case markers. This is due mostly to its lack of analytic ablative expressions, which makes it impossible to replace ABL or to substitute GEN by prepositions. Since there is no analytic alternative to ABL, and its occurrence is therefore not dependent on the Distribution Hierarchy, ABL in Lešaki may be placed in a higher position on the Stability Hierarchy than ACC, which does follow the Distribution Hierarchy (cf. Wentzel 1988:63). Thus, although Lešaki has abolished LOC completely, its case system is, compared to the other dialects, strongly oriented toward Layer I-II markers.

The Central dialect, spoken in the Czech and Slovak Republics and partly in Hungary, occupies the next position on the scale of synthetic case retention due to the relatively high productivity of ABL. It is followed by Bugurdži, where prepositions dominate in lower positions, but where synthetic ABL and LOC occur occasionally even beyond frozen or stereotype expressions. Lovari, representing the Vlach dialect group, appears to be the most advanced in replacing Layer I-II case markers. It rarely makes use of LOC with full nouns, it generally replaces ABL through prepositions, and it even shows tendencies toward a substitution of GEN.

Bearing in mind that the material considered in this study is limited to a number of sources representing individual varieties of the dialects concerned, the results point to the following pattern of retention of Layer I-II synthetic case markers across the various dialects:

(90)   *Layer I-II case retention in Romani dialects*:
       (Sinti) > Lešaki/Northern > Central > Bugurdži/Balkan > Lovari/Vlach

5. Conclusion

The hierarchies postulated in the preceding sections, apart from describing the pattern of current synthetic case retention in Romani, also serve to help trace the diachronic drift of the case system in the language from a postposed analytic structure (early New Indo-Aryan), via a predominantly postposed synthetic/ agglutinative structure (assumed for early Romani), toward a preposed analytic structure (contemporary tendency in Romani).

The connection between the distribution of Layer II markers and semantic-pragmatic properties of case-carriers such as animacy, prominence, and retrievability, which was found to determine the Distribution Hierarchy, may also be observed in subcontinental Modern Indo-Aryan (compare the distribution in Hindi of *ko*, or of Bengali *ke*). One cannot exclude the possibility that this hierarchical pattern of New Indo-Aryan was maintained in Romani throughout the period during which Layer II markers developed into agglutinated synthetic affixes. However, the fact that dialects of Romani differ in the degree of retention of Layer II markers as productive suffixes strengthens the assumption that the decline of synthetic case-marking began on European territory, and that the Distribution Hierarchy is drawn upon to help regulate the gradual drift toward an analytic case configuration.

The Stability Hierarchy shows that the shift to preposed analytic formation in the case system begins with categories which express basic spatial relations of location (Locative, Ablative), and continues from there to domains which may be expressed by analogy to spatial concepts (Dative, Genitive). In this very general respect there are similarities between the Stability Hierarchy and the universal hierarchy for inflectional case systems presented by Blake (1994:157-162). A number of typological particularities are nevertheless apparent. Blake's hierarchy of inflectional case runs as follows: NOM > ACC/ERG > GEN > DAT > LOC > ABL/INSTR; thus if a language shows inflectional case for a lower position, it is expected to display inflectional case for higher positions as well. Romani, with its complex system of case markers, possesses all of the positions named in Blake's scale, with the exception of Ergative, which is not applicable here. But the order of items on Blake's hierarchy does not completely match the Stability Hierarchy postulated for Romani in (89). Although ABL and LOC, the 'basic' spatial relations, are on both scales lower than ACC, GEN, and DAT, their order relative to one another is different. There is also a sharp contrast between the two hierarchies in the position of ACC, which is generally thought of as second in rank to NOM (cf. also Keenan & Comrie 1977:66). The lower position of ACC in Romani reflects its strong dependency on the Distribution Hierarchy; Romani, after all, does possess an inflectional ACC and, from a strictly structural viewpoint, ACC is a 'primary' case construed at the Layer I level, while the lower positions on Blake's hierarchy all appear in Romani as Layer II elements, and so are in a sense 'secondary'. The appearance of GEN, DAT or INSTR, but not of ACC, with lower elements on the Distribution Hierarchy (e.g. inanimates in non-prominent roles) might nonetheless be registered as a typological anomaly in Romani.

The position of GEN is in universal terms somewhat more ambiguous; it is second to ACC on Blake's (1994) scale, but lower than both Indirect Objects and Obliques on Keenan & Comrie's (1977) 'accessibility hierarchy'. The syntactic position of the Romani genitive contradicts Greenberg's (1966:110) second universal, which foresees that in languages with prepositions the genitive will generally follow the governing noun, while in languages with postpositions it will precede. The close interplay of genitive and possessive however leads to variation in this domain in many languages. The exceptional treatment of the Romani genitive is favored in addition by its particular structural feature of 'Suffixaufnahme' (see Plank 1995:11-13; Payne 1995:288-289), whereby the genitive affix agrees in gender and number with the head noun (cf. discussion in Grumet 1985; Friedman 1991:94-96). This in turn makes GEN available for derivational processes in many Romani dialects, especially of the Northern and Sinti group, which may account for its productiveness and so for its retention.

A further striking incongruency is the position of INSTR, which is lowest on Blake's scale, but present in all Romani dialects even with the lowest-ranking elements on the Distribution Hierarchy. Above it was implied that the lack of a native analytic alternative for INSTR is connected to the primacy of the basic spatial dimensions of location in the grammaticalization processes leading to the emergence of adpositions, which in turn makes it easier for the language to recruit material to substitute LOC and ABL, and by analogy also DAT and GEN. At the outcome of this development, Romani remains nonetheless an exception to the implicational hierarchies observed elsewhere, though as shown above the attempt to resolve the conflict between universal tendencies and the drift to analytic structures on the one hand, and the structural resources of the language on the other leads to the creation of a hybrid system in some dialects, with foreign or borrowed case marking being assigned to native elements.

References

Bernal, Jorge. 1994. 'The situation of the Gypsy language in Argentina and Brazil'. Paper presented at the Second International Conference on Romani Linguistics, University of Amsterdam, 8-10 December 1994.
Blake, Barry J. 1994. *Case*. Cambridge: Cambridge University Press.

Bloch, Jules. 1970 [1914]. *The Formation of the Marāthi Language*. Delhi: Motilal Banarsidass.

Boretzky, Norbert. 1993. *Bugurdži. Deskriptiver und historischer Abriß eines Romani-Dialekts*. Berlin: Harrassowitz.

---- 1994. *Romani. Grammatik des Kalderaš-Dialekts mit Texten und Glossar*. Berlin: Harrassowitz.

Bubeník, Vít. 1995. 'On typological changes and structural borrowing in the history of European Romani'. In: Yaron Matras, ed. *Romani in contact. The history, structure and sociology of a language*. Amsterdam: John Benjamins. 1-24.

Cortiade, Marcel. 1990. 'Let us finish the matter for good and all with the so-called seven cases of Romani nominal morphology'. In: *Konsultàcia vaś-i standardizàcia e ćhibăqiri*. Warsaw: Startonaj. 95-129.

Fillmore, Charles. 1968. 'The case for case'. In: Emmon Bach & Robert T. Harms, eds. *Universals in linguistic theory*. New York: Holt, Rinehart and Winston. 1-88.

Friedman, Victor. 1991. 'Case in Romani: old grammar in new affixes'. *Journal of the Gypsy Lore Society* 5:1-2. 85-102.

Givón, Talmy. 1984. *Syntax. A functional-typological introduction*. Vol. I. Amsterdam: John Benjamins.

---- 1990. *Syntax. A functional-typological introduction*. Vol. II. Amsterdam: John Benjamins.

Greenberg, Joseph H. 1966. 'Some universals of grammar with particular reference to the order of meaningful elements'. In: Joseph H. Greenberg, ed. *Universals of language*. Cambridge, Mass.: MIT Press. 73-113.

Grumet, Joanne. 1985. 'On the genitive in Romani'. In: Joanne Grumet, ed. *Papers from the Fourth and Fifth Annual Meetings: Gypsy Lore Society, North American Chapter*. New York: Gypsy Lore Society. 84-90.

Hancock, Ian. 1995. *A handbook of Vlax Romani*. Columbus: Slavica.

Holzinger, Daniel. 1993. *Das Rómanes. Grammatik und Diskursanalyse der Sprache der Sinte*. Innsbruck: Institut für Sprachwissenschaft.

Hopper, Paul J., & Elizabeth Closs Traugott. 1993. *Grammaticalization*. Cambridge: Cambridge University Press.

Keenan, Edward L. & Bernard Comrie. 1977. 'Noun phrase accessibility and universal grammar'. *Linguistic Inquiry* 8:1. 63-99.

Hübschmannová, Milena, Hana Šebková & Anna Žigová 1991. *Romsko-český a česko-romský kapesní slovník*. Praha: Státní pedagogické nakladatelství.

Masica, Colin P. 1991. *The Indo-Aryan languages*. Cambridge: Cambridge University Press.

Matras, Yaron. 1994. *Untersuchungen zu Grammatik und Diskurs des Romanes. Dialekt der Kelderaša/Lovara*. Wiesbaden: Harrassowitz.

---- 1995. 'Connective (VS) word order in Romani. *Sprachtypologie und Universalienforschung* 48:1-2. 189-203.

---- 1996. Prozedurale Fusion: Grammatische Interferenzschichten im Romanes. *Sprachtypologie und Universalienforschung* 49:1. 60-78.

Payne, John R. 1995. 'Inflecting postpositions in Indic and Kashmiri'. In: Frans Plank, ed. *Double case. Agreement by Suffixaufnahme*. New York: Oxford University Press. 283-298.

Plank, Frans. 1995. '(Re-)Introducing Suffixaufnahme. In: Frans Plank, ed. *Double case. Agreement by Suffixaufnahme*. New York: Oxford University Press. 3-110.

Sampson, John. 1907. 'Sar, 'with''. *Journal of the Gypsy Lore Society*, New Series 1. 95-96.
---- 1908. 'Tar, 'from''. *Journal of the Gypsy Lore Society*, New Series 2. 286-287.
---- 1926 [1968]. *The dialect of the Gypsies of Wales*. Oxford: Clarendon.
Singh, Ram Adhar. 1980. *Syntax of Apabhraṁśa*. Calcutta: Simant.
Tobin, Yishai. 1992. 'Semantic integrality: A universal semiotic feature of language in perception'. In: Michel Kiefer & Johan van der Auwera, eds. *Meaning and grammar: cross-linguistic perspectives*. Berlin: Mouton de Gruyter.
Wentzel, Tatjana. 1988. *Die Zigeunersprache*. Leipzig: Enzyklopädie.

Written data sources:

Giňa, Andrej. 1991. *Bijav. Romane priphende*. Praha: Apeiron.
Fabiánová, Tera & Milena Hübschmannová. 1991. *Čavargoš. Romaňi paramisi*. Praha: Apeiron.
Lacková, Elena. 1992. *Rómske rozprávky (Romane paramisi)*. Košice: Vychodoslovenské vydavateľstvo.
Matras, Yaron, ed. 1996. *Jekh, duj, trin ... romanes*. Hamburg: Verlag für Pädagogische Medien.
O latscho lab o Jesus Christusester (Markusevangelium Romanes). 1994. Florshain. [Missionary circulation].

OBJECT DOUBLING IN ROMANI
AND THE BALKAN LANGUAGES

VÍT BUBENÍK

Memorial University of Newfoundland, St John's

0. Introduction

Object doubling may be defined as the occurrence in the verb of the pronominal, most typically a clitic form, agreeing in gender, number and case with the patient (DO) or the recipient (IO). This strategy is one of the salient Balkanisms, which is usually discussed in an enumerative non-explanatory fashion in its pan-Balkan dimensions (e.g. Lopašov 1978, Vasilev 1979, Demiraj 1986:1089-98) with a glaring omission of the evidence of Romani. The overall situation in the central Slavic continuum of the Balkans stretching from Bulgaria to Macedonia to Albania was studied most recently by Friedman (1994). He described object reduplication in Bulgarian as a variable discourse phenomenon (in functional terminology as a phenomenon governed by the principles of pragmatics), in Macedonian as a syntactically grammaticalized phenomenon, and in Albanian as a syntactically or morphologically grammaticalized phenomenon. South of this belt, in Greek — as in Bulgarian — we are dealing with a syntactic phenomenon governed by the principles of pragmatics, and north of it, in Daco-Rumanian with a syntactically grammaticalized phenomenon.

1. The situation in the Balkan languages

To use a comparable sentence to exemplify these differences in the Balkan languages, let us examine a complex sentence with several clauses whose object has been assigned the pragmatic function of focus (in Dik's terminology, 1989:263 ff.). We may wish to look at the translation of Mark [9.37] with focal arguments capitalized:

(1)   'Whoever receives one child in my name receives ME; and whoever
        receives me, receives not ME but HIM who sent me'

In terms of communicative strategies the pronominal object in the first sentence
'receives ME' contains new information (completive focus); the same object in
the second sentence 'receives not ME' contains counter-presuppositional
information, i.e. 'he receives not ME but HIM' (called replacive focus). The
translation into Rumanian, Albanian and Macedonian is presented in (2), (3),
and (4), and that into Bulgarian and Greek in (5) and (6), respectively:

(2)   *Oricine primeşte pe unul din aceşti copilaşi in numele meu, mă primeşte
        pe MINE; şi oricine mă primeşte pe MINE, nu mă primeşte pe MINE, ci
        pe CEL ce m'a trimes pe MINE.* (Rumanian 1990)
(3)   *Kush e pranon një fëmijë të tillë, sepse ai më takon MUA. E kush më
        pranon, nuk më pranon vetëm MUA, por njëkohësisht edhe ATË që më
        dërgoi.* (Albanian, International Bible Society)
(4)   *Koj primi edno takvo dete vo moe ime, MENE me prima; a koj me prima
        MENE, ne MENE me prima, tuku ONOJ, koj me pratil.* (Macedonian
        1976)
(5)   *Kojto prieme edno otъ tĕzi dečica vъ moe ime, i MENE priema; i kojto
        priema mene, priema ne MENE, no TOZI kojto me pratil.* (Bulgarian
        1991)
(6)   *Opoios dexθēi héna mikròn paidíon hōsàn etoûto dià tò ónomá mou,
        EMENA déxetai; kaì hopoios dexθē eména, dèn déxetai EMENA, allà
        EKEÎNON hopoû mè ésteilen.* (Greek, Corfu Bible 1823)

Rumanian, Albanian and Macedonian present the grammaticalized version of
object doubling. In Rumanian and Albanian the focal pronominal patient is
anticipated by the proclitic (*mă* in Rumanian, *më* in Albanian); in Macedonian it
is resumed by the proclitic *me*. In syntactic terms, the definite patient in these
languages triggers obligatory doubling in the form of the pronominal proclitic
hosted by the verb. On the other hand, Bulgarian and Greek present object
reduplication as a discourse phenomenon. Significantly, the pronominal clitic
might be used in colloquial varieties of these two languages but it will be
avoided in their literary form (such as that used in biblical translations). Thus in
spoken/colloquial Bulgarian and Greek it is quite appropriate to say *MENE
priema* and *EMENA déxete* to express that the object is focal: 'he receives ME';
and *(mene) me PRIEMA* and *(eména) me DEXETE* (with or without doubling)
to express that the action is focal 'he RECEIVES me'.

The real difference between these two groups of Balkan languages is found in the expression of a focal object. This one has to be doubled if it is definite in Rumanian, Albanian and Macedonian, while this strategy is only used with non-focal objects in Bulgarian and Greek. To look again at our examples in (2) and (4), the clause 'and whoever receives me' contains a focal object which has to be doubled in Rumanian (*si oricine mă primeşte pe MINE*) and Macedonian (*a koj me prima MENE*); on the other hand, in colloquial Greek one would rather not double the object in these circumstances:... *EMENA me déxete; ke pu dexθí EMENA, den déxete EMENA, allá EKINON pu me éstile* (i.e. not *ke pu *me dexθí EMENA*).[1] The situation in Bulgarian is quite complex depending on one's location in the Bulgaro-Macedonian continuum. Here we are entering a grey area of geographic continuum but also, more seriously, in terms of linguistic categories, that of the secondary focus. To use again our data in (2), (3) and (4), one may observe that in the last clause 'who sent me' we are dealing with a definite but non-focal object. This one is doubled in Rumanian (*ce m'a trimes pe mine*) not in Macedonian (*koj me pratil*) and may or may not be doubled in Albanian (*që më dërgoi*).[2]

2. Object doubling in Romani according to Miklosich (1880)

The 19th century data in Miklosich (1880, Vol.XII) are perhaps the earliest recordings of this phenomenon in Romani. They are organized under the headings of Greek, Rumanian and Hungarian Romani. His Greek Romani data on the doubling of pronominal patients include the oblique form of the demonstrative pronoun *oda* 'this, that' resumed by the pronominal enclitic:

(7) a *óles   maradardó les*
      this:OBL killed   he:OBL
      'He killed him' (Miklosich 1880:9)
   b *ólen   čind'á(s) len*
      these:OBL cut:3SG   they:OBL
      'He cut them' (Miklosich 1880:9)

His examples involving nominal arguments display the patients as the left dislocands (or topics to use the terminology of Dik's FG) resumed by the pronominal enclitic:

(8)   *o pekó   mas biknéna   les*
       the roasted meat sell:3PL:PRES it:OBL
       'They are selling roasted meat' (Miklosich 1880:9)

The nominal patient appears normally to the right of the verb as in (9):

(9)   *me továv   la   i   bófča*
       I   wash:1SG she:OBL the press
       'I am washing the press' (Miklosich 1880:10)

In (8) the clitic is resumptive (or anaphoric), in (9) proleptic (or cataphoric).

    His Rumanian Romani examples of pronominal patients and recipients are
of considerable interest. Unlike the Greek ones, they involve the use of long and
short oblique forms of personal pronouns (cf. Hancock 1995:62 for the situation
in contemporary Vlax Romani):

(10)   *dikhliné ma   i   man*
       saw:3PL 1:OBL(short) also 1:OBL(long)
       (cf. Rumanian *și m'au văzut și pe mine*)
       'They saw also me' (Miklosich 1880:9)

If we take *i* (< Serbian 'and' (Conjunction) and 'also' (Adverb)) in its adverbial
function, we may interpret (10) as an instance of expanding focus 'they saw also
ME' (cf. Dik 1989:283), with the long oblique form in the position of focus; i.e.
the adverb *i* cannot be considered to be a phonological host in the phrase *i man*.

    The following examples show no formal distinction between the
pronominal patient and the recipient in the 1st and 2nd Pers Sg:

(11) a *lé   ma   man*
       take 1:OBL(short) 1:OBL(long)
       'Take me!' (= patient) (Miklosich 1880:9)
     b *de   ma   man*
       give 1:OBL(short) 1:OBL(long)
       'Give me!' (= recipient) (Miklosich 1880:9)
(12) a *tut   mudarъn tu*
       you:OBL(long) kill:3:PL you:OBL(short)
       'They will kill you' (= patient) (Miklosich 1880:9)
     b *dáua-tu   me tut*
       give:1SG-you:OBL(short) I   you:OBL(long)
       'I will give you' (= recipient) (Miklosich 1880:9)

Unfortunately, Miklosich did not make any observations on the pragmatics of his examples in (11) and (12). Thus one would like to know whether it was possible to say *dava tu me* 'I'll GIVE you' vs. *dava tu me tut* 'I'll give [it] to YOU (i.e. not to someone else)' with the contrastive focus placed either on the verb or on the extraposed pronominal recipient. Or is the meaning of *dava tu me tut* simply 'I'll give you' — as in Macedonian *ti davam na tebe* —(which would indicate that in this particular variant of Romani object reduplication could have appoximated the status of a syntactically grammaticalized phenomenon ?).

Miklosich's examples of Rumanian Romani nominal patients include a left dislocand appropriately (?) case marked; here one would like to know whether it was also possible to use the absolute form in this position (see below):

(13)   *ekhés   mukhlá-les   džuindó*
       one:OBL leave:PAST:3SG-he:OBL alive
       'He left one alive' (Miklosich 1880:10)

The most remarkable Rumanian Romani example is the translation of 'it seemed good also to him,' *videbatur etiam ei bonum* in Miklosich's Latin. Latin *etiam* corresponds to Serbian *i* in being both the conjunction 'and' the adverb 'also'. Interpreting (14) as an instance of expanding focus, Miklosich's notation remains puzzling (i.e., as in (10) one would expect stress to fall on the pronoun, *not* on the conjunction/adverb *i*):

(14)   *falá-les   í-les   mištó*
       seemed-he:OBL also-he:OBL good
       'It seemed good also to him' (Miklosich 1880:9)

Its counterpart *les fal-les* 'it seems to him' (*videtur ei*) with the resumptive pronoun hosted by the verb is modelled on the pattern of the possessive construction *les nas-les* 'he didn't have' (*non erat ei*) in Miklosich's data. Boretzky provides similar examples from contemporary Bugurdži (1993) and Kalderaš (1994) displayed in (15) and (16), respectively::

(15)   *a   les   te   mudaren e   manušes, kodle   čores*
       and he:OBL that kill:3PL the:OBL man:OBL that:OBL poor :OBL
       'And that they may kill the man, that poor (one).[3] (Bugurdži, Boretzky 1993:95)

(16)   *aj   lel   la   i   la   e lindri*
       and take:3SG she:OBL also she:OBL the sleep
       'And sleep overtakes also her' (Kalderaš, Boretzky 1994:153)

3. Contemporary treatments of object doubling in Romani

Turning our attention to contemporary treatments of object doubling,
Kostov (1962) in his observations on the syntax of Bulgarian Romani did not go
beyond listing some instances of what he calls "pleonastischer Gebrauch der
Pronomina". They are of the usual type with the topical patient as the left
dislocand and the resumptive pronominal clitic hosted by the verb. Unlike in
Vlax dialects, the pronominal patient appears to be case-marked and resumed by
the oblique pronominal form, to judge by his single example reproduced in (17):

(17)   *Tu   mán-da   li naští   te   pindžarés   man*
       you 1:OBL-too Q cannot COMP recognize:2SG   1:OBL
       'Even/also me you cannot recognize?' (Kostov 1962:140)

Kostov concluded that object doubling ("die doppelte Verwendung der
Pronomina bzw. Nomen plus Pronomen") is a characteristic feature of Romani
which is explainable through the influence of Bulgarian. As a reason for this
conclusion he mentions the fact that accusative marking in Romani shows the
signs of 'decay' ("eine gewisse Tendenz zum Zerfall") which is typical of
contemporary Bulgarian.
       Most recently, Boretzky in his treatment of object doubling in Bugurdži
(1993:94-6) and Kalderaš (1994:150-4) attempted a semantic analysis of it.
According to him its primary function is not to highlight the object ("das Objekt
hervorzuheben") but to focus on the verbal action or a certain element linked
with the verbal action ("vielmehr scheint in allen Fällen die Verbhandlung oder
ein mit der Verbhandlung verknüpftes Element fokussiert zu sein"). Thus in
(18), which displays the postverbal nominal patient and the proleptic clitic
hosted by the sentence-initial verb, focus is on the action:

(18)   *patozel les   o divi e   romes*
       crushed he:OBL the giant the:OBL man:OBL
       'The giant CRUSHED the man' (Bugurdži, Boretzky 1993:95)

For the patient or the recipient to be assigned secondary focus they have to be
moved into the marked pre-verbal position.

(19)   *man   o del na del   ma   kale   sabis*
       1:OBL the god not give3SG 1:OBL this:OBL baby
       '(But) to ME God does not give this child' (Bugurdži, Boretzky
       1993:95)

On the basis of similarly constructed examples Boretzky concluded that the left
dislocand may carry the sentential stress.
       As far as the case-marking of left dislocands is concerned, Boretzky
observes that in Bugurdži it is normal for the nominative (unmarked) form to
appear in this position (especially in the possessive construction):

(20)   *on   si len   svašta*
       they is they:OBL everything
       'They have everything' (Bugurdži, Boretzky 1993:94)
(21)   *ov nane   leske   interesantno*
       he isn't   he:OBL:DAT   interesting
       'To him it is not interesting' (Bugurdži, Boretzky 1993:96)

       The situation in Kalderaš is similar with the exception that the pronominal
objects have to be put into the oblique form; contrast (22) a with b:

(22) a *o   majpurano sî les   dešupanź*
       the   oldest   is he:OBL fifteen
       'The oldest one is fifteen years' (Kalderaš, Boretzky 1994:153)
     b *les   sî les   baro khər*
       he:OBL is he:OBL big   house
       'He has a big house' (Kalderaš, Boretzky 1994:153)

In (22b) — unlike in Bugurdži (20) — one cannot use the direct form (**vo sî les*
baro khər).
       Here Romani appears to be using the same strategy known from colloquial
varieties of other languages. For instance, in colloquial French one may say

(23)   *(Moi), ton frère, je-le-lui donne, le livre*

with the recipient as the left dislocand and the patient (object) as the right
dislocand; in adition, the recipient is resumed by the clitic *lui* and the object is
anticipated by the clitic *le* in the verb phrase. If, however, the recipient, *ton*
frère, is moved into the position of tail (in Dik's terminology, 'tail' is an

afterthought to the sentence) it must be appropriately case-marked with the preposition *à*:

(24)   *(Moi), le livre, je le lui donne, à ton frère*

This means that if *ton frère*, the recipient, is assigned the function of theme it may appear in the absolute (prepositionless) form, but in the position of tail it must be appropriately case-marked.

Kalderaš examples (such as 22b) which display case-marked left dislocands are thus best explained as due to the influence of coterritorial Rumanian. Similar examples in Bugurdži such as (25) with a case-marked beneficiary are rare:

(25)   *mange si mange dosta*
        1:DAT is 1:DAT enough
        'I have enough' (Bugurdži, Boretzky 1993:96)

On the basis of these and other similar examples one may conclude that topicalization strategies in Romani may trigger reduplication (as in Bulgarian and Greek), and that its status appears to be that of a discourse phenomenon governed by the principles of pragmatics.

4. *Object doubling outside the Balkan Sprachbund*

In the context of our French examples in (23) and (24), we should remind ourselves that topicalization strategies involving object doubling by means of pronominal clitics are not limited to the Balkan *Sprachbund*. They are certainly more widespread than their recognition in grammars of various languages would make one think so. It is worth mentioning that they are also found in the Asian Romani dialects, such as Nuri as described by Littman (1920) and Macalister (1914). They are of the type 'we buried him, the boy', 'I brought her forth, the wife', with the topical patient in the position of tail (right dislocand). An example for the extraposed object (left dislocand) is in (26):

(26)   *k̠autīrdēnd-săn kiyắkăn   t̠át̠e   zárēs   pardōs-is   k̠autár*
        stole-them   things:ACC fellahs boy:ACC took-him   hyena
        'The fellahs stole the things and the hyena took the boy' (lit. stole-them
        the things, the fellahs [and] the boy, took-him the hyena) (Macalister
        1914:22)

One may observe that the co-territorial Syrian Arabic may use both strategies of placing the topical object in the position of theme or tail (i.e. treating them as extra-clausal constituents) and that doing so will trigger object reduplication in the form of a pronominal clitic (cf. Bubeník 1979). To use a simple example of the question 'Do you know that girl?' with topical 'girl', one could say:

(27)   *Hal bənt, btaʕrəf-a   ʔənte?*
        that girl   2SG:know-her you
        'That girl, do you know her ?' (Syrian Arabic)
or: *btaʕrəf-a   ʔənte, hal bənt ?*
        2SG:know-her you,   that girl
        'Do you know her, that girl ?'

As in Bulgarian and Greek, we are dealing with a discourse phenomenon governed by the principles of pragmatics, because one can say also

(28)   *btaʕref ·   ʔənte hal BƏNT*
        2SG:know you   that girl
        'Do you know that GIRL' (Syrian Arabic)

with sentential stress on the definite object without the latter being doubled by means of the pronominal clitic.

In view of the above facts, I would like to pose a question of how much the strategy of object doubling in Romani is really influenced by its coterritorial languages as opposed to being governed by universal (?) principles of communicative strategies. Years ago, Littman (1920:135) saw the necessity of paying equal attention to both sides. To quote the original

> diese pleonastische Ausdrucksweise kann sich im erzählenden Stil bei Leuten, die auf ziemlich primitiver Sprachstufe stehen, selbständig herausgebildet haben. Doch ist es mir wahrscheinlich, daß hier im Nuri das Neuarabische zum mindesten mitgewirkt hat.

Omitting the comment about the language level of his narrators, Littman suggested that the internal dynamics of Nuri could lead to the development of object doubling strategy; in addition, the influence from the New Arabic adstrate which possesses the same strategy probably contributed to its appearance in Nuri.

5. Conclusion

From the preceding expose it appears that — with the exception of Boretzky's 1993 and 1994 monographs — the available Romanological literature on object doubling is not particularly extensive and informative. Further progress in this important area is impossible unless (i) our corpus of pertinent Romani data is larger and more reliable, (ii) we know more about the phenomenon of object doubling in Romani's coterritorial languages, (iii) and settle satisfactorily certain theoretical issues. A propos the latter point, the constituent called left-dislocand in North American linguistics corresponds to two different constituents in Dik's Functional Grammar (FG) (1989), namely Topic and Theme. I would like to mention that Theme and Tail have no formal counterparts in the Prague School analyses and that Sgall (1987:184) explicitly argues against this extension of the classical dichotomy of Theme and Rheme. Dik's FG defines the Theme as specifying the universe of discourse with respect to which the subsequent predication is presented as relevant; the Tail is characterized as an 'after-thought' to the predication, as information meant to clarify or modify some constituent in the predication. While the Topic is defined as what the utterance is primarily about, the Tail is only an 'after-thought' offset from the main predication by a short pause; it often appears in absolute form without any overt case marking (cf. our French example in 23). It should be made clear that the distinction between Topics and Themes is still in need of further refinement since in the languages of the Balkan *Sprachbund* with grammaticalized object doubling (Macedonian, Arumanian, Daco-Rumanian and Albanian) some Themes must be viewed as incorporated into the predication. This is the case of pronominal arguments which in the first and second person by definition refer to topical (or given) entities. Thus in Macedonian *(mene) mi reče* 'he told me' the speaker (always topical!) who is the beneficiary of the predication does not have to be encoded by the full form: *mi reče* is perfectly satisfactory. Similary, in Greek one would say *mu ípe* 'he told me'. If, however, the full form is used then it is to be taken as Theme: *eména, mu to ípe* 'as far as I am concerned, he told me'. In this case *eména* cannot be assigned focus (receive stress); only *eména mu to ÍPE* (Foc) 'as far as I am concerned, he TOLD me' is available (cf. Endnote 1).

Endnotes

In preparing the final version of this paper I profited from comments by Victor Friedman (University of Chicago) and Norbert Boretzky (University of Bochum, Germany).

1. The clitic pronoun presents the (pro)nominal argument as topical (given) information; consequently, these arguments cannot be assigned focus (cannot receive emphasis). Thus in Modern Greek one cannot say *to éfera to FÍLO mu* (Foc) 'I brought my FRIEND' (only *éfera to FÍLO mu* without object doubling is available); cf. Joseph and Philippaki-Warburton (1987:245).

2. In contemporary Albanian object doubling may vary all the way from a pragmatic function to a fully grammaticalized one in a dialectal continuum. Victor Friedman (University of Chicago) drew my attention to the (1980) translation in post-war Unified Literary Albanian (Kosovo variant) which reduplicates all the definite objects: *e kush më pranon mua, nuk më pranon MUA, por ATË që më dërgoi mua.* (Zagreb/Ferizaj: Krshcjanska Sadashnost/Drita). Compared with the International Bible Society, this version shows a greater degree of the grammatilization of object doubling. On the other hand, the (1930) translation in pre-war literary Korcha Tosk displays no doubling at all: *... që më ka dërguarë* (Korcha: British Foreign Bible Society).

3. The epithet *kodle čores* 'that poor' appears in the portion of tail (in Dik's terminology) as indicated by the pause separating it from the sentence. Similar examples appear only rarely in the available collections of data. There is another one from Drindari (Gilliat-Smith 1913/14:287): *Me túke kъká čhipás mothá túke* 'I will tell you of such and such an affair, to you'. One would like to know whether the speaker paused before the final *túke* 'to you'.

References

Boretzky, Norbert. 1993. *Bugurdži. Deskriptiver und historischer Abriß eines Romani-Dialekts.* Berlin: Harrassowitz.
---- 1994. *Romani. Grammatik des Kalderaš-Dialekts mit Texten und Glossar.* Berlin: Harassowitz.
Bubeník, Vít. 1979. 'Thematization and passivization in Arabic'. *Lingua* 49. 295-313.
Demiraj, Shaban. 1986. *Gramatike historike e gjuhes Shqipe.* Tirana: Shtëpia Botuese "8 Nëntori".
Dik, Simon C. 1989. *The theory of Functional Grammar.* Dordrecht: Foris.
Friedman, Victor. 1994. 'Variation and grammaticalization in the development of Balkanisms'. In: Katherine Beals et al., eds. *Variation and grammaticalization in the development of Balkanisms. Papers from the 30th Regional Meeting of the Chicago Linguistic Society, Vol. 2: The Parasession on Variation in Linguistic Theory.* Chicago: Chicago Linguistic Society. 101-115.
Gilliat-Smith, Bernard. 1913/14. 'The dialect of the Drindaris'. *Journal of the Gypsy Lore Society* 7. 260-298.
Hancock, Ian. 1995. *A handbook of Vlax Romani.* Columbus: Slavica.
Joseph, Brian D. & Irene Philippaki-Warburton. 1987. *Modern Greek.* London: Croom Helm.

Kostov, Kiril. 1962. 'Aus der Syntax der Zigeunersprache Bulgariens'. *Balkansko Ezikoznanie* 4. 131-146.

Littman, Enno. 1920. *Zigeuner-Arabisch. Wortschatz und Grammatik der arabischen Bestandteile in den morgenländischen Zigeunersprachen.* Bonn & Leipzig: Kurt-Schroeder.

Lopašov, Yu.A. 1978. *Mestoimennye povtory dopolnenija v balkanskix jazykax.* Leningrad: Nauka.

Macalister, R.A. Stewart. 1914. *The language of the Nawar or Zutt: The nomad smiths of Palestine.* Edinburgh: Constable.

Miklosich, Franz. 1872-1880. *Über die Mundarten und die Wanderungen der Zigeuner Europas.* Wien: Karl Gerold's Sohn.

Sgall, Petr. 1987.'Prague functionalism and Topic vs. Focus'. In: R. Dirven & V. Fried, eds. *Functionalism in linguistics.* Amsterdam: Benjamins. 169-90.

Vasilev, Christo. 1979.'Die Konvergenz der pronominalen Klitika in den Balkansprachen'. *Zeitschrift für Balkanologie* 15. 208-212.

SUPPLETIVE FORMS OF THE
ROMANI COPULA: '*OVEL/AVEL*'

NORBERT BORETZKY
Ruhr-University, Bochum

0. *Introduction*

In Romani, the copula is one of the few elements that have preserved strong suppletion. Among verbs, the only other suppletive element is 'to go', with its present stem *dža-* and past *gel-*. With this behaviour Romani follows a universal trend according to which the most frequent items (lexemes, grammatical markers) and items that occupy a central position either in human language in general or in the language of a particular society, tend to develop or to maintain irregular or even suppletive forms. Thus it is not astonishing that there is no tendency in Romani to give up suppletion with 'to be/to become', although morphological innovations have occurred. *te si* 'if ... is' and *te sas* 'if ... were' occur as conditionals alongside *te ovel/avel* and *te ovelas/avelas*, and in the dialect of Prilep (Macedonia), future tense is formed with both *si* and *ovel* (*ka sinum* and *ka ovav*; see below 3.); but this does not mean that one of the roots will necessarily replace the other.

The aim of this study is to give an overview of the forms and their distribution among dialects, as well as to clarify the historical relation between *ovel* and *avel*. Occasionally attention is drawn to the theories of Naturalness and Grammaticalization, but no attempt is made to provide a full account of these theories. More on this issue can be found in Boretzky (1995), where the development of all copula forms is discussed, including the history and the diversification of the indicative *si*, the evolution of *sine* as a past form, the use of both copula stems *s-* and *ov-* for grammaticalization, etc..

1. The present stem

Along with the present stem *s-* (*som san si* etc.) covering the indicative or factive domain, there exists another stem *ov-/av-*, which has subjunctive or non-factive functions. It is used in the formation of the so-called subjunctive, in the infinitive of the Central dialects[1], in the future tense, in the imperative, and partly in the conditional (see Figure 1):

	subjunctive	future	infinitive
1.sg.	*te ovav/te avav*	*ka ovav/ovava/avava*	
2.sg.	*te oves/te aves*	*ka oves/ovesa/avesa*	*te ovel/te jel*
3.sg.	*te ovel/te avel*	*ka ovel/ovela/avela*	

	conditional	imperative
1.sg.	*te ovava(s)/ te avava(s)*	
2.sg.	*te ovesa(s)/te avesa(s)*	*ov!; oven!*
3.sg.	*te ovela(s)/te avela(s)*	

Figure 1: The non-factive present copula

The similarity between *ovel* and *avel* might induce the reader to establish a ge-netic connection between the two forms. However, and this will be discussed below, there is only an indirect historical relation leading from *ovel* to *avel*. At any rate, *ovel* cannot be derived from *avel* by postulating a late process of as-similatory labialization.

The future makes use of this second form as well. This is due to the fact that it is derived from a volitive construction *kamav te ovav* 'I want to be/become', which has its parallels in the Balkan languages, but is not necessar-ily copied from them. However, the transition of modal *kamav te ovav* to future tense through semantic reinterpetation and reduction of the form took the same way as in the Balkan languages; cf. Greek θέλω νά πάω lit. 'I want that I go' > θά πάω 'I'll go', Bulgarian *xăštă da idă* > *šte idă*, Rumanian *voi merge* or *voi să merg* > *o să merg*, and Albanian (Tosk dialect and standard) *do të shkoj* for both 'I will/want to go' and future tense (for the Balkan details see Asenova 1989:155-172, and for the Romani-Balkan connections concerning subjunctive constructions see Friedman 1985). It can be taken for granted that Greek and the other Balkan languages provided the model for this process in Balkan Romani, since the Central and other dialect groups of Romani do not have this type of future. What one needs to explain, therefore, as a process of increasing gram-maticalization in terms of grammaticalization theory (cf. Lehmann 1982:13 for a general model, and Heine, Claudi, & Hünnemeyer 1991:170ff. for the devel-opment from volition to future) is the development in older stages of the Balkan languages. With regard to Romani we may speak of borrowed or mediated grammaticalization. From this it follows that the use of the alloform *ovel/avel* in the Romani (Balkan) future form is only connected indirectly with the semantic characteristics of the future in general.

The above forms can be translated by 'to be' and/or 'to become'. In addition to the forms belonging to the non-indicative sphere there is another independent paradigm meaning 'become (something or somebody)' or 'change/turn into', and in the past 'became' or 'happened', and in some dialects even 'to be born' (see Figure 2-3):

	sg.	pl.
1.	*ovav(a)/avav(a)*	*ovas(a)/avas(a)*
2.	*oves(a)/aves(a)*	*oven(a)/aven(a)*
3.	*ovel(a)/avel(a)*	*oven(a)/aven(a)*

Figure 2: The present of 'become'

	sg.	pl.
1.	*uljom/aviljom*	*uljam/aviljam*
2.	*uljan/aviljan*	*uljen/avilen*
3.	*ul-o/-i (ulja/ulilja)*	*ule (ulile)/avile*
	/avil-o; -i	

Figure 3: The past of 'become'

Whereas the present forms *som san si* etc. cannot be traced back to Old Indic *asmi asi asti* etc. without considerable difficulties (see Boretzky 1995: 3ff. for details), the derivation of the regular inflected forms *ovel* and *ulo* from Old Indic does not pose serious problems. The base of present *ovel* is the Old Indic root *bhav-* 'to become' (cf. Sampson 1926: vocab. 17), which in its development to Middle Indic forms (cf. Fahs 1985:322f., Pischel 1973:350, Jacobi 1967:LII) underwent irregular sound changes, especially reductions (see Figure 4):

	sg.	pl.
1.	*bhavāmi > -bhomi > homi*	*bhavāmaḥ > homa*
2.	*bhavasi > -bhosi > hosi*	*bhavatha > hotha*
3.	*bhavati > -bhoti > hoti > hoi*	*bhavanti > honti/hunti*

Figure 4: The present of 'become' in Old and Middle Indic

As a rule, older and younger forms co-occur in Middle Indic. In this verb *-ava-* appears to have been contracted to *-ō-* (a sound change not met with generally in the history of Indic), and a further reduction of *bh-* to *h-* has taken place (a process that is typical of internal aspirates but normally does not occur in word-initial position). Since both stems of the copula, *s-* and *ov-*, have their roots in Old Indic, and since at least some of the functions appear to have been preserved from Old Indic times, suppletion need not be explained as a change that occurred in the history of Romani, but as a much older process. In many languages the copula stem has characteristics of the imperfective aspect only, which means that another stem has to be used in order to form aorists, future forms, etc. ('became', 'will become'). Nearly the same forms are found in Nuri (Middle Eastern Gypsy), with the function of an independent present-future (see Figure 5; cf. Macalister 1914:35). As is often the case with function words, a further reduction took place in Romani: initial *h-* disappeared. It is possible that a *-v-* was inserted between the root *o-* and the personal morphemes in order to obviate the hiatus, thus giving rise to the paradigm shown in Figure 6.

	sg.	pl.		sg.	pl.
1.	*hōmi*	*hōmi*	1.	*ov-av*	*ov-as*
			2.	*ov-es*	*ov-en*
3.	*hōri*	*hōndi*	3.	*ov-el*	*ov-en*

Figure 5: The copula in Nuri   *Figure 6: The conservative present form of 'become'*

But this is only one possibility of historical reconstruction. Perhaps we should not stick too strictly to the Middle Indic forms, but instead base our reconstruction directly on the Old Indic ones shown in Figure 7:

	Old Indic	Middle Indic	Middle Indic	Romani
1.sg.	*bhavāmi* >	**bhovāmi* >	**hovāmi* >	*ovav(a)*
2.sg.	*bhavasi* >	**bhovasi* >	**hovasi* >	*oves(a)*
3.sg.	*bhavati* >	**bhovati* >	**hovati* >	*ovel(a)*

Figure 7: The reconstruction of present 'become' from Old Indic forms

Figure 7 suggests that we would simply need to assume labialization of *a* > *o* (as e.g. in Old Indic *java-* > Romani *džov* 'oats, barley'), without loss of intervocalic *-v-*.

The variant *ovel* occurs in two dialectal zones, namely: i. in South-Balkan, i.e. in all dialects originally spoken south to the Vlach zone, in particular in Arli and related dialects[2], in Erli, in Bugurdži and some varieties of Drindari, furthermore in the European Romani dialect of the Zargari of Northern Persia (Windfuhr 1970), and possibly in other dialects, but of course not in the southern Vlach (Gurbeti, Džambazi, Vlach of Greece and Turkey); it is absent from the dialect of the Sepečides of Izmir (Turkey, see Heinschink 1994; Cech & Heinschink, this volume), although the dialect is quite similar to Arli and Erli; and ii. in subdialects of the Central group, i.e. in the Romungro of Hungary (including Vend), of the Austrian Burgenland, of northern Siovenia (Prekmurje), and partly in Slovakia[3], but not in Czechia or southern Poland.

The variant is missing in Sinti as well as in other dialects spoken north of it. There may be a closer historical relation between the South-Balkan and the Central dialects, as was suggested by M. Heinschink as early as 1978.[4]

	Arli	Erli	Bugurdži	Kalajdži	Paspatian dial.	Vend
1.sg.	ovav/ovava	ovav	ovav/ovava	ojav(a)	uvav(a)	ova/ovā
2.sg.	ove/oveja	oves	oves/ovsa	ojes(a)	uves(a)	oveh/oveha ?
3.sg.	ovel/ovela	ovel	ovel/ovla	ojel(a)	uvel(a)	ōl/ōla(ovla)
1.pl.	ova/ovaa	ovas	ovas/ovasa	ojas(a)	uvas(a)	ovah/ovaha
2.pl.	oven/ovena	oven	oven/ovna	ojen(a)	uven(a)	oven/ovna
3.pl.	oven/ovena	oven	oven/ovna	ojen(a)	uven(a)	oven/ovna

Figure 8: Short and long forms of present 'to become' in some dialects

In most of the southern dialects (Figure 8) the *a*-forms represent present tense, but in Erli (Sofija) the rare long forms have future function (Gilliat-Smith 1910-1914). In Kalajdži (Gilliat-Smith 1940 & 1944), *ojela* etc. has come about via *oela* (which also exists) < *ovela*. In the closely related Drindari (Kotel) this verb is used rather seldom, but forms like *oil(a)* can be found. According to Kenrick (1969:175) it has been borrowed from another dialect, the normal verb being *ačh-*, which has lost its original meaning 'to remain'. (This is a case of renewed suppletion, i.e. the loss of *ov-* did not lead to the abandonment of suppletion itself.) In other varieties of this dialect, however, *ov-* seems to be in normal use:

(1)   *t' eel (< te   ov-el)   ma kisalu žāmutrú!*
       SUBJ   become-3rd.SG me such   son-in-law
       'I wish I had such a son-in-law!' (Gilliat-Smith 1931:80)
(2)   *na   diš–ila   kaj mu o-ela   phira-du*
       NEG appear-3rdSG that FUT become-3rdSG open-PARTIC
       o   cirus
       ART.MASC time
       'It doesn't seem like the weather will clear up!' (Gilliat-Smith 1913/14, 283; a variety spoken near Kotel)

In these varieties of Drindari *ačh-* did preserve its old meaning 'remain'. Therefore, I prefer to assume that *ov-* is an indigenous element in Drindari, and its replacement in the subdialect of Kotel a rather recent development. Drindari is not the only dialect that has incorporated *ačh-* into the copula paradigm; there are also Central dialects of Slovakia which use this stem:

(3)   *but   roma   ča   vaš oda   kam-en   te   ačh-ol   šerutnen-ge,*
       many Roma only for that want-3rdPl SUBJ remain-INF leader.PL-DAT
       kaj....
       that...
       'Many Roma want to be/become leaders only for the reason that ...'

The *u* in *uvava* etc. (in the Paspatian dialect, cf. Paspati 1870:80f.) may have
been introduced by analogy to the past tense form *ulo* (cf. below), but it may
also be due to the confusion between [u] and [o] in unaccented (especially pre-
accent) syllables (cf. *vordon ~ vurdon* 'waggon', *opre ~ upre* 'above', *zoralo ~
zuralo* 'strong', but only *zor* 'strength'), reinforced by the compound influence
of northern Greek and eastern Bulgarian. As for the Central group, *ovel* is
documented for the following dialects: for Vend (Vekerdi 1984), for the dialect
of Liebing as well as for the Romungro of the Burgenland in general (both in
Knobloch 1953), and for various varieties spoken in southern Slovakia where
the main language is Hungarian, but not in the dialect of Humenné in eastern
Slovakia (Lípa 1963). This verb appears to be missing in the dialect of southern
Poland as well, at least I was not able to find any instances of it in the texts of
Kopernicki (1930). For Czechia (Bohemia), Ješina (1886:43f.) does not
mention *ovel*, but somewhere in his data *ulo* 'was born' occurs. The paradigm
given by him resembles the Sinti forms (cf. Finck 1903:13), and one cannot
exclude that these forms belong to a Sinti variety spoken in Bohemia at the time
(see Figure 9; cf. also note 10):

Bohemian		Sinti	
sg.	pl.	sg.	pl.
1. *vaba*	*vaha*	1. *vava*	*vaha*
2. *veha*	*vena*	2. *veha*	*vena*
3. *vela*	*vena*	3. *vela*	*vena*

Figure 9: The future of the copula in Bohemian and in Sinti

In all likelihood *vava /vaba* etc. goes back to *avava* etc., i.e. to forms which
are present in the Slovak group of Central dialects, e.g. in Humenné; cf. also the
Sinti imperative form *av!, ab!* (Holzinger 1993:109). The Bohemian forms
could have been reduced from *ovava* etc., but since past forms like *vejom* 'I became' and *vejomes* 'I had become' (Ješina 1886; again identical with the Sinti
past) must be derived from **aviljom* and **aviljomas* respectively, not from
uljom, uljomas, the entire paradigm should continue original *av-*.
Some functions of *ovel* are illustrated by the following sentences:

i. Future/subjunctive of 'to be':
(4)   *uzar tu-e   ov-ā*
       with you(SG)-LOC become- 1st SG
       'I will be with you' (Vend)

ii. Future/subjunctive of 'to become':
(5)   *terno t' isi, mo phral   t'-ov-el,   phuro t'isi, mo   dat*
       young if is   my brother SUBJ-become-3rdSG old   if is my father
       t' -ov-el
       SUBJ-become-3rdSG
       'If he is a young man, let him be/become my brother; if he is an old man,
       let him be/become my father' (Gilliat-Smith 1912-13:15; Erli)
(6)   *odoles-kr-o   ov-la   ratjaha o   pek-o*
       that-GEN-MASC become-3rdSG early   ART.MASC steaked-MASC
       masor-o
       meat- MASC
       'He will get the roasted meat early tomorrow' (Romano Hangoro 1993,
       90)
(7)   *ténar   vitieždj-a ov-na   andare len-der*
       at least hero-PL   become-3rdPL from   they-ABL
       'At least they will become heroes ' (Liebing; in Knobloch 1953)

iii. Specialized 'to belong to':
(8)   *dehát kas-keri   te   ō-l?*
       but   who-GEN.FEM SUBJ become-3rdSG
       'But to whom shall it belong?' (Vend; cf. Vekerdi 1984)

iv. Future with epistemic function (rare):
(9)   *oda ov-na   odo-la kamašl-i*
       that become-3rdPL that-PL shoe-PL
       'That will be those shoes' (Romano Hangoro 1993:55)

   Parallel to *si te* 'must, has to' there is a necessive construction with *ovel te* :

(10)   *te man-ge o   dat o   gad-a   kin-la   hat ov-la*
       if I-DAT ART father ART cloth-PL buy-3rdSG then become-3rdSG
       ništa   te   počin-el   miste o   siklibe
       nothing SUBJ pay-3rd.SG for   ART learning
       'If my father buys the clothes for me, nothing will have to be paid for the
       class' (Burgenland Romungro)

In addition, *ovel* is used to form a passive, thus repeating a development that led to the inherited passive (*umbladjo(ve)l* < **umbladi-ovel*); cf. the passive future:

(11)   okor taha   ratja-ha   umla-do   ov-eha
           then tomorrow night-INSTR hang-PARTIC.MASC become-2ndSG
           'Then tomorrow morning you will be hanged' (Liebing; in Knobloch 1953)

It is likely that in the Burgenland Romungro this passive construction arose under the influence of German, much like the development in Sinti; cf. from Finck (1903:15) *vela phendlo* 'is said', *vejas phendlo* 'was said', *hi phendlo* 'has been said' and *his phendlo* 'had been said', and from Holzinger (1993:139):

(12)   o   čavo vaj-as   (fon) kol   phuri romia-ter
           ART boy become-PAST.3rd.SG from that-OBL old   woman-ABL
           dre klide-men
           in lock- PARTIC
           'The boy was locked up by that old woman'

Such constructions are rare in dialects outside the German contact sphere. For there, the passive *umblad(j)ol* is used, and if the passive form of a given verb has become obsolete recourse is taken to the reflexive, e.g. *kerel pe(s)* 'is (being) made'. Constructions made up of the main verb participle and the copula, as *si kerdo* 'is made', are rare, but when they occur they have perfect value ('has been made', not 'is being made'). Lípa (1963) does not even mention the possibility of constructing a passive with the aid of *avava* 'become', but in southern Poland (Kopernicki 1930:8) a similar construction seems to be possible:

(13)   tajsa   trit-ona   hodzina-ke av-la   zaveš-imen
           tomorrow third-OBL hour-DAT   become-3rdSG.FUT hang- PARTIC
           'Tomorrow at three o'clock he will be hanged'

In this case, Polish *zostanie (będzie) zawieszony* may have been the model for the Romani passive future.

    In Vlach, the second copula stem is possible after *te*, e.g. *te avel kerdo* 'if it is made' along with *te si kerdo*, but a future *avela kerdo* or *ka avel kerdo* would hardly be used, and **avilo kerdo* 'it has been made' is impossible. Some Central dialects distinguish between present *ovav* and future *ovav-a*, whereas others use *ovava* indiscriminately for both tenses, but even in the first group the distinction does not seem to be clear-cut. In the same way, in some Vlach dialects *avav-a* has future value.

According to the general rules of Romani, an imperfect is formed based on the present paradigm[5]; its meaning is '(usually) became', sometimes 'was going on', and together with *te* 'if' it forms a conditional 'if I were/if I became' (see Figure 10):

	Bugurdži	Romungro	Paspatian
1.sg.	*(te) ovavas*	*ovāhi < *ovavahi*	*uvavas*
2.sg.	*(te) ovsas*	*ovehahi*	*uvesas*
3.sg.	*(te) ovlas*	*ovlahi*	*uvelas*

Figure 10: The imperfect (conditional) of the copula

Example (14) shows a sentence from Burgenland Romungro with iterative meaning (from contexts like these the meaning 'to be born' may have developed):

(14)   *sako berš la*   *Bubaj ovla-hi*   *džek čavoro*
        every year ART.FEM.OBL Bubaj become-IPF.3rdSG some child
        'Every year Bubaj gave birth to a child' (literally: "it became to her";
        Knobloch 1953:30)

In Arli no imperfect ending in -*as* or -*a* has been preserved, but there is a periphrastic form made up from the present of the main verb and uninflected 3rd.p. *sine* 'was'. It is quite possible that this new imperfect is also formed from *ovava* (*ovava sine* etc.), but I have no information about it.

2. The past stem

The present stem *ov-* has an irregular, weak suppletive past *ul-*, which most probably goes back to the past participle of the verb *bhav-/bhū-*. For phonological reasons, one cannot link it to the present stem *ov-*. From Old Indic and Pali *bhūta-* (-*hūta*) we arrive at Prakrit *bhūa-/hūa*, but since this cannot be the ancestor of Romani *ul-*, we have to depart from *bhūta-*, and arrive at *ul-* through regular sound change and the loss of *h-*: *bhūta- > hūta- > hūla- > ul-*.[6] The personal forms, e.g. 1st sg. *uljom/ulom*, *ujom*, (Figure 11) have come into being by adding the copula *s-* to the past stem, i.e. *uliom < *uli-hom* and perhaps < *ul-isom through irregular sound change, in the same way the past of other verbs was formed (see Boretzky 1995:19ff., esp. fn. 17).

	Arli/Erli	Bugurdži	Kalajdži	Vend	Romungro	Paspatian
1.sg.	uljom/ulom	ujom	ojom	ūjum	uljan	uniljan/unilan
2.sg.	uljan/ulan	ujan	ojan	ūjal	uljan	uniljan/unilan
3.sg.	ulo & uli	ulo & uj	ojas	ūlo & ūli	uljas; ulo & uj	uniljas/unilas

Figure 11: Past forms of 'become' in some dialects

The forms given in Paspati (1870:81) may have come about by metathesis from *ulino, an expanded participle to ulo. It is less convincing to derive them from a reshaped Middle Indic present -bhuṇāti instead of -bhoti. In Drindari ulo might be a borrowed element being used but rarely (cf. ov- in this dialect). The meaning of these past forms is 'I became, I have become', and in the 3rd person they also mean 'it happened'. In subdialects of Romungro (Hungary, Burgenland and southern Slovakia) this verb replaced bijandol, bijandilo 'to be born' (the latter being preserved for animals). The Vend paradigm shows that the gender-inflected forms of the 3rd person singular have been preserved, which makes this dialect very similar to Arli and Bugurdži.[7]

For the functions of ulo consider the following:

(15)   kaj   ulj-an,   sinko, ta   našavdj-ilj-an?
        where become-PAST.2nd.SG son   and lose-PASS-PAST.2nd.SG
        'Where have you been, my son, did you get lost?' (Gilliat-Smith 1912:88; Erli)

One might assume that the meaning of this uljan is simply 'you have been', but here it can be interpreted as an action, not necessarily as a stative: 'where did you get (to)?'. The two meanings are closely related, however, as demonstrated by the following example:

(16)   ul-o   kaj   ul-o   jek
        become.PAST-3rdMASC that/where become.PAST-3rdMASC one
        xoraxaj
        Turk
        'Once upon a time there was a Turk' (Gilliat-Smith 1912:85)

This might be conceived of as a shortening or a contamination of lit. 'what happened - happened, (there was) a Turk' (cf. Gilliat-Smith 1912:85), but since this formula is interchangeable with *sine kaj sine* 'it was that/where it was', we may accept the first version as well. Note that in this dialect *áčhol ačhilo/ašlo* 'remain' is used for 'become, turn to' as well (like in Drindari and in dialects of Slovakia):

(17) *ukud-inj-as   l-es,   áčh-ol   manuš*
     read.spell-PAST-3rdSG he-OBL remain-3rdSG man
     'She cast a spell over him, he became a human being'
(18) *ma   dža,   sinko, kaj ka   ačh-os   bařes-te*
     NEG.IMP go-IMP son   that FUT become-2ndSG stone- LOC
     'Don't go, my son, for you will turn into a stone' (Gilliat-Smith 1945:23)
(19) *oho, sinko, so   šukar   ačh-il-o   t-o*
     oh son   what beautiful remain-PAST-3rdMASC your(SG)-MASC
     kher
     house
     'Oh son, how beautiful your house has become!'

It is not clear which of the subdialects of Erli display both *ov-* and *ačh-*, and what the functional distinction between them is like.
    Comparable forms appear in the Central dialects:

(20) *te afka ul-o*
     and so   become.PAST-MASC
     'And so it happened'
(21) *fiti   ul-i   i   kaša*
     ready become.PAST-FEM ART porridge
     'The porridge was ready' (Vend; Vekerdi 1984)
(22) *hat ul-o   ratja-ha   taj al-i   i*
     then become.PAST-MASC night-INSTR and come.Past-FEM ART
     ura hotj...
     hour that
     'Now it became night, and there came the hour that ...' (Liebing; in Knobloch 1953)

The meaning 'to be born' is restricted to Central dialects:[8]

(23) *upr-o   them al-i   o   šovardeš-to berš kada*
     on-ART world come.PAST-FEM ART 60-th   year when

ul-i
born.PAST-FEM
'Into the world she came in the 60th year, when she was born'
(Knobloch 1953:34; Burgenland)

(24)   *taj   pisin-d-e   hodj u-l-e   l-a   duj   žukial-a*
       and write-PAST-3rdPL that become-PAST-3rdPL she-OBL two dog-PL
       'And they wrote him that she gave birth to two dogs' (ibid. 46)

(25)   *me ul-il-om   andr-o   17.11.1924*
       I   born-PAST-1stSG in-ART
       'I was born in ...' (Romano Džaniben 1, 1994:30)

A new past stem *ulil-* occurs alongside *ul-*, and a new present *uljol* has been shaped from it by back formation. The sources we have to rely upon are not explicit enough to show the precise distribution of *uljol, ulilja*, but it seems to be lacking in Hungary (absent from Vekerdi's dictionary 1983). At any rate it is used in southern Slovakia. There is another possibility to derive this word: it might continue Vlach *huljel* (Bugurdži *uhjel*), past *hulisto/*hulilo* (Bugurdži *uhilo/uhicilo*) 'to descend', which semantically reminds us of German 'niederkommen', lit. 'come down', i.e. 'to give birth to'; cf. also *uljol tele* 'to go down' in Slovakia (Hübschmannová et al.1991). For the moment, at least a contamination of the two stems cannot be excluded. To me, the latter assumption seems more likely than to derive it from *huljel* exclusively, because there are examples for the short forms *ulo* and *uli* meaning 'was born', which one could not explain if this verb continued *huljel* 'descend'. Also, the passive of *ker-* 'make', which in many dialects is used for 'become', additionally acquired the meaning 'be born', and this corroborates the assumption made with regard to the semantic transition with *ul-*.[9]

Apparently, not all Central dialects that substituted *av-* for *ov-* with the meaning 'to be, become, happen' (see below), also preserved *ul-* for the meaning 'to be born', and the adjective *ulo* for the meaning 'ripe, cooked'. In Ješina (1886) an isolated *ulo* 'born' is mentioned, but it may be taken from another dialect or misunderstood by the author.[10] In Lípa (1963) no *uljom* etc. 'I was born' can be found, but in another text from Humenné (Gejza Demeter in Romano Džaniben 2/1994:37f) *ulil-* is used for 'to be born' (dialect mixing?). The following distribution seems to hold for at least some varieties of this dialect: 'to be, to become': pres./fut. *avava, aveha, jela* etc.; cond. *avavas, avehas, jelas* etc., past *uljom, uljan, uljas* etc., plup. (cond.) *uljomas, uljalas, uljahas* etc.; 'to happen, to become (profession)': *ačhol (pes), ačhola (pes), ačholas (pes), ačhilja (pes)*; 'to be born': pres. *uljol*; past *ulilja* (different from the past of 'become'); noun *ulipen* 'birth'. Some examples follow:

(26) *sar ulj-ol   o   čhavoro, ker-en   les-ke bonja*
      as   born-3rdSG ART child   make-3rdPL he-DAT baptizm
      'When the child is born, he is baptized'
(27) *angl' oda midig o   čhavo ul-ij-a*
      before this always ART child born-PAST-3rdSG
      'Before the child was born'

In some Balkan dialects the vocalism of the present form was influenced by that of the past (see above), and the same analogy leveling took place in the opposite direction, resulting in past forms like **oljom* or **oviljom*, which in the dialect of the Varna Tinners (Kalajdži; cf. Gilliat-Smith 1944) gave *ojas < *oljas* or **oviljas*. In Cortiade (1992:35) a form *ondilo* is given, which is characteristic of the Mahadžcr dialect (Southern Serbia). This form reminds us of the Paspatian *unil-*; apparently, a form related to *unil- < ulino, -i* has been extended by the past tense morpheme *-d-*.

3. The replacement of ov- and ul-

In Vlach as well as in many dialects spoken north of it *av-* has been substituted for *ov-*. Sampson (1926: vocab. 17) seems to view this *av-*, but not *av-* 'to come', as a reflex of Old Indic *bhav-* ("a weakened form of Continental Gypsy *uv-*, *ov-*"), i.e. as a development of *bhavati > *havati > avel*, that has taken place in some of the dialects, whereas in others the change resulted in *ovel* (< **hovel < bhavati*; see above). The divergence is considered to be an old one, and *av-* I and *av-* II are thought to have merged by mere coincidence. But this view can be proven wrong for several reasons. If Sampson were right, it would not be understandable why in Vlach and other dialects no past form *ulo <* Old Indic *bhūta-* has survived, and the past of *av-* II 'to come' *avilo* is in use for the meaning 'he became' as well. Furthermore, there would be no plausible explanation for the fact that in many Central dialects we have mixed paradigms going back to both *ov-/ul-* and *av-*. Last but not least, the development of a distinct verb 'to be born', or at least of isolated forms such as the adjective *ulo* 'ripe, cooked' would remain unexplained.

There is another reason for regarding *ov-* as the oldest element once present in all dialects of Romani: the formation of passive forms as *kerdj-ovel* 'is made' and *barj-ovel*, 'grows, becomes big' made up of participles or adjectives + *ov-el* (lit. 'made it-becomes' and 'big it-becomes' respectively).[11] No doubt all this points to the fact that *avel* 'he becomes' and *avilo* 'he became' are etymologically identical with the homophonous forms of 'to come'. What has taken place here is a grammaticalization of *av-* 'to come' (as well as a regrammaticalization or renewal of the concept of non-indicative 'to be, to become') and a subsequent replacement of *ov-* and *ul-*. This development was favoured by the phonological similarity of *ov-* and *av-*, but also by the semantic characteristics of the verb 'to come', as demonstrated by the following sentences:

(28)   *bar-e lov-e   amen   av-na*
       big-PL money-PL we.OBL come-3rdPL
       'We will get/have much money' (Kopernicki 1930:11)
(29)   *av-il-o   man-ge pharo*
       come-PAST-MASC I-DAT difficult
       'It became difficult for me' or 'it came to me as a difficulty' (Kalderaš;
       Boretzky 1994)

Constructions like these show that 'come' and 'become' are semantically related; cf. also the etymological relatedness in English. Apparently, future is seen as something to come in many cultures (this is widespread in West African languages; cf. Welmers 1973:353, Boretzky 1983:122ff.; in Swedish a certain future tense is formed by *komma att* INF 'come to'). On the other hand, there are instances of *ovel* and *ulo* for which the most natural translation is 'to come', not 'to be' or 'to become', perhaps a proof that the opposite path of change is possible as well. This is the case in Bugurdži and in Erli:

(30)   *i   o   raklo ul-o   pes-ke   an po*
       and ART boy   become.PAST-MASC REFL-DAT in REFL.POSS
       berš-a
       year-PL
       'And the boy became older' (lit. 'came in his years') (Boretzky
       1993:191)
(31)   *tu   te   čhaj-a   dži kaj na   l-es   palal,*
       you(SG) your daughter-ACC until that NEG take-2ndSG behind
       te   no   ov-el   mamuj man nisav-i,   me
       so that NEG become-3rdSG in.front.of me no.one-FEM I
       tu-ke   řomni n' ov-av
       you(SG)-DAT wife   NEG become-1stSG
       'As long as you do not send your daughter away so that no one comes before me, I will not be a wife to you' (Gilliat-Smith 1912-13:86)

As is often the case in grammaticalization, a lexeme can be utilized to form more than one grammatical concept in different languages and sometimes even within one language (cf. Heine et al. 1993:40ff., where for 'come' 21 different grammaticalizations are listed), and different lexemes may give rise to the same category ("multiple paths"; cf. Hopper & Traugott 1993:112f). As mentioned above, there are mixed paradigms, obviously the result of the gradual replacement of *ov-/ul-*. This process may be observed in some Central dialects, taking into account all data available. This is even less compatible with the reconstruction suggested by Sampson. Vend preserved present *ovā* etc. and conditional *ūjomahi*, but the simple past *ūjom* has become obsolete. In Slovak Romani the present stem is taken from *av-* throughout, and for the conditional old *ujomas* and new *avljomas* (Hübschmannová et al. 1991:633) are competing; the East-Slovak dialect of Humenné (Lípa 1963) does not have the variant *avljomas* for the conditional, and the simple past *uljom* etc. is used only after *šaj/našti* 'can/cannot':

(32)   *ajso rom   šaj ulj-a   godjer   a   šaj*
        such Rom   may become.PAST-3rdSG intelligent and may
        pretho-dj-a
        translate-PAST-3rdSG
        'There may have been such an intelligent Rom who could have translated this' (p.113)

Hübschmannová et al. (1991) provide the paradigm reproduced in Figure 12:

	future	condit.pot.	past (restricted)	cond.irrealis
1.sg.	*avava*	*avavas*	*uljom*	*uljomas/avljomas*
2.sg.	*aveha*	*avehas*	*uljan*	*uljanas/avljanas*
3.sg.	*(j)ela*	*(j)elas*	*ulja(s)*	*uljahas/avljahas*

Figure 12: Forms of 'become' in Slovakia

Sentence (33) is an example for the pluperfect (irrealis):

(33)   *na   ulj-ah-as   feder kol-a   kaxnj-a   takoj*
        NEG become-PLUPERF-3rdSG better that-OBL.FEM hen-OBL at once
        te   čhin-el ?
        SUBJ cut-INF
        'Wouldn't it have been better to kill that hen at once?' (Romano Džaniben 1994/2, 48)

Innovations, as hinted above, did not result in the total leveling of the copula paradigm, e.g. in the domination of the root *s-* in all tenses and moods. There is certainly quite a frequent conditional *te si* 'if it is' or *te sas* 'if it were' besides *te ovel* and *te ovelas*, but in general *ovel/avel* has been preserved for the subjunctive and the future. The only other exception I know of is Prilep, where *ka sinum* 'I will be' and *ka ovav* 'I will become' are distinguished, at least formally, apparently according to the Macedonian model *k'e sum* and *k'e bidam* (Bulgarian *šte săm* and *šte băda*), which are not distinguished consistently (cf. Koneski 1954, II:209 for Macedonian, and Stojanov 1993:340 for Bulgarian).

In the dialects that have substituted *av-* for *ov-* we observe tendencies to differentiate the full verb *av-* 'to come' from the copula *av-* by phonetically reducing the latter ("split" or "divergence" in grammaticalization theory; cf. Hopper & Traugott 1993:117): i. in varieties of Slovak Romani (cf. for instance Lípa 1963) we have 3rd persons future *jela* and *jena*, subjunctive *te jel* and *te jen*, and conditional *te jelas* and *te jenas* contrasting with *avela, te avel, te avelas* etc. for 'to come'; ii. in southern Gurbeti (e.g. in Kosovska Mitrovica) as well as in Džambazi (Kumanovo) *av-* intruded the domain of the past 'was', but only in the negative forms: *sa* 'was', but *n'avlo/n'avli* 'was not, there was not; did not have' (competing with *naj-sa*). Consider the following examples:

(34) *n' avl-i   i   familija khoni   la-sa*
      NEG become.PAST-FEM ART family   somebody she-INSTR
      'No one of the family **was** with her'

(35) *n' avl-o   bući, n' avl-o*
      NEG become.PAST-MASC work NEG become.PAST-MASC
      khanči
      something
      'There was no work, there was nothing'

(36) *oj lj-ol   pe av-il-i   akari k-i   Germanija*
      she take-3rdSG REFL come-PAST-FEM hither to-ART Germany
      'She set out (and) **came** hither to Germany' (Džambazi from Kumanovo, Macedonia)

It is not clear whether in Kalderaš or in the Vlach of Ajia Varvara reduced forms like *t' ael, kam ael* or even *t' el* instead of *te avel, kam avel* are used for 'be, become' exclusively or if they occur indiscriminately with both meanings as alegro forms.

4. 'to have' and 'to obtain' in Romani

In dealing with the copula, expressions for 'to have' in various dialects have been mentioned. Here we want to represent and to supplement these data. An independent verb 'to have' exists only in some South-Balkan dialects, especially in the Paspatian dialect (Paspati 1870) and in the dialect of Prilep (my own recordings): *ther-*, which in other dialects means 'to get, to obtain' (in varieties of Kalderaš, cf. Boretzky 1994) and 'to hold', the latter apparently being the oldest meaning (cf. Old Indic *dharati/dhārayati*).

The bulk of the dialects makes use of a construction containing 'to be': *si man, si tut, si les* etc., which because of its generality must be of old age. Contrary to what one might expect, 'is' is not combined with the dative (*si mange* 'it is to me') or the locative (*si mande* 'it is with me') of the personal pronoun or the noun (at least not when meaning 'have'), but with the accusative. It is very likely that this construction stems from a time when the secondary case system of Romani was not fully developed and the form of the accusative represented a general oblique case displaying more functions than the modern accusative, among others that of a genitive. Note that the oblique form of Romani continues the Old Indic genitive. Thus, *si ma* may have meant once 'it is of me/it is mine'. Other modern Indic languages lacking a special verb for 'to have', such as Hindi or Punjabi, also use the copula, but combine it with various postpositions (*kā* 'of' for permanent possession or relationship, *ke pās* 'at, beside' for actual possession in Hindi; *da* 'of', *nuŋ* 'to' or *koḷ* 'beside' in Punjabi). Thus we have the following forms in Hindi:

(37) *zamīndār k-e   do gāmv th-e*
      land owner POSS-PL two village be.PAST-PL
      'The land owner owned two villages' (McGregor 1972: 52)
(38) *us-ke   pās   paisā nahīm hai*
      he/she.OBL-POSS beside money NEG is
      'He has no money' (McGregor 1972: 51)

In Punjabi we have:

(39) *muṇḍ-e da   bəut vəḍḍa syr si*
      boy-OBL POSS very big   head was
      'The boy had a very big head' (Shackle 1974:65)

One of the possibilities to express 'have' in classical Persian agrees with the Romani construction in nearly all details:

(40)   *ma-râ dar šahr dust-ân   besyar-and*
       I-OBL in   town friend-PL many- copula.3rd.PL
       'I have many friends in the town'

Note that *-râ* has a history comparable to that of the Romani oblique morpheme. In the older language it served to mark the indirect object and other case relations, but in the modern language it has become the marker of the definite direct object. More research is necessary in order to clarify the origin of the Romani construction, but it is most likely that it was already there when the Roma came into contact with European languages including Greek.

On the whole, the copula-form of the 'have'-construction and the general copula of a given dialect are identical, but in dialects where emphatic and enclitic copula-forms exist, the emphatic form is preferred for the 'have'-construction. Thus we have in Vend *si ma* 'I have', but *hi* 'is'; in Arli *isi man* 'I have', but unstressed enclitic-*i/-j* 'is' (in all varieties?); in Kalajdži *sine man* 'I have' (present!), but unstressed *si/isi* (in this dialect from Rusčuk the past is *sias* - as in the Drindari-group); in Ajia Varvara *ninaj man* (*inaj man*) 'I don't have' and *ninas man* 'I didn't have', but unstressed *naj* 'is not' and *nas* 'was not' (Igla 1996:49). For the positive, no distinction is made between 'have' and 'is'.

It is only southern Gurbet and Džambazi that have the reversed distribution: *sa ma* 'I had', but partially *sasa* 'was' and pl. *sesa* 'were'. The first, more widespread distribution of the weak and strong forms appears to match the assumptions of the Naturalness Theory (cf. Mayerthaler 1981), since 'to have' can be considered the more marked category of both, but other interpretations are possible as well (e.g. phonetic reduction of all expressions undergoing grammaticalization).

Parallel to *si man* the suppletive constructions *ovel man/avel man* occur, meaning 'to get, to obtain' in addition to 'to have'; consider the following constructions in some dialects: Southern Balkan and Romungro (*ovel ma*), *te ovel ma*, *te ovelas ma* ; Vlach dialects *avela ma*, *te avel ma*, *avelas ma*; Central dialects *(j)ela ma*, *te (j)el ma*, *ulja ma*, *uljahas ma* . The following provide some examples:

(41)   *obavezno t'   ov-ol   tu   sarma*
       absolutely SUBJ become-3rdSG you(SG).OBL sarma
       'At any rate you will get sarma' (Arli, Baručisko)
(42)   *t'   ov-el   ma odoriga tumači*
       SUBJ become-3rdSG me there   interpreter
       '... that I get an interpreter' (Bugurdži; Boretzky 1993:174)

(43)   *numa 'k   mija   marke t'   av-el   amen   po śon*
         only   one thousand marks SUBJ become-3rdSG we.OBL on month
         'If we had/obtained at least one thousand marks a month' (Kalderaš;
         Boretzky 1994:204)

(44)   *kaj mr-e   čav-en   te   ha-l*
         that my-PL child-PL.OBL SUBJ eat-3rdSG(=INF)
         t'   ou-l
         SUBJ become-3rdSG
         'That my children have/get to eat' (Burgenland; Knobloch 1953)

In Hübschmannová et al. (1991) I was not able to find instances of 'to get'; apparently, only *lel* 'to take' and *astarel* 'to grab' are used for this meaning:

(45)   *el-a (avela)   tu-t   tajsa   časos?*
         become-3rdSG you(SG)-OBL   tomorrow time
         'Will you have time tomorrow?'

(46)   *jekh l-es   našti   ulj-a   čačo*
         one   he-OBL cannot become.PAST-3rdSG right
         'In one thing he couldn't be right'

Nevertheless, in some contexts a connotation of 'get' can be identified:

(47)   *mi tu   j-el (avel)   bari baxt!*
         let   you(SG).OBL become-3rdSG great luck
         'May you have (get) good luck!'

The meaning 'to get, to obtain' seems to occur exclusively with the present stem *ovel/avel*, and the past stem *ulo/avilo* cannot be used for this purpose.

5. *Conclusion*

The Romani copula displays a set of properties that appear to be typical of elements with a high degree of grammaticalization: The copula has more variants (allomorphs) than any other element of the language, both inter- and intradialectally. It is also one of the few elements that have developed suppletive forms; in addition to the stem *s-* (imperfective) a stem *ov-* (perfective) was in existence since Old Indic times.

Suppletion has not been abandoned in any of the dialects; on the contrary, another stem *ačh-*, originally meaning 'remain', has taken over functions similar to those of *ov-*. There seem to be dialects where all three stems are in use, but it is not clear whether *ov-* and *ačh-* acquired clearly distinctive functions or not. In the Vlach dialects and other dialect groups north of them *ov-* has been replaced by *av-*, originally 'come'. There are dialects in which this process did not come to an end, thus resulting in mixed paradigms. Beside *ov-* and *ačh-* many dialects use the passive of *ker-* 'make', *kerdjol, kerdilo* 'be made; feign' for expressing 'become' and even 'be born', but in no dialect has this stem acquired the neutral meaning of 'is, was', i.e. 'will be' cannot be expressed by *ka kerdjol* but only by *ka ovel/avel* and perhaps in some dialects (Drindari?) by *ka ačhol* too.

The basic stem *s-* has an atypical inflection, thus diverging from all other verbs: the present inflection parallels the past inflection of other verbs, and the inflection of the imperfect is identical with the pluperfect inflection of other verbs. This irregularity is explained by the fact that the past of normal verbs is the result of a grammaticalization process. The copula has been utilized in such grammaticalization processes. This is seen with the present of *s-* in the formation of the past tense, the old imperfect *asi* in the formation of the imperfect, both elements combined in the formation of the pluperfect, and the stem *ov-* in the formation of the passive. Both copula stems provided the material for a construction meaning 'to have'.

Historically, the Old Indic stem *as-/s-* underwent a number of irregular sound changes as well as analogical changes before giving rise to the actual forms of the individual dialects. Since the history of *s-* is outside the scope of this paper, we will restrict ourselves here to the discussion of *ov-*, especially the problems connected with suppletion and grammaticalization. Romani is not exceptional in having two stems. There are many languages displaying a variety of stems with the copula, e.g. English with *is, be* and *was*. In some language groups the distinction of more than one form is based on semantic factors (e.g. in West African languages), but in Indo-European languages suppletion is (or was) triggered by aspectual properties. Apparently, the basic stem *s-* did not qualify to express perfective (aorist) meaning; moreover, it could not even be used for rendering ongoing events or actions, but was restricted to expression properties, dispositions, and states. Whenever perfective or progressive meanings had to be expressed, other stems carrying connotations like growing, becoming, and similar meanings had to be adduced. Such elements can be found in the Balkan languages as well, and often more than one root has been associated with the original copula.

Thus we have Greek γίνομαι, έγινα 'to become, to happen', and στέκο–μαι, στύθηκε 'to stand' - a rather new suppletion. Rumanian has an infinitive *a fi*, subjunctive *să fie*, aorist *fu/fuse*, participle *fost*, a second stem inherited from Latin and not in use for the present. It is no longer aspectually distinctive from

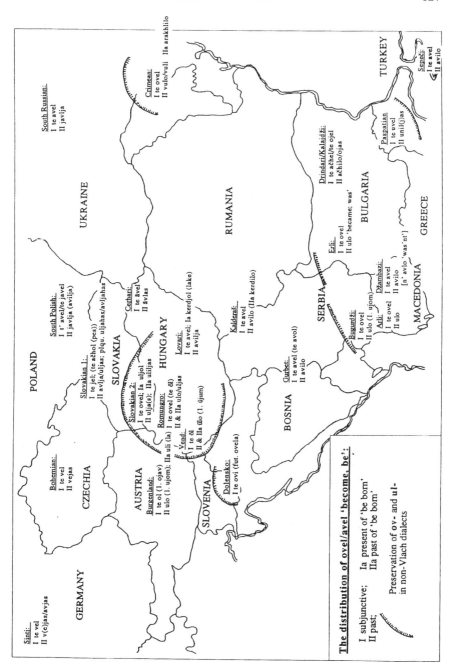

The distribution of ovel/avel 'become, be':

I subjunctive;   Ia present of 'be born'
II past;   IIa past of 'be born'

Preservation of ov- and ul-
in non-Vlach dialects

the basic stem *sînt* (*ieste*), i.e. it has become suppletive in the strict sense of the term. Therefore, other verbs have been added to fill the gap: *a se face* 'to be made' = 'to become', *a deveni* (< French), *a ajunge* 'to reach' etc.. Further examples are the Albanian aorist *qe* 'was, became' and participle *qënë*, and further passive *bëhet, u bë* < 'be made', again a rather recent formation; and Bulgarian *bǎde*, aorist *bidne* (the latter is rare), a very old element going back to Indoeuropean **bhū*, and more recent *stava, stana*. Comparable formations can be found in other Slavic languages.

Some linguists may not be prepared to accept all these forms as suppletive in the technical sense of the word, since the new stems cannot be used with precisely the same functions as the copula proper 'is, was'. However, if we take into account that other verbs normally have both an imperfective and a perfective stem, the relation between the two stems of the copula can be seen as an instance of functional suppletivism. Moreover, in some cases the functional distinction between the two stems is already blurred (as with Bulgarian *e* and *bǎde*).

The existence of at least two stems in the Balkan languages may have contributed to the preservation of two stems in Romani too, but the main reason has to be sought in language-universal, functional factors. As for the distribution of *s-* and *ov-*, parallels can be drawn to Greek and the other languages, but in the details Romani differs considerably from its Balkan surroundings. In my view, the development of *kerdjol* 'be made' > 'become' can also be explained by universal factors rather than by interference. The reinterpretation of *ačh-* 'remain' as 'become' seems strange, but it is by no means singular in Europe; thus we have Polish *zostać* to remain' and 'to become', and Swedish *bli(va)* with the same meanings.

When *av-*, originally 'come', replaced *ov-*, a rather complex process was taking place. First, *av-* must have been reinterpreted (see Hopper & Traugott 1993, especially chapters 3-4) in ambiguous contexts to mean 'become' instead of 'come' (cf. examples 28 and 29), and later transferred to non-ambiguous contexts. Then, *ov-* must have receded until it fell out of use. The existence of mixed paradigms containing both *ov-* and *av-* proves that the development took this pathway; nothing speaks in favour of a scenario where *ov-* was abandoned first, and the gap then had to be filled by *av-*. But this is only part of the story. We are faced with the fact that there already existed an element *ov-* suppletive to *s-* fulfilling its functions not worse than the new *av-*. Moreover, it was not as ambiguous as the new *av-* is. All this suggests that the motive for the renewal was not increase of informativeness, but a tendency towards greater expressiveness by the substitution of an element with a concrete lexical meaning. (For renovation as opposed to innovation cf. Lehmann 1982:20ff., and for the motives of renewal cf. Hopper & Traugott 1993:121ff.).

Such 'emotional' forces must be of considerable strength; in our case they resulted in the replacement of an element that already was suppletive, and one should recall again that *av-* remained ambiguous, notwithstanding the fact that there are tendencies to differentiate *av-* 'come' from *av-* 'become, be' morphologically. On the whole, suppletive items tend to preserve or to renew suppletivism, even when the functional distinction has become weak or is given up altogether.[12]

Endnotes

1. Hancock (1995:32f) subsumes under this term the non-Vlach dialects of Hungary, Slovakia, Czechia, and Southern Poland. The Sinti groups living in these countries are not included. Hungarian (Romungro and closely related dialects) constitutes a group of its own. This new classification corresponds rather well to the distribution of *ovel* and *avel*.

2. The data for Gurbeti, Džambazi, Arli, and the Prilep dialect are taken from my own recordings.

3. Lípa (1979) divides the non-Vlach dialects of Slovakia into two groups: a smaller Hungarian group spoken to the South of a line connecting Bratislava, Zvolen, and Rimavská Sobota, and a greater indigenous Slovak group spoken to the North. This line corresponds roughly to the Slovak-Hungarian linguistic boundary.

4. Heinschink (1978) identifies some other common features that speak in favour of a common ancestry: *uzar* 'from' (besides *uze* 'at, by, to') < Serbian *uz* (much less frequent in Serbian than *u* 'in', *kod* 'at' and others), which takes the place of *ke/kaj* in other dialects; *pedar* 'upon' < *upreder*, enclitic *tov*, *toj* 'he, she'. An archaism of Romungro is the 3rd person singular past in *-o* masc. and *-i* fem. with verbs of motion.

5. The imperfect marker *-as/-ahi* goes back to Old Indic *āsīt*, Middle Indic *āsi*, ipf. of *as-* 'to be' (cf. Sampson 1926:192; Bubeník 1995:10). Apparently, this element was facultatively combined with the present forms of the verb forming something like an imperfect, and later on became agglutinated to the inflected verb. This explanation makes more sense than to derive *-*asi* from pres. *asi 'is' < Old Indic *asti*, especially for semantic reasons.

6. Bloch (1932:32) also derives Nuri 3.sg.past *hră/hri* directly from *bhūta-*. This is unproblematic as far as *-t-* > *-r-* is concerned, but not with regard to the loss of long *ū*!

7. Gender forms of the 3rd sg. survived with other verbs too, cf. Vend *gelo* 'went', *alo* 'came', *mulo*, 'died', *bešto* 'sat', and Liebing (Knobloch 1953) *gielo*, *pielo* 'fell'.

8. With this meaning, *ulo* seems to be absent from the Balkan dialects. At least, I was not able to detect it in any of the publications on these dialects known to me or in my own recordings. M. Cortiade (Courthiade), who is known for his profound knowledge of the southern dialects, confirmed my assumption (personal communication).

9. In the Vlach of Ajia Varvara (Athens) active *ker-el* 'makes' is also used for 'gives birth to' (Igla 1996), but this seems to be a calque from Greek κάνει (παιδιά).

10. As Grant (1995) has shown, both Ješina and Finck plagiarized other authors, which means that we cannot be sure about the correct dialectal and geographical affiliation of these forms.

11. While there seems to be no doubt about the general origin of the past, it is not clear whether (and if so, why) the nominal element represents a feminine form or not. In the

same way, the past passive *kerd-ilo* and *barilo* can be derived from **kerdi-ulo* and **bariulo* by phonetic reduction. For another suggestion cf. Boretzky (1995: 19ff).
12. In Modern Greek and Albanian the verbs showing suppletive forms are largely the same, although they do not agree etymologically (cf. Boretzky 1991:20ff.). This means that there should be properties (of frequency, or semantic ones) of rather universal dimensions that cause individual items to remain suppletive. The reason why lexemes develop suppletive forms seems to be "psychological nearness" rather than token frequency, and, for function words, it is the central role they play in sentence structure and in grammaticalization processes (cf. Bittner 1990:230ff).

References

Asenova, Petja. 1989. *Balkansko Ezikoznanie. Osnovni problemi na Balkanskija ezikov săjuz.* Sofija: Izdatelstvo Nauka i Izkustvo.
Bittner, Andreas. 1990. 'Eine unendliche Geschichte? Nochmal zum Verhältnis von Suppletion und Natürlichkeit'. In: N. Boretzky, W. Enninger, & T. Stolz, eds. *Spielarten der Natürlichkeit - Spielarten der Ökonomie. Beiträge zum 5. Essener Kolloquium über "Grammatikalisierung: Natürlichkeit und Systemökonomie" 1988 in Essen.* 227-247. Bochum: Brockmeyer.
Bloch, Jules. 1932. 'Quelques formes verbales du Nuri'. *Journal of the Gypsy Lore Society* 3:11. 30-32.
Boretzky, Norbert. 1983. *Kreolsprachen, Substrate und Sprachwandel.* Wiesbaden: Harrassowitz.
---- 1991. 'Sprachstruktur und Sprachwandel - Zur Rationalität ihrer Erklärung'. In: N. Boretzky, W. Enninger, & T. Stolz, eds. *Kontakt und Simplifikation. Beiträge zum 6. Essener Kolloquium über "Kontakt und Simplifikation" 1989 an der Universität Essen.* Bochum: Brockmeyer. 3-27.
---- 1993. *Bugurdži. Deskriptiver und historischer Abriß eines Romani-Dialekts.* Berlin: Harrassowitz.
---- 1994. *Romani. Grammatik des Kalderaš mit Texten und Glossar.* Berlin: Harrassowitz.
---- 1995. 'Die Entwicklung der Kopula im Romani'. *Grazer Linguistische Studien 43.* 1-50.
Bubeník, Vít. 1995. 'On typological changes and structural borrowing in the history of European Romani'. In: Yaron Matras, ed. *Romani in contact: The history, structure and sociology of a language.* Amsterdam: Benjamins. 1-24.
Cortiade (Courthiade), Marcel. 1992. *Dialectological inquiry.* Béziers/Besièrs: Agéncia Occitana de Comunicacion.
Fahs, Achim. 1985. *Grammatik des Pali.* Leipzig: VEB Verlag Enzyklopädie.
Finck, Franz N. 1903. *Lehrbuch des Dialekts der deutschen Zigeuner.* Marburg: Elwert.
Friedman, Victor. 1985. 'Balkan Romani modality and other Balkan languages'. *Folia Slavica* 7:3. 381-389.
Gilliat-Smith, Bernard J. 1910-1914.'Bulgarian Gypsy folk-tales (Erli)'. *Journal of the Gypsy Lore Society* 4:2. 142-151; 5:1. 1-13; 5:4. 279-282; 6:1. 3-19; 6:1. 33-34; 6:2. 85-90; 7:1. 37-44; 7:2. 111-116; 7:3. 214-223.
---- 1931. 'A Drindari folk-tale'. *Journal of the Gypsy Lore Society* 10. 76-86.
---- 1940. 'The ballad of Lady Rose'. *Journal of the Gypsy Lore Society* 19. 146-152.

---- 1944. 'A Bulgarian Gypsy tale (Ali Üstas)'. *Journal of the Gypsy Lore Society* 23. 14-21.
---- 1945. 'Two Erlides fairy tales'. *Journal of the Gypsy Lore Society* 24. 1-2, 17-25.
Grant, Anthony. 1995. 'Plagiarism and lexical orphans in the European Romani lexicon'. In: Yaron Matras, ed. *Romani in contact: The history, structure and sociology of a language.* Amsterdam: Benjamins. 95-124.
Hancock, Ian. 1995. *A handbook of Vlax Romani.* Columbus: Slavica.
Heine, Bernd, Ulrike Claudi, & Friederike Hünnemeyer. 1991. *Grammaticalization. A conceptual framework.* Chicago & London: University of Chicago Press.
---- et al. 1993. *Conceptual shift. A lexicon of grammaticalization processes in African languages.* Institut für Afrikanistik, Universität zu Köln.
Heinschink, Mozes. 1978. 'La langue tsigane parlée en Autriche et en Yougoslavie'. *Etudes Tsiganes* 24:1. 8-20.
---- & Fatma Zambakli-Heinschink. 1994. 'Izmirští Romové - Sepetdžides'. *Romano Džaniben* 2/94. 2-15.
Holzinger, Daniel. 1993. *Das Ròmanes. Grammatik und Diskursanalyse der Sprache der Sinte.* Innsbruck: Institut für Sprachwissenschaft.
Hopper, Paul J. & Elizabeth Closs Traugott. 1993. *Grammaticalization.* Cambridge: University Press.
Hübschmannová, Milena, Hana Šebková, & Anna Žigová. 1991. *Romsko-český a česko-romský kapesní slovník.* Praha: Státní pedagogické nakladatelství.
Igla, Birgit. 1996. *Das Romani von Ajia Varvara. Deskriptive und historisch-vergleichende Darstellung eines Zigeunerdialekts.* Wiesbaden: Harrassowitz.
Jacobi, Hermann. 1886 [1967]. *Ausgewählte Erzählungen in Maharashtri.* Leipzig: Hirzel [Darmstadt: Wissenschaftliche Buchgesellschaft].
Ješina, Josef. 1886. *Románi čib oder die Zigeunersprache.* Leipzig: List und Francke.
Kenrick, Donald S. 1969. *Morphology and lexicon of the Romani dialect of Kotel (Bulgaria).* Ph.D. dissertation, SOAS, London.
Knobloch, Johannes. 1953. *Romani-Texte aus dem Burgenland.* Eisenstadt: Landesarchiv und Landesmuseum.
Koneski, Blaže. 1954. *Gramatika na Makedonskiot literaturen jazik.* II. Skopje: Prosvetno delo.
Kopernicki, Izydor. 1930. *Textes tsiganes.* Warsaw: Polska Akademia Umiejętności. (Mémoires de la Commission Orientaliste Nr. 7.)
Lehmann, Christian. 1982. *Thoughts on grammaticalization. A programmatic sketch.* Vol. I. AKUP. Arbeiten des Kölner Universalienprojekts. Nr. 48. Köln: Institut für Sprachwissenschaft, Universität zu Köln.
Lípa, Jiří. 1963. *Příručka Cikánštiny.* Praha: Státní pedagogické nakladatelství.
---- 1979. 'Cases of co-existence of two varieties of Romani in the same territory in Slovakia'. *International Journal of the Sociology of Language* 19. 51-57.
Macalister, Stewart. 1914. *The language of the Nawar or Zutt - the nomad smiths of Palestine.* (= Journal of the Gypsy Lore Society, Monographs No. 3). Edinburgh: Edinburgh University Press.
Mayerthaler, Willi. 1981. *Morphologische Natürlichkeit.* Wiesbaden: Athenaion.
McGregor, R. S. 1972. *Outline of Hindi grammar.* Oxford: Clarendon.
Paspati, Alexandre G. 1870 [1973]. *Études sur les Tchinghianés ou Bohémiens de l'Empire Ottoman.* Constantinople: Koroméla. [Osnabrück: Biblio].

Pischel, Richard 1900 [1973]. *Grammatik der Prakritsprachen*. Strassburg: Trübner.
Romano Džaniben. 1994. Časopis romistických studií (ed. by M. Hübschmannová). 1-4. Praha.
Romano Hangoro. 1993. comp. by Dezider Banga. Bratislava: Gold Press.
Sampson, John. 1926 [1968]. *The dialect of the Gypsies of Wales*. Oxford: Clarendon.
Shackle, C. 1974. *Punjabi*. London: St. Paul's House.
Stojanov, Stojan. ed. 1993. *Gramatika na săvremenija bălgarski knižoven ezik*. Tom 2: Morfologija. Sofia: Izdatelstvo na Bălgarskata Akademija na Naukite.
Vekerdi, József. 1983. *A Magyarországi Cigány nyelvjárások szótára*. Dictionary of Gypsy dialects in Hungary. Pécs: Janus Pannonius University.
---- 1984. 'The Vend Gypsy dialect in Hungary'. *Acta Linguistica Academiae Hungaricae* 24. 381-389.
Welmers, William W. 1973. *African language structures*. Los Angeles & London: University of California Press.
Windfuhr, Gernot L. 1970. 'European Gypsy in Iran: A first report'. *Anthropological Linguistics* 12. 271-292.

CAUSATIVES IN SLOVAK
AND HUNGARIAN ROMANI

MILENA HÜBSCHMANNOVÁ
Charles University, Prague
and
VÍT BUBENÍK
Memorial University of Newfoundland, St. John's

0. Introduction

In Romani the grammatical categories of the causative and factitive and their diathetic counterparts (the passive, inchoative and reflexive) are most often expressed synthetically (morphologically). This state of affairs is at variance with that prevailing in most Indo-European languages spoken outside India, where the passive voice is usually expressed analytically (periphrastically), and causation analytically or lexically.

The following suffixes will figure in our account: *-av* deriving causatives, *-ar* deriving factitives, and *-uv/-ov* (with the allomorph *-o*) passives. Figure 1 displays these categories derived from the root *dar-* 'fear':

	intransitive verb	transitive (1st causative)	intransitive (passive, reflexive)
Romani:	*dar-a-l*	*dar-a-(a)v-el*	*dar-a-(n)d'-o-l*
	'fear, be afraid'	'frighten'	'get/be frightened'
		transitive (2nd causative)	
Hungarian		*dar-a-av-av-el*	
Romani (only):		'make X frighten Y'	

Figure 1: Causative and passive categories

The stem of the intransitive verb *te daral* 'to fear' is *dara-* (*-a-* is a thematic vowel, *dar* is the nominal root 'fear'). The suffix *-av* changes the intransitive verb into a transitive (causative) verb with the resulting meaning 'to frighten' (i.e. cause somebody to be afraid). The third form, the synthetic passive, is marked by -*o*, the allomorph of the suffix -*uv*. This suffix is attached to the stem of the past participle of the causative: *dara-(n)d-*.

In Hungarian Romani another suffix -*av* may be attached to the stem of the 1st causative, *darav*-, turning it into the 2nd causative. In what follows we will argue that the category of the 2nd causative, typical of many Indo-Aryan languages, could have been preserved in Hungarian Romani as a result of its contact with Hungarian which causativizes extensively (by the suffix -*tet/tat*). Another suffix which serves the purpose of verb formation is -*ar*. It derives verbs from nouns, adjectives, and more rarely from the stems of the past participle. The suffix -*ar* is used to derive factitives, or exceptionally also causatives. While -*av* does not cause any phonetic change in the preceding stem-final consonants, -*ar* and -*uv/-ov(-o)* entail palatalization; for instance in East Slovak Romani we encouner forms *pekel* 'to bake', (regional *pekavel* 'to bake'), *peťarel* 'to be hot (about spices)' and the passive *peťol* 'to be baking' (cf. Bubeník (1995:17) for the historical treatment of this palatalization).

The category of voice (diathesis) in Romani is grammatically encoded in morphosemantic patterns of verbs derived from the same word-base (not necessarily from the same stem) by suffixes which operate as distinct voice-markers. Derivational paradigms with three or four members as in Figure 1 are typical of all Romani varieties. In this respect Romani manifests great similarities with the derivational paradigms of other Indo-Aryan languages, such as Hindi displayed in Figure 2 below. This is true especially of those Romani dialects where the 2nd causative (*to have something done by somebody, i.e. to make X do Y*) is preserved.

The above derivational suffixes are also interesting and important as a means of enlarging the lexicon. They are very productive and can thus serve as an efficient device for producing new lexical items which are essential if Romani is to be developed and serve adequately in new social and cultural functions, in accordance with the ethno-emancipational aspirations of Roma. In fact, the lexical aspect of the deverbative verb-forming suffixes will be our main concern here.

At this point a note on terms which are understood and used differently by different authors is in order. The term *diathesis* (*diathetic*) will be used for *voice* in accordance with Czech and German linguistics (e.g. Boretzky 1993, 1994). *Factitives* (factitive verbs) are defined in Czech linguistic literature as "Effective verbs expressing the action of an agent who brings about the state or action of another agent" (our free translation of "Účinné sloveso vyjadřující činnost činitele působícího stav nebo činnost podmětu jiného" according to Brabcová & Martinová 1992). In Romani it is useful to differentiate between *factitives* and *causatives* for morphological (as well as semantic reasons) in that each of them is derived from a different lexical category by a different suffix. Factitives are derived mostly from nouns and adjectives, while causatives are derived from verbal roots. This has an impact on the resulting meaning (see below). There is no ambiguity in the term *causative* as the verb form expressing the notion of causation (Comrie 1981). However, there is no unanimously accepted term for the notion 'to make X do Y', 'to have Y done by X'. Pořízka (1963) in his text-book of Hindi uses the term *2nd causative*. Comrie (1981) speaks of causatives of *higher valency* and Shibatani (1976) operates with the term *double causative*. We will follow Pořízka in his use of the term *2nd causative*.

A full treatment of the verbal derivational morphology in Romani would surpass the space limits of this paper. Consequently, we decided only to concentrate on one issue: the semantic value and morphotactic restrictions of the suffix *-av* in the Eastern (ESR) and Western (WSR) varieties of the so-called 'Slovak Romani', and in Hungarian Romani (HR), spoken in the territory of Southern Slovakia in the Hungarian-speaking environment. The main informant for the West-Slovak Romani was Bartoloměj Daniel, a Romani historian from Šaštín; for information about Hungarian Romani we are most indebted to Hilda Pášová and Tera Fabiánová from Vlčany (near Nové Zámky).

1. Historical origins of the causativizing suffix -av

In Old Indo-Aryan (Sanskrit) the causative was formed by the suffix *-aya* attached to the lengthened root, e.g. *kṛ* 'make' ---> *kār-aya-* 'make X make Y'. In the case of vocalic roots the suffix *-aya* was preceded by an epenthetic conso-nant *-p-*, e.g. *sthā-* 'stand, stay' ---> *sthā-p-aya-* 'place, put'). This epenthetic *-p-* became a source of Middle Indo-Aryan *-v-* and was inherited into all dialects of European Romani: *sthā-p-aya-ti* > *thā-v-et* > *tho-v-el* 'place, put' (for the change of *p* > *v* cf. Old Indo-Aryan *api* 'also' > Middle Indo-Aryan *(a)vi* > Vlach Romani *vi*). In all modern Indo-Aryan languages it is possible to derive causatives from simple verbs and by repeating this process to derive second causatives. For instance, Hindi derives its causatives by the suffix *-ā* placed after the root (e.g. *ban-nā* 'be made, exist' ---> *ban-ā-nā* 'make', or by lengthening the radical vowel (*mar-nā* 'die' ---> *mār-nā* 'beat, kill'). The suffix *-vā* placed after the root derives second causatives as shown in Figure 2 (see Bubeník 1987 for a full treatment of causatives in Old and Middle Indo-Aryan languages):

bannā	*banānā*	*banvānā*
'be made, exist'	'make Y'	'get Y made by X'
(Y exists)	(make Y exist)	
marnā	*mārnā*	*marvānā*
'die'	'beat, kill Y'	'have killed, arrange the killing of Y by X'
(Y dies)	(make Y die)	
dikhnā	*dikhānā*	*dikhvānā*
'be visible'	'show Y'	'get X show Y'
(Y is visible)	(make Y be visible)	

Figure 2: Hindi first and second causatives

The first causative increases the valency of the simple verb by assigning the function of the *causee* to the erstwhile subject:

(1) *maĩ āpko   patr dikh(l)āũgā* (Hindi)
  I you:DAT/ACC letter see:CAUS:1SG:FUT
  'I will show you the letter' (i.e. will make the letter visible to you)

The second causative increases the valency of the derived causative by adding another (second) causee to it; this one is marked by the postposition -*se*, glossed instrumental in (2):

(2) *maĩ āpko   mantrī -se patr dikhvāũgā* (Hindi)
  I you:DAT/ACC secretary-INSTR letter see:CAUS:1SG:FUT
  'I will get the secretary to show you the letter'

As distinct Romani dialects have undergone (and are undergoing) different developments, the suffix -*av* has also acquired different semantic as well as morphotactic properties crossdialectically. Though by its origin -*av* is a causativizing suffix - and predominantly it functions like that even now - in some dialects it has lost this primary function in some circumstances; consequently, its morphotactic possibilities became restricted also. This will be demonstrated in what follows.

2. The suffix -av in Slovak Romani

The suffix -*av* attached to the root of the *lost primary verbs* (Sampson 1926) functions as a marker of transitives (causatives) in all the three regional varieties of Romani which we deal with. The dialect-index will denote the verbs in the following examples only when the use of the respective verb is not general: *(h)aravel* 'pull down', *bašavel* 'play music', *bičhavel* 'send', *čalavel* 'move, strike, touch', *gundžavel* (ESR) 'excite sexually (only about men)', *nakhavel* 'swallow', *prasavel* (ESR) 'mock, nickname in a mocking way', *pharavel* 'tear, split', *phosavel* 'sting', *phukavel* (ESR) 'accuse, complain', *sikhavel* 'show, teach', *tasavel* 'strangle', *umblavel* 'hang (somebody)', *unglavel* 'light on fire', etc..

While in some Romani dialects the primary verbs have been lost, some other dialects retain them. For example the verb *nakhel* 'pass away' is no longer found in any dialect spoken on Czech and Slovak territory; however, it is current in Kalderaš, Bugurdži and other Balkan dialects. Also the primary verb *bašel* 'to sound' is no longer used in Slovak Romani, but it is current in Hungarian Romani, in Kalderaš and other dialects.

The former existence of the lost primary verbs can also be proven by the morphological structure of their passive counterparts which some of the above mentioned causatives possess. The passivizing suffix *-uv/-ov (-o)* is joined to the past participle stem of the primary (underived) verbs, while the suffix *-av* is attached to the root. Hence the morphosemantic model capturing different diathetic (voice) values (for the Eastern variety of Slovak Romani) is as presented in Figure 3 (only the main meanings of the verb *sikh-av-el* 'show, teach' are given):

sikh-el	*sikh-av-el* 'show, teach'	*sikh-a(v)-do* 'shown, learned'
sikh-l-o 'used to'	*sikh-ľ-o-l* 'get used to, learn'	

Figure 3: Diathetic values in ESR

The primary verb is preserved in Hindi *sīkh-nā* 'learn' (< Middle Indo-Aryan *sikkhe-i*) where it also forms the causative *sikh-ā-nā* 'teach'.

In WSR it is exceptionally possible to derive causatives by either *-av* or *-ar* from the word-base (not from the same stem, though, as *-av* is attached to the verbal root while *-ar* to the stem of the past participle). The resulting causatives represent two different expressions with two different meanings, as shown in Figure 4:

*sikh-el	sikh-av-el 'show'	sikh-a(v)-do 'shown'
sikh-l-o 'used to'	sikh-l-ar-el 'teach'	sikh-l-ar-do 'learned, teacher'
*tas-el	tas-av-el 'strangle'	tas-a(v)-do 'strangled'
tas-l-o 'drowned (by accident)'	tas-l-ar-el 'drown (somebody)'	tas-l-ar-do 'drown (intentionally)'

Figure 4: Causative in WSR

It should be observed that in WSR the *-l-* is never palatalized which is apparently due to the influence of the West-Slovak regional varieties where *l'* does not exist.

The suffix *-av* attached to a consonant-ending root of intransitive verbs derives transitives (causatives). In Slovak Romani pairs of such primary and derived verbs with different diathetic value are rare. They are much more frequent in Hungarian Romani, as seen in Figure 5:

Primary verb (intransitive)	Causative	Passive derived from the Intransitive verb	Passive derived from the Causative verb
(de)našel 'run, flee'	*našavel* 'lose, destroy'	*našl'ol* 'disappear'	*našad'ol (ESR rare)* 'get lost'
perel 'fall'	*peravel (HR)* 'fell'	---------	---------
phirel 'walk'	*phiravel* 'wear'	---------	---------

Figure 5: Diathetic derivations in ESR and HR

It should be observed that in Slovak Romani only the form *denašel* exists. (This form is a unique compound of the imperative form *de!* 'give!' and the noun *naš* 'flight, escape').

In the same fashion the suffix *-av* attached to the stem (in *-a*) of intransitive verbs causativizes the basic verb. The class of the *a*-stem verbs includes a limited number of members. They are marked not only morphologically (by the thematic vowel *-a*) but they also share similar semantic characteristics. Most of these verbs express some lasting psychic states: *asal* 'laugh', *daral (pes)* 'be afraid, fear', *izdral* 'shiver', *ladžal (pes)* 'be ashamed', *tromal* 'venture', etc. The only transitive verbs among them are *chal* 'eat', and *ledžal* 'carry'.

3. Morphophonemic properties of the suffix -av

The initial *a* of *-av* is elided when attached to the thematic *-a: dar-a-l* > *dar-a-v-el*. In the past participle as well as in the preterite tense the terminal *v* of the *-av* is omitted: *dar-a-(v)-d-o* 'frightened', *dar-a-(v)-d'-om* 'I frightened (somebody)'. As far as *dar-a-ň-om* is concerned, it is the preterite form of *daral* 'be afraid', meaning, 'I was afraid, I was frightened (by somebody)'. In Slovak Romani the following derivatives are common: *daral* >*daravel* 'fear > frighten', *asal* > *asavel* (WSR) 'laugh > make laugh', *izdral* > *izdravel* 'shiver > shake', *dukhal* > *dukhavel* (ESR) 'ache > hurt'. In Hungarian Romani the scope of *-av* includes also *ladžan* and *han*: *ladžan* > *ladžaven* 'be ashamed > make somebody be ashamed', and *han* > *havaven* 'eat > feed'.

4. Causative derived from transitive verbs

The meaning of the resulting derivative differs in Hungarian Romani from that in Slovak Romani. In Hungarian Romani the resulting verbs are 2nd causatives expressing the notion of *causing an action to be performed by somebody (i.e. making X to do Y)*. Thus, these *-av* derivatives in Hungarian Romani have higher valency than similar forms in Slovak Romani, since they assign the function of the causee to the former agent. While in HR *keren* > *keraven* means 'do, make' > 'have somebody make something', in some regional varieties of Slovak the form *keravel* does not exist at all, and in some it is only a marked form of *kerel* meaning the same, that is 'do, make'. Examples from Hungarian Romani include: *anen* >*anaven* 'bring > make somebody bring something, order something to be brought', *maren* > *maraven* 'to have somebody beaten by somebody':

(3) a *and'om*   *mange*   *habe*
        bring:PRET:1SG   I:DAT   food
        'I brought my food'
     b *anad'om*   *mange*   *habe*
        bring:CAUS:PRET:1SG I:DAT   food
        'I ordered my food (i.e. I had the food brought to me)'
(4) *I*   *sasuj*   *šoha*   *na*   *marlahi*   *pra*
     the   mother-in-law never   not   beat:3SG:IMPF   her:ACC
     bora   *korkori*   *de*   *maravlahi*   *la*
     daughter in law self   but   beat:CAUS:3SG:IMPF she

pre   *čhaveha.*
her:OBL   boy:INSTR
'The mother-in-law never used to beat her daughter-in-law herself but
had her beaten by her son'

It should be noted that the causee is in the instrumental as in Hindi in (2).

In Slovak Romani 2nd causatives are expressed periphrastically, as in Czech
or Slovak; thus (4) would be translated into Slovak Romani as follows: *E sasvi
šoha na marlas peskera bora korkori, al'e kerlas upre peskere čhas, kaj la te
marel.* 'The mother-in-law was never beating her daughter-in-law herself, but
she made her son to beat her' (Lit: ...but she instigated her son that he beat her).

5. Semantic changes in the suffix -av

In Slovak Romani the suffix *-av* deriving verbs from the stem of the transitives has changed its function and semantic value. The following cases may be
distinguished:
The derivative marked by *-av* is synonymous with the unmarked verb from
which it has been derived: *demel/demavel* 'hit, strike'. These cases are rare.
The derivative marked by *-av* has acquired meaning quite distant from the
basic one: *bolel > bolavel* 'dip > baptize', *thovel > thovavel* 'put > be jealous':

(5)   *thovavel   man pro   murša*
        put:CAUS:3SG I:ACC on   men
        'He envies me over (my relation with) men'

These instances are also rare.
The derivative marked by *-av* is used only in idiomatic constructions:

(6)   *čhinavel   droma*
        cut:CAUS:3SG roads
        'He wanders, roams' (lit. 'he cuts roads')

Example (6) is found in the song *'Devla Devla so me kerd'om/ raňa romňa khere
mukl'om/ lubňoraha drom čhinad'om* 'God, what did I do/ I left a noble wife at
home/ and went wandering with a whore'.
In Northern varieties of ESR *-av* is synonymous with the iterative suffix
-ker. Iterative forms derived by *-ker* are sometimes fully synonymous with those
derived by *-av*, sometimes their meaning is slightly different. Often both suf-

fixes are strung together which intensifies the iterative meaning. In such cases *-av* always precedes *-ker: čhiv-el* > *čhiv-av-el/čhiv-ker-el* > *čhiv-av-ker-el* 'throw > be throwing all the time (frequently)':

(7)   *Ola duj princesi   čhivavkernas   somnakuňa*
        those two princesses throw:ITER:ITER:3PL:IMPF golden:FEM:OBL
        lobdaha
        ball:FEM:INSTR
        'The two princesses were throwing a golden ball (i.e. playing with a golden ball)'

While in some regional varieties of ESR *-av* can derive iteratives along with the primary iterative suffix *-ker,* in the Sepečides Romani spoken in Izmir in Turkey *-ker* derives causatives from verbs with the stem in *-av: gil-av-ker-* 'make somebody sing' (Cech & Heinschink 1997 & this volume). In Slovak Romani *gil'-av-ker-el* is an iterative form 'to sing often, to be singing all the time'.

As far as the relationship between causativity and iterativity is concerned, one may observe that the multiplicity of action (iterativity and distribution) and causativity are somehow linked. Assuming that the causativity was the original meaning of the form (Old Indo-Aryan *-p-aya* > Middle Indo-Aryan-*av)* during the ancestral Middle Indo-Aryan stage, the iterativity would develop out of it in the Carpathian area where the double causative *-av-av* has not developed (as in Hungarian Romani where it was apparently reinforced by the same category in Hungarian).

On typological grounds one may observe that this semantic shift is not uncommon. For instance in Semitic languages the form with the reduplication of the second radical expresses the notions of intensity, iterativity, distribution, factitivity and causativity seen in Arabic *kattaba* 'he made X write Y' and Hebrew *kittēb* 'he wrote zealously'. Or to use the notorious Indo-European example, the PIE verbal suffix **-sk'* is used in Latin to mark inchoatives, in Hittite duratives or iteratives (in both present and preterit), and in Tocharian and Armenian causatives. In addition, *-sk'* is used in Latin, Greek, Indo-Iranian and Tocharian to form the present stem of certain verbs. A number of scholars have explained these forms from an original iterative or durative function (e.g. Rix 1986, Szemerényi 1990). But Kuryłowicz (1964) and Meillet (1937/1964) are reluctant to ascribe a precise meaning to this suffix in PIE. Thus the relationship between multiplicity of action and causativity remains an open problem to whose solution the study of Romani dialects may contribute.

6. *Morphosyntactic restrictions on the deverbative suffix -av*

In Hungarian Romani the grammatical category of the 2nd causative (derived by the reduplication of the suffix *-av*) has been preserved while in Slovak Romani it has been lost. In Slovak Romani *-av* may only derive 1st causatives or it may function in cases which have been described in 5. Here the range of the morphosyntactic possibilities of the suffix *-av* is more restricted than in Hungarian Romani. In fact, *-av* has become an inseparable part of the stem of the derived verbs. It can only be followed, not preceded, by other suffixes (e.g. *-ker*). On the other hand, in Hungarian Romani *-av* can be separated from its root by other suffixes.

In Slovak Romani the suffix *-av* cannot be used after the stem in *-av* of primary lost verbs. For instance, the forms **bičhavavel, *bašavavel,* etc. are not possible even in those regional varieties where *-av* can express the iterative aspect in free variation with *-ker*.

In Hungarian Romani the suffix *-av* can follow the stem in *-av* provided that there are no semantic restrictions, as in (8):

(8)   *Ola   čhaja   bašavavnahi*   *pumare   d'íja*
      The   girls   play:CAUS:CAUS:3PL:IMPF their:ACC   songs
      pumare   piranenca
      their:OBL   lovers:INSTR
      'The Romani girls had their songs played by their lovers' (lit.' ...had their lovers play their songs')

In Slovak Romani the suffix *-av* cannot be used in those compound verbs where *del* 'give' is the second member of the compound: *cirdel* 'pull, draw', *čhandel* 'vomit', *kidel* 'collect', *kikidel* 'press', *phurdel* 'blow', *čhungardel* 'spit', *khandel* 'stink', etc.. In Hungarian Romani, on the other hand, this is possible: *ciden > ciddaven, keden > kedaven, phudden > phuddaven, čhanden > čhandaven,* etc:

(9)   *Kana   mri   daj   pal   gavende   phirlahi,   o*
      When   my   mother on   villages:LOC   walk:3SG:IMPF   the
      dad   phuddavlahi   *o   pišot   amenca*
      father blow:CAUS:CAUS:3SG:IMPF   the   bellow   we:INSTR
      ole   čhavenca.
      the:OBL   children
      'When my mother was roaming from village to village (to earn a living) the father had us children blow the bellow'

In Slovak Romani *-av* cannot be combined with the factitivizing suffix *-ar*. In Hungarian Romani, the sequence of these two suffixes, *-ar-av*, is found: *kal-o > kal'-ar-en > kal'-ar-av-en* 'black > make Y black > make X make Y black':

(10)   *Kaljara(va)d'om*   *mre*   *topanki*
        black:CAUS:(CAUS):PRET:1SG   my:PL   shoes
        'I had my shoes coloured black'

While in Slovak Romani the suffix *-av* cannot follow the iterative suffix *-ker*, in Hungarian Romani it is possible. (The allomorph of *-ker* is *-inger* only in HR). The morphosyntactic and semantic differences between the derivatives of *bikenel* 'sell' in ESR and HR may be surveyed in Figure 6:

ESR	*bikenel*	*bikenkerel*	*bikenavel*	*bikenavkerel*
	'sell'	'sell often'	'sell usually/often'	'sell usually & often, do business, deal with'
HR	*bik(i)nen*	*bikingeren*	*bikinaven*	*bikingeraven*
	'sell'	'sell often'	'to have something' sold by somebody	'to often have something sold by somebody'

Figure 6: Derivatives of 'bikinel' in ESR and HR

These derivations are exemplified in expressions such as the following: *cinav-kernas u bikenavkernas balen* 'they were (all the time, always) buying and selling pigs' (ESR); *t'inkeravnahi taj bikingeravnahi ole bálen čore gádženca* 'they had the poor gádžos buy and sell (all the time) pigs for them' (HR). Further examples are *ušt'en > ušt'ingeren > ušt'ingeraven* 'jump' > 'jump all the time' > 'let somebody jump all the time', as in *ušt'ingeravlahi nasvale čhavore ari!* 'she let (past imperfective) an ill child jump (jumping) outside!' (HR); *dikhen > dikhingeren > dikhingeraven* 'see' > 'see often' > 'has seen by a doctor', as in *kana som nasváli, dikhingeravel man pre baráteha, ávre orvošiha* 'when I am ill he always has me seen by his friend, another doctor'.

In Hungarian Romani (the Vlčany regional variety) *-av* can, but need not, follow the Hungarian causative-marker *-tet-/-tat-* (in Hungarian loan-words): *ňirinen > ňirinaven/ňirtetinen/ňirtetinaven* 'cut' > 'have something cut, have somebody to cut'. In the regional variety of Hungarian Romani spoken in Klenovec we observed that the Hungarian causativizing suffix *-tat/-tet* (combined with the marker of borrowings *-in*) can follow the suffix *-av*. Thus the 2nd causative becomes marked by reduplicated causative markers (the first

Romani, the second Hungarian); e.g *čhid-en* > *čhid-av-en/čhid-av-tat-in-en*
'throw' > 'have somebody to throw something, have something be thrown (by
somebody)'.

7. Conclusion

The suffix *-av* is a marker of causatives. In Slovak Romani only the 1st
causatives are formed by this suffix while the 2nd causatives are expressed analytically (periphrastically). In Hungarian Romani the category of the 2nd
causative is realized morphologically and the suffix *-av* functions as its exponent. In Slovak Romani *-av* derives the 1st causatives of some intransitives; it
can also be attached to the transitive verbs but the semantic value of these
derivatives is not that of the 2nd causatives. The absence of the 2nd causatives in
Slovak Romani can be partially explained by its absence in Slovak, its coterritorial language. Thus the morphosyntactic possibilities of the suffix *-av* and its
productivity as a device of word-formation in Slovak Romani are severely restricted. On the other hand, in Hungarian Romani where the existence of the category of the 2nd causative can be partially explained by its existence in
Hungarian the range of morphosyntactic possibilities of the suffix *-av* is much
broader. Unlike in Slovak Romani, here the suffix *-av* is a productive means of
word formation.

References

Boretzky, Norbert. 1993. *Bugurdži. Deskriptiver und historischer Abriß eines Romani-Dialekts*. Berlin: Harrassowitz.
---- 1994. *Romani. Grammatik des Kalderaš Dialekts mit Texten und Glossar*. Berlin: Harrassowitz.
Brabcová, Radoslava & Olga Martinová. 1992. *Současný český jazyk. Slovník lingvistické terminologie*. Praha: Karlova Univerzita.
Bubeník, Vít. 1987. 'Passivized causatives in Sanskrit and Prākrits'. *Linguistics* 25. 687-704.
---- 1995. 'On typological changes and structural borrowing in the history of European Romani'. In: Yaron Matras, ed. *Romani in contact. The history, structure, and sociology of a language*. Amsterdam: Benjamins. 1-24.
Cech, Petra, & Mozes F. Heinschink. 1997. *Sepečides-Romani*. Munich: Lincom.
Comrie, Bernard. 1981. *Language universals and linguistic typology*. Chicago: University of Chicago Press.
Kuryłowicz, Jerzy. 1964. *The inflectional categories of Indo-European*. Heidelberg: Winter.
Meillet, Antoine. 1937 [1964]. *Esquisse d'une histoire de la langue latine*. Paris: Klincksieck.

Pořízka, Vincenc. 1963. *Hindština - Hindi language course*. Praha: SPN.
Rix, Helmut. 1986. *Zur Entstehung des urindogermanischen Modussystems*.
Innsbruck: Institut für Sprachwissenschaft der Universität Innsbruk.
Sampson, John. 1926 [1968]. *The dialect of the Gypsies of Wales*. Oxford:
Clarendon.
Shibatani, Masayoshi. 1976. *Causativization*. New York: Academic Press.
Szemerényi, Oswald. 1990. *Einführung in die vergleichende Sprachwissenschaft*.
Darmstadt: Wissenschaftliche Buchgesellschaft.

THE ROMANI DIALECT OF THE RHODOPES

BIRGIT IGLA
St. Kliment Ohridski University, Sofia

0. Introduction

The dialect considered here is spoken in the Rhodope and the Rila mountains in Bulgaria.[1] The majority of the Roma in this area are Muslims and have preserved their language, while a great part of the Muslim Roma in Bulgaria have lost Romani and use Turkish as their mother tongue. The language shift from Romani to Turkish probably took place during the time of the Ottoman Empire. Interestingly, it still continues nowadays, long after Turkish has lost its status as a prestige language in Bulgaria.[2]

In many towns and villages in the region the percentage of Roma in the overall population exceeds the general figure of 6-10% given for Bulgaria as a whole. In the town of Velingrad for example there are 5-6000 Roma, or 18-20% of the population; Rakitovo has a population of 8000, 3000 of whom are Gypsies, that is nearly 40%. In the area under consideration several groups of Roma live. Here we shall deal with a dialect of the *Erli* group (from Turkish *yerli* 'settled'; a Non-Vlach dialect[3]), which seems to be the most important variety of Romani in this part of the country. *Erlis* (pl. *Erlides*) is the self-appellation of the group; the dialect is called *Erliski*. One should, however, note that this name may be used for various groups, either as an in-group or as an out-group designation. It is generally used for groups that had already been living in a place when another group arrived there. This seems to be true for the whole of the Balkan area. In Greece, for example, nomadic Roma use *Erlides* as an (out-group) name for settled Gypsies who have replaced Romani with Greek. The self-appellation of this group is *yifti* (Greek *yifti* 'Gypsies'). In the town of Plovdiv Turkish-speaking Gypsies are called *Erlides* by those who refer to themselves as *Bugurdži* and who speak a dialect of Romani which is very similar to the dialects of other groups who use the word *Erlides* as an in-group name. Most of the Romani-speaking Erlides in Bulgaria share their neighbourhoods with the so-called Vlach-groups who probably only arrived after the abolition of serfdom in Rumania during the second half of the 19th century.

Here I shall be using *Erli* as a cover-term for varieties of Romani spoken in Bulgaria which seem to be structurally closely related. To my knowledge most, but not all speakers of dialects referred to here as *Erli* use *Erlis/Erlides* as an ingroup name. It is therefore worth while to discuss reference conventions. The most exhaustive description of a variety of this group is Kostov (1963), which is mainly based on the language of the Erlides from Sofia. The Sofia variety of Erli has served as a basis for a dictionary by Malikov (1992) and a translation of the New Testament by Metkov (1995). Atanasakief's translation of the Gospel according to Matthew (1932) uses an Erli variety as spoken in the town of Pazardžik. Historically, the dialect of the Roma of the Rhodopes is clearly related to the varieties of the Erlides from Pazardžik, Plovdiv, and, to a lesser degree, Sofia and probably other places as well. The dialect of the Rhodopes shows a number of peculiar features which have not been observed in other dialects.[4] Language transmission as a whole is, according to my observations, functioning quite well, at least when compared to the situation in the Romani communities of the *mahallas* (Gypsy neighbourhoods) of the big cities where Romani is steadily being replaced by Bulgarian as an everyday means of communication even within the family.

1. Lexicon

In the Romani dialect of the Rhodopes the inherited lexicon is preserved quite well, comprising words that are no longer known in the majority of the other dialects of the country, such as *ričhini* 'bear', *angušto* 'finger', *alindž* 'field', *cicaj* 'cat'. The dialect also shows some words of Greek origin which do not appear in other dialects. Besides the Greek words for the numerals 7, 8, 9, 30, 40, 50, which exist in Romani dialects all over Europe, the Rhodope dialect has *eksinda* '60' (Gk. *eksinda*), *eftanda* '70' (Gk. *evðominda*), *oxtonda* '80' (Gk. *oxðonda)* and *eninda* '90' (Gk. *eneninda*). The word *eksinda* is identical with the Greek form, whereas *eftanda* and *oxtonda* have a regularized form, and *eninda* has been simplified. These words do not occur in the related Erli dialects; those, however, have Greek *dekapende* '15' (Gk. *ðekapende*), which is absent in the Rhodope dialect.

As for Bulgarian loans, apart from words belonging to Standard Bulgarian, there are many items taken from the local Bulgarian dialects, such as *gəlčínaf*, *razgəlčínaf* 'to speak, to talk' (Standard Bulgarian *govorja, razgovarjam*), *dripes*[5] 'clothes' (Standard Bulgarian *drexi*) or *polena* 'meadow, field' with a special phonetic form (Standard Bulgarian *poljana*). The word *laxana* 'cabbage', though ultimately of Greek origin, might have been borrowed from the local Bulgarian (or Turkish) dialects where it is present as well.

Like other Bulgarian Romani dialects or, more generally, Romani dialects that are influenced by Slavic languages, the dialect makes use of the Slavic verbal prefixes: *po-dikhles lən* 'he looked at them (slightly)'; *za-žakərdə* '(they) waited'; *do-rəstə o Roma* 'the Roma came'; *do-pələ* 'they happened to'; *za-sutə* 'they fell asleep'.[6] There are many cases where the prefixed verb is calqued on a concrete Bulgarian verb, but there are also instances where no such verb is to be found, but rather the pattern as such was copied. In some instances the verbal prefixes are added without any change in meaning: *bistrav* 'to forget' has changed to *za-bistrav* 'to forget' in analogy with Bulgarian *za-bravja*. While here the analogy is formal, there are other cases where the prefix changes the verb semantically: *nakhav* 'to pass', by taking the prefix *za* (*za-nakhav*), changes its meaning to 'to leave'. This pattern is a semantic calque on Bulg. *minavam* 'to pass' - *zaminavam* 'to leave'. As in Bulgarian prefixation in Romani can be used to modify a verb with respect to aspect or manner of action, but it is used neither as regularly nor as consistently as in the model language.

Turkish is nowadays hardly spoken in the area under consideration, but the loan-words in the Romani dialect, remarkably common in legends and fairy-tales, as well as some of the non-lexical features of the dialect point to its former presence.[7]

I will confine myself here to discussing the main phonetic and morphosyntactic pecularities of the Rhodope dialect that justify its separate position among the Bulgarian Romani dialects.

2. Phonetics

2.1 The vowel system

The vowel system of the dialect has undergone many changes which make it unintelligible at times to speakers of other Romani dialects. Many of these changes are highly regular; for others it hardly seems possible to discover rules. We find dialect-internal differentiation with forms varying from one village or one mahalla to another and even from one family to another. The main regular processes are discussed in the following sections.

2.1.1 é > ə́ (e > ə)

Stressed *e* has been changed to a centralized vowel [ə] in all instances; the same process in unstressed syllables is less regular. When *e* occurs in stressed syllables it results from another change, namely *-já > e* (see below). The schwa has phonemic value in this dialect. The outcome of this process affects some roots (*divə́s < divés* 'day'; *dovə́l < devél* 'god'; *phənlés < phenljás* 'he/she said'), but it mainly results in an altered phonetic form of rather many grammatical morphemes: e.g. 2nd and 3rd person present tense in *əs < es, əl < el, ən < en*, 3rd pl. past tense *-(d)ə < -(d)e*. The abstract noun ends in *-ibə* (< *-ibe*), the participle of borrowed verbs in *-imə* (< *-ime*). In words borrowed from Bulgarian stressed *é* sometimes remains unchanged, e.g. *plémes* 'tribe' < *pleme*. It is not clear to what extent this corresponds to the local varieties of Bulgarian, or whether there is influence from Standard Bulgarian.

With the case endings for dative, locative and genitive unstressed *e* has been changed to *ə*. Thus we find the endings *-kə/-gə -tə/-də* and *-kəro/-gəro < -ke/-ge, -te/-de* and *-kero/-gero*. Compare the corresponding forms in the Rhodope dialect and the forms used in Sofia (Figure 1):

Rhodope Romani	Erli from Sofia	
resə́s, rəsə́l	*resés, resél*	'you arrive/ he arrives'
restə́	*resté*	'they arrived'
phirə́las	*phirélas*	'he walked'
ekhə plemestə	*ekhe plemeste*	'to a tribe' (locative)
rovibə	*rovibe*	'search'
obeštajmə phuv	**obeštajme phuv*	'promised land'[8]

Figure 1: Forms in Rhodope and Erli (from Sofia)

2.1.2 já (ja) > é (e)

Another important change is the one from *ja > e*. This change again occurs mainly with stressed syllables (*tasé < tasjá* 'tomorrow', *počorel < počorjál* 'secretly'), but sometimes with unstressed ones too (*sigerən < sigjaren* 'they hurry', *kalerdə < kaljarde* 'they blackened' *xolenəl < xoljánel* 'is angry'). This change affects the 3rd person singular and the 1st plural of the preterite paradigm, which end in *-es* and *-em* (< *-jas* and *-jam*) respectively, feminine nouns which have have the plural marker *-é* (< *-já*), and the oblique case marker *-é-* (< *-já-*): *naštes < naštjas* 'he fled'; *dines < dinjas* 'he gave'; *nakhles < nakhljas* 'he ran away'; *beštem < beštjam* 'we sat'; *bare < barja* 'gardens'; *dines lən armane* [9] < *dinjas len armanja* '(he) cursed them'; *phuvetə < phuvjate* 'on the earth'; *ratetə < ratjate* 'in the night'. In the instrumental case masculine and feminine are not distinguished, and both have *-esa: o ro(j)ésa < e rojása* 'with the spoon', *xolésa* < *xoljása* 'with anger'. The Turkish loan *barémi* 'festivity' shows metathesis: *barémi* < **barjámi* < Tk. *bayram*. In the same way the pluralia tantum *xálke* 'people' suggests **xalkja* (sg. **xalki*) from Tk. *halk*.

Although the changes from *e* > -ə- and *ja* > *e* have some impact on morphology, grammatical distinctions have not been blurred extensively. Only after the change *e* > -ə́ had taken place, -*ja*- could develop to -*e*-. Thus a collapse of *e* < *ja* and old *e* is prevented. Minimal pairs *e:ə* have come into existence, cf. the nominative plural and the instrumental sing. of 'boy' and 'girl' in the Rhodope dialect and in the Erli dialect of Sofia (Figure 2):

Rhodopes	Sofia	
raklə́	raklé	'boys'
raklé	rakljá	'girls'
raklə́sa	raklésa	'with (a) boy'
raklésa	rakljása	'with (a) girl'

Figure 2: Plural and instrumental

Rhodopes	Sofia	
o raklə́	o raklé	'the boys'
o raklé	o rakljá	'the girls'
o raklə́sa	e raklésa	'with the boy'
o raklésa	e rakljása	'with the girl'

Figure 3: Definite articles

2.1.3 e (i) > o

The change of /e/ and /i/ to /o/ only affects unstressed syllables. In some cases it can be interpreted as regressive assimilation, resulting in vowel harmony: *tornó* 'young' < *ternó*; *goló* 'he went' < *geló*; *poló* 'he fell' < *peló*. Not all cases, however, allow for such an interpretation, cf. *dovəl* 'god' < *devél*. Through the development of *e/i* > *o* the distinctions between the masculine and the feminine plural forms, and between the nominative and the oblique form of the article have collapsed (cf. Figure 3).

Most (or at least many) of the Balkan Romani dialects belonging to the non-Vlach-branch use *o* for the plural, but have *i* for the feminine sg. (vs. *e* in Vlach-dialects) and *e* for the oblique cases. The use of *o* for fem.sg. instead of *i* in the related dialects is somewhat odd. It is not clear whether one has to assume *i* or *e* as the underlying form. In the first instance we would have to assume that an isolated change (*i* > *o*) has taken place only with the article, since no further instances of *i* > *o* are recorded. This would be supported by the form of the related dialects. On the other hand *e* > *o*, although not a regular sound-change, is found in some other items as well in this dialect.

2.1.4 en > an

The change from *en* > *an* is met in unstressed syllables exclusively and has no impact on the morphological system: *panžaraf* 'to know, to be acquainted with' < *pendžarav*, *anjé* 'nine' < *enjá*, *phanjé* 'sisters' < *phenjá*. As can be seen from *eninda* 'ninety' it is not without exception.

2.2 The system of consonants

The retention of a retroflex *r* is known as a pecularity of Bulgarian Non-Vlach dialects of Romani. In the Rhodope dialect it is still present. In many other dialects the distinction between retroflex *r* and flapped *r* has ceased to exist: the retroflex has merged with the flapped sound.

The development from *dž* > *ž*, which has taken place in many of the Romani dialects belonging to the non-Vlach branch in Bulgaria, is a completely regular sound change in the Rhodope dialect.[10] This process can easily be understood as an internal sound change, i.e. simplification in the sense of a loss of one articulation mode (the plosive). One should, however, not exclude the possibility that the change is induced by the influence of the contact language: Slavonic does not possess an affricate *dž* and where it exists in Bulgarian nowadays, it is found mainly with words of Turkish origin. But even in such instances there is a tendency in Bulgarian, too, to simplify *dž* > *ž*, cf. the pronunciation [pazaržik] instead of the normative [pazardžik].

With respect to the phonetic changes that have taken place in the dialect of the Rhodopes, I have only mentioned such developments that are not common among Bulgarian Romani dialects. Also, only those processes were mentioned for which some regularity could be detected. As is the case with other Bulgarian Romani dialects,[11] there is variation especially in the vowel system. Most of the changes cannot be explained by the influence of Standard Bulgarian. Thus the common Bulgarian 'reduction' of unstressed vowels (*a* > *ə*, *o* > *u*, *e* > *i*) is found only in single instances. On the other hand, a comparison with the local Bulgarian dialects shows that the influence of the contact language must have played a major role and that at least some of the phonetic processes, if not all, should be viewed in comparison with the local Bulgarian dialects.

The development from *ja* > *e* is quite common for some of the Bulgarian Rhodope dialects, which show *e* not only in place of Old Bulgarian Ѣ ('jat'), common for Western Bulgarian and Macedonian dialects, but also in place of Я ['a], cf. *polena/ poléna* for Standard Bulgarian *poljana* 'field'; *zanaet* for *zanajat* 'handicraft', *jebəlka* for *jabəlka* 'apple'.

The change from *-ja-* > *e* has been discussed by Gilliat-Smith (1935) in his review of the translation of St. Matthew by Atanasakief into a Romani dialect spoken in villages of the Pazardžik district, some twenty miles to the west of Philippopolis (Plovdiv). This dialect, however, with its marked affinity to Drindari, is different from our Rhodope variety. Only some of the phonetic features coincide, while others do not, and the morphological system is quite different. Gilliat-Smith (1935:28) writes about that dialect:

As in Drindari there is a general tendency for all vowels to lose their original value ...; As regards the phonetics, one of the most characteristic phenomena to be found ... appears to be the extraordinary prevalence of the rule '*ja* becomes *e*'. ... nowhere is the rule so generally applied to all parts of speech as in the dialect we are considering.

Keeping in mind that the dialect of the Pazardžik district described by Gilliat-Smith and the Rhodope dialect considered here are spoken in the same area, and, although they do not belong to the same dialectal group, they share some important phonetic innovations, we may conclude that these features are the result of linguistic convergence in an area. Studying the distribution of important linguistic features in more detail hopefully will enable us to make up for (relative) chronologies, that is to decide whether features shared by different dialects point to parallel developments in the distant past or to more recent convergence.[12]

Most of the instances of *e > o* listed, though not all, look like a result of vowel harmony. Although this is not at all a regular process, the Old Bulgarian so-called *jer malək* (ь), which has turned to *e* or *ə* in most Bulgarian dialects, appears as *o* in some Rhodope dialects, including in the area under consideration: *loko, tomno* instead of Standard Bulgarian *leko, təmno* 'light', 'dark'. As far as can be seen from the Bulgarian dialect atlas (Stojkov 1974), however, in Bulgarian this has taken place in stressed syllables only, whereas in Rhodope Romani it applies to unstressed syllables.[13]

3. Morphosyntax: case expressions

3.1 Postpositions

There is a rather interesting syntactic phenomenon which, to my knowledge, has not yet been described for any other Bulgarian Romani dialect. Along with the inflected case expressions and their prepositional equivalents the dialect sometimes uses postpositions to express case relations. Thus, we have three alternative constructions for case marking (Figure 4):

NOUN + OBLIQUE ENDING (ABLATIVE)	*o vošestar*	
PREPOSITION + NOUN	*katar o voš/ isko*[14] *voš*	'from the forest'
NOUN + POSTPOSITION	*o voš katar*	

Figure 4: Alternative constructions for case marking

All these forms actually occur. The given example - all three constructions with the same word - suggests that the case marking distribution does not depend on the choice of the lexical item. However, my corpus is too small to exclude the possibility that there are certain preferences conditioned by the chosen lexeme. It also does not allow for claims concerning the frequency of the respective constructions. My assumption is that the use of postpositions has been caused by Turkish influence. This can be backed by the following arguments: Though no longer of any importance synchronically, the Turkish presence had once been very strong in the entire area. More important in this context is the fact that the use of postpositions, quite uncommon for European Romani dialects, also occurs in Finnish Romani,[15] that is, in another dialect in contact with a language of the postpositional type.

3.2 Accusative of inanimate direct objects

With inanimate nouns, Romani does not distinguish morphologically between direct objects and subjects (see Figure 5; cf. also discussion in Matras, this volume):

	'brother'	'place'
NOM	*phral*	*than*
ACC	*phrales*	*than*
DAT	*phraleske*	*thaneske*

Figure 5: Case declension: Animate and inanimate

One might say that the nominative and accusative case forms of inanimate nouns are identical, or that inanimate nouns do not possess a morphologically marked accusative but have an oblique stem which serves as a base for other oblique cases, but which is never used independently. In Rhodope Romani, however, it is possible to mark inanimates functioning as direct objects by an independent accusative, as in (1). Of course this is only one possibility of encoding the direct object. As in other dialects the (formal) nominative can be found in this position (2):

(1)   *po-lošanerəla o   ekh-ən* (< *jakhen*; other dialects: *jakha*)
       more-pleases ART eye-PL:ACC
       'It is...more pleasant to the eye' (Nounev 1994:57)

(2)   *soskə phənlan ...   tə thovən ... lulude* (other dialects: *luludja*)
       why   you said ...   they plant ... flower:PL:NOM
       'Why have you ordered flowers to be planted' (Nounev 1994:57)

In (1) one cannot exclude the possibility that the choice of the accusative was affected by the fact that the noun denotes a part of the body. The phenomenon is
widespread in Bulgarian Romani dialects.

3.3 Prepositions

    Prepositions in Romani usually govern the nominative case with nouns and
the locative case (in *-te/-de*) with pronouns.[16] While this is quite a strict rule in
most dialects, the Rhodope dialect allows for some further possibilities. First,
prepositions can take the accusative case, both for (animate and inanimate)
nouns (3) and for pronouns (4):

(3)   *ek šoro na   məkles pə thanəs* (other dialects: *pe thaneste*)
       one head NEG he left   on place:ACC
       'Not a single head remained in its place' (Nounev 1994:55)
(4)   *gəlí   paš   ləs* (other dialects: *paš leste*)
       she.went towards he:ACC
       'She went to him' (Nounev 1994:57)

    Second, not only pronouns, but also nouns can appear in the locative case
after prepositions (5-6):

(5)   *ži ˙ ekhə   purte-tə*
       up to one   bridge-LOC
       'Up to a bridge' (Nounev 1994:48)
(6)   *paš   ekhə plemes-tə*
       towards one tribe-LOC
       'Towards a tribe' (Nounev 1994:57)

There seem to exist no rules governing the distribution of accusative vs. locative
after prepositions:

(7)   *ži ekhə purte-tə   paš   ekhə plemes-tə*
       up.to one bridge-LOC towards one   tribe-LOC
       'Up to a bridge near a tribe'

(8)   *ži   ekhə thanəs   paš   pə   xalken*
       up.to one   place:ACC towards his:REFL people:ACC
       'Up to a place near his people'

Third, prepositions may combine with *ko*. In this case the noun is always in
the nominative form. The doubling of prepositions corresponds to the Modern
Greek prepositional system and confirms Boretzky's (forthcoming) hypothesis
on the Greek influence on the development of the prepositional system in
Romani. As illustrated by (9) and (10), the expression PREP + *ko* + NOM is
functionally equivalent to PREP + NOUN + LOC (7) or PREP + NOUN +
ACC (8):

(9)   *ži   k-o   purt*
       up.to to-ART bridge:NOM
       'Up to the bridge'
(10)   *paš   k-o   xalke*
       towards to-ART people:NOM
       'Towards the people' (Nounev 1994:53)

Occasionally the verb *del* 'give' which usually governs the accusative case
both for the direct and for the indirect object, takes a prepositional phrase *ko* +
nominative (11). Since semantics allow for a locative, it is impossible to decide
whether the prepositional phrase has replaced the accusative or the locative:

(11)   *dinesla   k-o   phuro*
       he.gave.it   to-ART old man
       '[God] gave [the Romani alphabet] to the old man' (Nounev 1994:53)

4. Conclusion

The variation in the case system gives the impression of a dialect in a re-
structuring phase. The other possibility is that we are faced with a stable system
that allows for several variants. In order to make claims about the direction of
the development it is necessary to have a more detailed description of the dialect
which takes into consideration the frequency of the competing constructions and
their distribution among speakers of different generations. While the phonetic
pecularities are very specific to this dialect, in morphosyntax we find parallel
phenomena in many other Romani varieties.

Endnotes

1. The data are partly taken from the legends collected in Rakitovo by Yosif Nounev. If no source is given, the data stem from my own (B.I.) inquiries made during the years 1994/95 in the villages of Velingrad, Rakitovo and Bansko.
2. Since the end of World War II there has been a tendency of abandoning Romani in favour of Bulgarian. Parents prefer to use Bulgarian with their children in order to avoid discrimination which results from being identified as a Gypsy by an accent when speaking Bulgarian.
3. The terms 'Vlach' and 'Non-Vlach' are used in the tradition of Gilliat-Smith (1915-1916) to distinguish Romani dialects according to the degree of Romanian influence. Contrary to Non-Vlach, Vlach dialects have been influenced by the Rumanian language.
4. Talking about a Romani dialect/ variety of the Rhodope and the Rila mountains - or even just of the area of Velingrad - means neglecting some minor differences existing e.g. between Velingrad and Rakitovo or even between the different parts of Velingrad.
5. In Standard Bulgarian *dripi* means 'rags', whereas in the Rhodope dialect of Bulgarian it is used for 'clothes'.
6. Examples from Nounev (1994). I use 'ə' for the centralized vowel (instead of 'â' used by Nounev).
7. There are however no signs of the adoption of Turkish verbal morphology as known from Eastern Bulgarian dialects. For the use of Turkish verbal morphology in Romani dialects, see Igla (1988, 1991).
8. Nounev (1994:49).
9. Nounev (1994. 52).
10. This change is not to be confused with a similar development in Kalderaš dialects. As can be seen from many varieties of Kalderaš, *dž* and *čh* have developed to palatal sounds - like *ź* and *ś* in Polish. In most Kalderaš dialects there is a distinction between *ź* and *ž* (*ś* an *ś*), in some varieties *ź* and *ž* (*ś* and *ś*) have merged into *ž* (*ś*). Historically one mus assume two different processes.
11. This is especially true for the varieties belonging to the Drindari group, cf. Gilliat-Smith (1913) and Kenrick (1967).
12. This general question is discussed in Boretzky (1995).
13. One also has to take into consideration that there were movements of the Bulgarian population throughout the centuries of the Ottoman empire; the same is certainly true for the Romani population.
14. The preposition *isko* is composed of Slavic *iz* 'from' and Romani *ko* (= *ke* + article). In Bulgarian, however, *iz* as an ablative preposition has been replaced by *ot*. It must therefore be a rather old loan in Romani.
15. For the development of postpositions cf. Boretzky (forthcoming).
16. The form in *-te/-de* is therefore sometimes called prepositional case, following Russian grammar. Since most dialects have the possibility of using the *-te/-de* marker for an independent locative too, and since the use of the marker is hardly ever confined to nouns governed by a preposition, I prefer the term "locative" rather than "prepositional".

References

Atanasakief, A. 1932. *Somnal Evangelie (Il) Matejatar.* Sofia: Pridvorna Pečatnica.
Boretzky, Norbert. 1995. 'Interdialectal interference in Romani'. In: Y. Matras, ed., *Romani in contact. The history, structure and sociology of a language.* Amsterdam: Benjamins. 69-94.
---- forthcoming. 'Grammatical interference: Loan formation for foreign categories'. *Acta Linguistica Hungarica*
Gilliat-Smith, Bernard J. 1913. 'The dialect of the Drindaris'. *Journal of the Gypsy Lore Society* 7. 260-298.
---- 1915-1916. 'Report on the Gypsy tribes of north-east Bulgaria'. *Journal of the Gypsy Lore Society* 9. 1-55; 65-108.
---- 1935. 'The dialect of the Moslem Kalajdžis (Tinners) of the Tatar Pazardžik district'. *Journal of the Gypsy Lore Society* 14. 25-43.
Igla, Birgit. 1988. 'Kontakt-induzierte Sprachwandelphänomene im Romani von Ajia Varvara (Athen)'. In: N. Boretzky, W. Enninger, & T. Stolz, eds. *Vielfalt der Kontakte. Beiträge zum 5. Essener Kolloquium über "Grammatikalisierung: Natürlichkeit und Systemökonomie".* Bochum: Brockmeyer. 67-81.
---- 1991. 'On the treatment of foreign verbs in Romani'. In: P. Bakker & M. Cortiade, eds. *In the Margin of Romani. Gypsy languages in contact.* Amsterdam: Institute for General Linguistics. 50-55.
Kenrick, Donald S. 1967. 'The Romani dialect of a musician from Razgrad'. *Balkansko Ezikoznanie* 11:2. 71-78.
Kostov, Kiril. 1963. *Die Zigeunersprache Bulgariens.* Ph.d. dissertation, Humboldt Universität, Berlin.
Malikov, Jašar. 1992. *Cigansko-Bǎlgarski rečnik.* Sofia: Otvoreno obštestvo.
Metkov, Suljo. 1995. *O Nevo Zaveti.* (The new testament. Translated by Suljo Metkov). Sofia: Sǎjuz na cǎrkvite na adventistite ot sedmija den v Bǎlgarija.
Nounev, Yosif. 1994. 'Legends'. In: E. Marushiakova & V. Popov, eds. *Studii Romani,* Vol. I. Sofia: Club '90.
Stojkov, Stojan, ed. 1974. *Bǎlgarski dialekten atlas III: Jugozapadna Bǎlgarija.* Sofia: Izdatelstvo na Bǎlgarskata Akademija na Naukite.

THE DIALECT OF THE BASKET-WEAVERS (SEPEČIDES) OF IZMIR

PETRA CECH and MOZES F. HEINSCHINK
Austrian Academy of Sciences, Vienna

0. Introduction

With the exception of Paspati's (1870) book on the non-Vlach Romani dialect spoken in the Turkish/Greek area of Rumeli, there exists little literature about the dialects of Turkish Romani groups. Publications so far deal with appearance, work, social life, and music of the Roma, but not their languages.[1] Moreover, the present situation shows a rapid decline of Romani competence among the Roma. Nonetheless the existence of approximately 120 hours' recordings collected by Mozes Heinschink during the last 27 years in Turkey (mainly in the districts of Izmir, Manisa, and Aydin in Western Anatolia) enables us to investigate at least one of the Romani dialects of Turkey - that spoken by a non-Vlach group of basket makers (Sepečides) originating from northern Greece. A first contribution on the group and its language was presented by Heinschink (1989). In the meantime the transcription of the recorded material has been completed at the Phonogram Archive of the Austrian Academy of Science in Vienna (See Fennesz-Juhasz 1996). The dialect has been codified and outlined in a comprehensive grammar (Cech & Heinschink 1997). This paper presents some of the main characteristics of Sepečides Romani.

1. The basket makers of Izmir

The Sepečides of Izmir are a group of sedentary non-Vlach Gypsies. Until around 1920 they travelled in the area of Saloniki; their traditional profession was the production and selling of baskets. They were Muslims and spoke Greek and Turkish alongside Romani. During the Greek-Turkish war those Sepečides willing to adopt the Orthodox religion remained in Greece and are now scattered

in various villages in northern Greece. The largest group settled in Volos. Those
who favored their Muslim tradition moved to today's Turkey. After several
years of migration they arrived at Mersin, where they stayed for about three
years. Sepečides settled in Malatya and in the area of Mersin in Adapazar,
Tarsus and Adana. In Mersin and Adana there are still settlements of at least several hundred speakers. However, there exist no records of their dialect so far.
From Mersin several families migrated to Izmir and settled in Çırpıköy,
Arapçıköy and Çıplaköy, villages in the region of Izmir. Later, many of them
moved to Izmir, to the Gypsy quarter Gültepe, and finally to the district
Ballıkuyu. This was around 10 years after they had left Greece. In the urban
surroundings their traditional profession of basket making disappeared. Now the
women work as cooks or cleaning women; the men occasionally work in service
industries, e.g. at filling stations, or trade with food and dry goods in small
shops or at the markets. However, they still refer to themselves as 'Sepečides',
while the Turks traditionally call them *mübadele mahacır* 'exchange immigrants'.

Language competence has decreased considerably among the younger people. In the middle-aged generation only a few have full competence. The children generally attend school, which favors their second language, Turkish.
Frequent contact with non-Gypsies leads to an increasing number of exogamic
marriages, mostly among the young men. Because of these tendencies the young
Roma undergo an assimilation process that seems irreversible; Turkish is their
main language now. There is no information about the Sepečides groups living
in Mersin and Adana, but a similar situation is to be expected.

The Greek Sepečides used to call themselves *sevlengere Roma* 'basket
Roma'. Basket weaving, however, has disappeared in Greece, as it has in the
area of Izmir. But unlike their relatives in Izmir, the Sepečides of Volos have
engaged in another stable profession - carpet trading. The girls and women work
in weaving factories and are paid half in money, half in goods. Their carpets are
sold by the men. Although the families are sedentary all year, their business
forces the men to travel with small trucks all over northern Greece. These people
are more conservative, as can be seen from the clothing of the women and,
above all, in maintaining Romani, which is the main language of the group both
at home and at work. Even the children talk Romani with each other. The dialect, which is about to disappear among the Turkish groups, is still alive in
Greece.

2. Phonological features of Sepečides Romani

2.1 Vowels

The phonological system of Sepečides Romani shows the characteristic features of other non-Vlach dialects. There are no long vowels except in Turkish proper names; there is no lowering of intervocalic /v/ or /j/ resulting in long vowels, as in other dialects. Long vowels in loanwords that are incorporated into Romani grammar are shortened.

Apart from the inherited vowels /u/, /i/, /o/, /e/, /a/ and the Turkish vowels /ü/ and /ö/ there exist two different schwas, an intermediary vowel between /e/ and /o/, and the Turkish central /ı/ ; the latter occurs regularily in loanwords of Turkish origin as well as sometimes in Iranian words: *sır* < Persian *sir* 'garlic', *hazıri* < Turkish *hazır* 'ready'. Central /ê/ also occurs in a few early Iranian loanwords, e.g. *xêr* 'donkey' or *pêr* 'stomach'. The Turkish phonological rules of vowel harmony are generally not transferred into Romani. However, there is a tendency to pronounce the loanverb marker *-din- (-tin-)* with a central vowel if applied to stems with *-a-: anlatınava* 'to explain', or *jazdınava* 'to write' with the central vowel vs. *-i-* in *bejendinava*, 'to like'. Another example is the combination of names and the Turkish diminutive+1st person possessive suffix *-džim* (Turkish *ciğim*): The vowel of the suffix is allomorphic according to the phonological context: *dajo-džum* 'my mother' vs. *dade-džim* 'my father'. Pronunciation however varies among speakers and among utterances of single speakers, not allowing to describe the phenomenon as a phonological rule.

There is a tendency to replace /e/ by /o/ in many words: *Devel >Dovel, Dovol* 'God', as well as *nevo > novo*, feminine *nevi* 'new', *pherdo > phordo* 'filled', *brekh > brokh* 'breast', *memeli > momeli* 'candle' , *šero > šoro* 'head'; even in proper names, e.g. *Rebeka > Robeka*. Another feature is the frequent diphthongization of /e/ and /u/ to /ej/ and /uj/ in final position, as in several Turkish/Greek Romani dialects. Especially the words *me* 'I', *tu* 'you', *khere* '(at) home' and locatives ending in *-te* tend to have a diphthong, both in narration and in songs.

2.2 Consonants

The inventory of consonants includes the consonants known from other non-Vlach dialects; all aspirate stops are distinctively and properly pronounced: *čor* 'thief' vs. *čhora* 'beard', *kher* 'house' vs. *ker!* 'do!', *pherava* 'to fill' vs. *perava* 'to fall', *thut* 'milk' vs. *tut* 'you' (acc.); palatalization of guttural stops or sibilants does not occur; as in Turkish all voiced stops and sibilants appear voiceless in final position, with the exception of final /z/. We therefore transcribe them as voiceless, disregarding their voiced realization in non-final position: *drap - draba* 'poison', *dat - dades* 'father' (acc.), *jak - jaga* 'fire'. A preceding nasal stops final de-voicing: *pandž* 'five', but *lač* 'shame'.

The phoneme /v/ is often omitted before /k/, but not necessarily: *ladžakerava* or *ladžavkerava* 'to blame', *našakerava* or *našavkerava* 'to kidnap', but *xavkerava* 'to feed', *gilavkerava* 'to make someone sing'.

Turkish /h/ is usually dropped when Turkish words are used in Romani. Thus we find *(h)ič* 'nothing' (Turkish *hiç*), *(h)ep* 'all, always' (Turkish *hep*), *(h)er* 'every' (Turkish *her*), *(h)odžas* 'Hodža' (Turkish *hoca*). This /h/ is generally pronounced in formal speech.

The consonant clusters /st/ and /xt/ in final position still exist, but with a strong tendency to be reduced to /s/, /x/: *grast* vs. (more frequent) *gras* 'horse', *vast* vs. *vas* 'hand'; In *gešt* 'brother-in-law', and *baxt* 'luck', final /t/ is entirely dropped.

2.3 Sepečides Romani in Volos, Greece

The few recordings of Sepečides in Volos so far show few differences in phonology. Older and middle-aged people had all the sibilants including /čh/. Compared to Vlach speakers from Dendropotamos near Saloniki, whose dialect shows a strong influence of Greek and lacks /š/, /č/, /čh/, and /ž/, even the children of the Sepečides in Volos produce full sibilants, but with a tendency to drop aspiration; in consequence /čh/ and /č/ sound alike. Furthermore, some informants had palatalized guttural stops, e.g. *khéra*, 'houses'; *h*-drop as well as final diphthongization of *-e* > *-ej* and *-u* > *-uj* was also recorded. In fact the two groups are very interesting for comparative investigations, as they originally spoke the same dialect, and the time of their division is known. It should therefore be possible to determine several layers of loanwords, that is, older Greek combined with modern Turkish influence, compared to older Ottoman combined with modern Greek influence.

3. Morphological features

3.1 Non-Vlach characteristics

As a non-Vlach dialect Sepečides Romani has the typical non-Vlach features in its morphology - long forms of the 3rd person possessive pronouns (fem. *lakoro, lakiri, lakere*, 'her'; masc. *leskoro, leskiri, leskere*, 'his') and the genitive of nouns (sing. *romeskoro, romeskiri, romeskere*, 'man's'; pl. *romengoro*, 'men's'):

(1) *Mahmer isi leskoro anav*
        is his   name
    'His name is Mahmer'

(2) *Mi dadeskoro dat   sevlja na   kerelas*
    my father:GEN father:NOM baskets NEG made:3SING
    'My father's father did not make baskets'

(3) *Mi dajakere   dajakiri   phen na   geli*
    my mother:GEN mother:GEN sister NEG went:3SING
    'The sister of my mother's mother did not go'

The copula has a long form with initial *i-* : *isinom, isinan, isi* 'I am, you are, he/she is':

(4) *Sar isinan,   lačhes?*
    how be:2SING well
    'How are you? Well?'

(5) *Isine   ma ka sine,   isine   jek*
    was:3SING NEG if was:3SING was:3SING ART.INDEF
    phuro   da jek   phuri
    old man and ART.INDEF old woman
    'There was, if there was not, there were an old man and an old woman'

There are no plurals in *-ora* or *-ura* like in Vlach dialects. The preterite 1st singular ends in *-om: džava, gelom* 'go, went' , *xava, xalom* 'eat, ate':

(6) *Othe gelom,   athe avilom!*
    there went:1SING here came:1SING
    'There I went and here I came!'

Apart from these general non-Vlach features the dialect fits into the group of south-west Balkan dialects together with the Arli dialects of western Bulgaria, Macedonia and Cosovia; there is also a resemblance to the non-Vlach Ursari dialect of Rumania and Moldavia as well as to that of the Krim-Gypsies in the northern Caucasus (L. Tcherenkov, personal communication). Characteristic features common to all these dialects are a) metathesis of /k/ in certain pronouns and adverbs, as in *asavko* for *kasavo* 'such one', or *adikas* for *kadia* 'so, such'; b) future tense with the particle *ka* + inflected subjunctive form, corresponding to the analytic future tense in Greek, Bulgarian and Macedonian:

(7)   *Ka-praxunav   tut,   ka-mudarav   tumen!*
        FUT-bury:1SING you:OBL.SING FUT-kill:1SING you:OBL.PL
        'I'll bury you, I'll kill you!'

c) at the lexical level, there are typical words like the indigenous verb *therava* 'to have, to hold', apart from the common periphrastic construction *isi man* 'I have'; d) in syntax the doubling of subjects and objects expressed by a pronoun or double possessive pronouns in a sentence (see also Bubeník, this volume):

(8)   *Adalen   isi len   duj čhave*
        these:OBL is they:OBL two sons:NOM
        'They have two sons'
(9)   *I   čhaves   našti   ti   vakeren les   'Rom'*
        ART boy:OBL cannot COMP tell:3PL him:OBL Gypsy
        'The boy, they cannot tell he is a Gypsy'
(10)   *Tindri ti   daj   kana k'avel?*
        your   your mother when FUT-come:3SING
        'When will your mother come?'

One of the few linguistic studies of Greek/Turkish dialects concerns the non-Vlach Romani spoken in the district of Rumeli in north-eastern Greece (Paspati 1870). The dialect of the Sepečides partly resembles the Romani of Rumeli, but the two cannot be regarded as closely related. Apart from shared, general non-Vlach features there are some characteristic forms that separate both the Romani of Rumeli and that of the Sepečides from other southwest Balkan dialects, such as *valval* 'wind' for *balval* , or the *i-* in initial position in words like *ištar* 'four'. In both dialects present tense verb inflection ends in *-a*: *phirav-a, phires-a, phirel-a* etc. 'walk, travel'. In the subjunctive the final *-a* is omitted. One remarkable difference compared to the dialects described by Paspati is the replacement of *ovola (uvola)* 'to become', past participle *ulo*, by *avela*, past participle *avilo* in Sepečides Romani (cf. Boretzky, this volume).

The most closely related dialect outside of today's Greece or Turkey is the dialect spoken by the Arli of Prilep, Macedonia. Apart from a strong phonological resemblance there are identical suffixes for loan verbs in both dialects as well as a strong congruence in the inventory of Turkish lexemes. One big difference is the more 'conservative' character of Sepečides Romani with its full use of all morphological cases, compared with the dialect of Prilep, where some cases such as locative are replaced by prepositional constructions (cf. discussion in Matras, this volume).

3.2 Nominal Inflection

Sepečides Romani is a conservative dialect in phonology, morphology and lexicon. As in most Romani dialects animate and inanimate nouns differ in their accusative form (cf. Figure 1): for animate nouns the accusative has the oblique form, for inanimates accusative and nominative are morphologically identical. There is a strict distinction between indigenous and borrowed words (Figure 2). The latter have stem accent in the nominative and inflect in their own declension classes (cf. Bakker, this volume).

	Masc.sing.	pl.	Fem.sing.	pl.
nom.	-C,-o	-a,-e	-C,-i	-(j)a
acc.	-C,-o/-es	-a,-e/-en	-C,-i/-ja	-(j)a/-(j)en
dat.	-eske	-enge	-ake	-enge
abl.	-estar	-endar	-atar	-endar
instr.	-esar	-endžar	-asar	-endžar
loc.	-este	-ende	-ate	-ende
gen.	-eskoro/i/e	-engoro/i/e	-akoro/i/e	-engoro/i/e
voc.	-a,-eja	-alen	-(j)e,(-o)	-(j)alen

Figure 1: Inflection of indigenous (thematic) nouns (animates follow -/-)

	Masc.sing.	pl.	Fem.sing.	pl.
nom.	-i,-is,-os,-as	-ja,-i(o/a)des	-a	-es
acc.	-i,-as/-is,-os,-as	-a/-en	-a	-es/-en
dat.	-iske	-enge	-ake	-enge
abl.	-istar	-endar	-atar	-endar
inst.	-isar	-endžar	-asar	-endžar
loc.	-iste	-ende	-ate	-ende
gen.	-iskoro/i/e	-engoro/i/e	-akoro/i/e	-engoro/i/e
voc.	-a	-alen	-e	-(j)alen

Figure 2: Inflection of borrowed (athematic) nouns (animates follow -/-)

Like in all Romani dialects, dative, instrumental, ablative, genitive and locative are formed from the oblique case by suffixation. The suffixes represent grammaticalized case morphemes, but diachronically they are postpositions (cf. Friedman 1991; see discussion in Matras, this volume). Apart from these cases there are old locatives as well as ablatives still in use as adverbs. Some are common in many dialects: *ekhe thane* 'together', cf. *ketane* in Lovari, *ketni* in Sinti, *kitane* in the dialect of Rumeli (Paspati); *dural* 'from afar', common in many dialects, *kheral* 'from home', and *khere* 'home, at home'. The following are more or less unique to Sepečides-Romani and unknown in the dialect of Prilep: *dondolal* 'around' (cf. Turk. *dön-* 'turn, switch'), replacing *trujal* (or *trušal*) in other dialects. This form appears in dialects with strong Turkish influences, such as some Erli ones. It is not mentioned by Paspati. Further, *gave* 'in(to) the village', *gaval* 'from the village' are mentioned by Miklosich (1880), as is *dromal*, which is not used by the Sepečides, but is understood by them.

All inflectional cases are still in use. There is, however, a tendency to replace locatives and ablatives by *ko, ki ,(katar) ko, (katar) ki* (which derive from *ke* + article and *katar ke* + article respectively) or *kako, kaki* before an isolated noun. Unlike the dialect of the Arli from Prilep and many other less conservative dialects, where in such cases the analytical construction is obligatory, in Sepečides Romani it is optional. The inflectional cases can also be used. The analytical form is rarely used in combination of the noun with either an adjective, a possessive, or a demonstrative pronoun. In example (11) both forms are combined in one sentence:

(11)   *Džana   ko   doktori, kale doktoriste*
        go:3PL   PREP doctor   this doctor:LOC
        'They go to the doctor's, to this doctor'

(12)   *Astardas   la   izdrani   katar ki   dar*
        grabbed:3SING her:OBL shiver:NOM PREP PREP fear
        'She started to tremble in fear'

· 3.2.1 Turkish influences on nominal morphology

The agglutinating character of Turkish morphology reinforces the full use of the inflectional cases in Sepečides Romani. Unlike other Balkan Romani dialects, the Turkish ones are not subject to the influence of prepositional constructions by the contact language spoken by the *gadže* (non-Roma). However, interference with the Turkish nominal or verbal paradigm does occur even in the speech of competent speakers. Sometimes a Turkish plural is used for a loanword in narrative speech, and turkisms abound especially at the morpho-semantic and the syntactic levels. Turkish syntax strongly influences the choice of case in a Romani sentence:

(13) ablative for locative or accusative:
  Čumidava   tumare   jakhendar tumen
  kiss:1SING your:PL eyes:ABL you:OBL.PL
  Turkish: *Gözler-in-den   öperim*
          eyes-POSS-ABL kiss:1SING
  'I kiss you on your eyes'
(14) locative for dative:
  Adale čhajate   opral   izdrana
  this   daughter:LOC above fear:3.PL
  Turkish: *Kızın üstünde   titriyorlar*
          girl   above:LOC fear:3.PL
  'They fear for this daughter'
(15) instrumental for accusative:
  Me dinom   les   tüfekisar!
  I   gave:1SING him:OBL gun:INSTR
  Turkish: *Verdim   ona   tüfekle*
          gave:1SING him:DAT gun:INSTR
  'I shot him'('I gave him (a blow) with the gun')
(16) instrumental for nominative:
  Adale   bašnesar   adaja khajni sine   but phure
  this:OBL cock:INSTR this   hen   were:1PL very old:PL
  'This cock and this hen were very old'

Indigenous words can be combined with Turkish suffixes: *akana-dan* 'from now on' cf. Turk. *sora-dan* 'from then on'. Turkish suffixes are also applied to Turkish proper names and nouns in Romani: The Turkish 1st person possessive suffix *-(V)m* is affixed to the nominative or vocative of a Romani noun:

(17)   *Tu   džasa   tuke,   dadoreja-m,*
you:SING go:2SING you:DAT father:DIM:VOC-TURK.1POSS
dikhava   pala   tute!
look:1SING PREP you:LOC.SING
'You are leaving, my father, I follow you with my eyes!'
(18)   *Ax, bre Šajin-im,   phabardan   mo jilo!*
oh dear Šajin-TURK.1POSS burnt:2SING my heart
'Oh, my dear Šajin, you have burnt my heart!'

As can be seen from the examples, the Turkish language has only slightly influenced Sepečides Romani phonologically, but Turkish influence is deep at the morpho-semantic and syntactic levels. The further development of prepositional structures (see for instance Vlach dialects in Greece or Macedonia, where there exists a large inventory of prepositions) decelerates under the influence of Turkish.

3.3 Verb inflection

The preterite suffixes are *-d-* or *-l-* , as in other dialects. The passive is formed with the preterite stem, to which the suffixes *-j-, -iv-* or *-indiv-* are added for indigenous verbs, and the suffix-*iv-* for loanverbs. Figure 3 provides an overview of the verb inflection system.

	present	pret.	imperf.	pluperf.	pass./intransitive	imp.
Sing.						
1.	*-ava*	*-om*	*-avas*	*-omas*	*-ava*	
2.	*-esa,-asa*	*-an*	*-esas,-asas*	*-anas*	*-osa*	*-Ø*
3.	*-ela,-ala*	*-as*	*-elas,-alas*	*-asas*	*-ola*	
Pl.						
1.	*-asa*	*-am*	*-asas*	*-amas*	*-asa*	
2.	*-ena,-ana*	*-en*	*-enas,-anas*	*-enas*	*-ona*	*-en,-an,-on*
3.	*-ena,-ana*	*-e*	*-enas,-anas*	*-enas*	*-ona*	

Figure 3: Verb inflection

The copula has long forms throughout its paradigm, as seen in Figure 4. Initial *i-* is frequently dropped after a word ending in a vowel.

	present	negation	preterite	negation
Sing.				
1.	isinom	na sinom	isinom-as	na sinom-as
2.	isinan	na sinan	isinan-as	na sinan-as
3.	isi	nane	isine	na sine
Pl.				
1.	isinam	na sinam	isinam-as	na sinam-as
2.	isinen	na sinen	isinen-as	na sinen-as
3.	isi	nane	isine	na sine

Figure 4: The copula

Borrowed verb stems take the suffix *-in-*. They all inflect uniformly, using *-d-* for preterite. With loanverbs of Greek or Slavic origin *-in-* is attached to the present verb stem; with Turkish ones the preterite stem is suffixed:

(19) Slavic *moliti* , Romani *mol-in-* 'to ask for, prey'
 I džamba molindas i Devles ti kerel amen
 ART frog asked:3SING ART God:OBL COMP make:3SING us
 Roma
 Roma
 'The frog asked God to create us as Roma'

(20) Greek ψωνίζω, Romani *ipson-* 'to go shopping'
 Ki čaršija gelom t' ipsoninav
 PREP market went:1SING COMP shop:1SING
 'I went to the market to go shopping'

(21) Turkish *acı-* , Romani *adži-d-in-* 'feel sympathy, feel pity'
 I khamnjake amen adžidinasa but duje gendžar
 ART pregnant:DAT we feel sorrow:1PL much two souls:INSTR
 'For a pregnant woman, with two souls, we feel much sympathy'

The use of tenses corresponds to what is known from other dialects. An outstanding characteristic of verb morphosemantics is the frequent use of causative and inchoative intransitive verbs, partly serving as a means of lexical enrichment. These are discussed below.

3.3.1 Turkish influence on verb morphology
In the Romani dialect of Ajia Varvara described by Igla (1996) Turkish verbs are used with Turkish inflection, that is, the verb inflection system includes both a Romani verbal paradigm and an entirely Turkish one. In Sepečides Romani this phenomenon does not occur, either for verbs of the current contact language or for those of the former one (Greek). However, Turkish loanverbs

can be used with Turkish inflectional suffixes. The proper incorporation of loanverbs into the Romani inflectional system requires suffixation with *-in* (cf. Bakker, this volume).Rather long verb forms may therefore result, especially with Turkish verb stems of more than one syllable. Their corresponding Turkish inflected forms are much shorter and probably preferred for this reason, above all by less competent speakers. The use of Turkish forms is restricted to past tenses, including the past participle:

(22)   *But beğendi   la   o   geralo!*
         much was:fond:of:3SING her:OBL ART bald:man
         'The bald man was very fond of her!'

The Turkish verb stem *beğen-* appears as *bejend-in-* in Sepečides-Romani. The proper Romani form of the preterite 3rd singular would be *bejend-in-d-as*. Instead, the shorter Turkish preterite *beğend-i* is used. In (23) we have Turkish *bayılmak* 'to faint':

(23)   *Ka   dikhlas   so   si ko   kher, bayıldı   polo*
         when saw:3SING what is PREP house fell.PRET.3.SING fell:PART
         o   raklo
         ART boy
         'When the boy saw what there was in the house, he fell unconscious'

The length of the verb root seems to influence the choice of a Turkish or Romani inflected form. The following examples originate from the same story, told by one speaker. Turkish and Romani inflected forms alternate. Turkish *gir -* 'enter' appears in (24), Turkish *zehirlen-* 'be poisoned' in (25), and Turkish *namaz kıl-* 'to pray' in (26):

(24)   *Linde   pes   othar,   girdinde   ko   saraj*
         took:3PL REFL there:ABL entered:3PL PREP palace
         'They started from there and went into the palace'
(25)   *I   rakli (...) zehirlendi*
         ART girl   was poisoned:3SING
         'The girl was poisoned'
(26)   *Voj namazi kıldı .   Adala rakle ka   barile,   von   da*
         she prayer made:3SING these boys when grew up:3PL they also
         namazi kıldınde
         prayer made:3PL

'She said the prayer. These boys, when they grew up, said the prayer too'

4. Derivational processes

Several derivational processes are still productive (or reinforced by the influence of Turkish) in Sepečides Romani.[2] They are either hardly known or not used in other dialects. Even the closely related dialect of the Arli of Prilep has a restricted use of causatives and lacks a productive derivational process for forming inchoative intransitive verbs.

4.1 Causatives

For deverbal derivation we present the frequent and productive formation of morphological causatives. Morphological causatives occur in Lovari, where they are still productive. In Balkan dialects such as the dialects of the Kalderaš and Gurbet there exist fossilized causative forms. With the exception of Hungarian Romani as described by Hübschmannová & Bubeník (this volume) and Austrian Lovari (younger group), in no dialect morphological causatives are as abundant as in Sepečides Romani. There are several formants that can apply to the same verb. For loanwords only one suffix is used; the loanverb causative suffix however can be applied to indigenous verbs as well. Thus there are often several variants of the causative.

There are three types of causative suffixes for indigenous verbs. The suffix-*ar*- attaches to the preterite stem; the base verb may be transitive or intransitive. The derived verb has a general causative meaning:

(27) *Vov na   vakerd-ar-elas   amen 'loli loli xurbuzi'*
      he NEG say-CAUS-3SING.PAST us   red red water melon
      'He would not let us say "red red water melon"'
(28) *Resela, Devla-m,   javer ma   čid- ar   man!*
      enough God-POSS other PROH suffer-CAUS:IMP me:OBL
      'It is enough, my God, don't make me suffer any further!'
(29) *Jekh   lil   tu   lind-ar-dan   les*
      ART.INDEF book you:SING bring-CAUS-PRET2SING him:OBL
      mande
      me:LOC
      'You made me get a book'

Deadjectival intransitive verbs are also causativized by applying -ar- to the verb stem:

(30)   *Ka   čhinena   mandro, tumaro   vast   na*
       when cut:2PL   bread   your:PL hand NEG
       čalj-ar-ela   dženen   sigo
       be satisfied-CAUS-3SING men:OBL   quick
       'When you cut bread, your hand does not satiate people quickly'

In the dialect of the Arli from Prilep causatives are formed with -ar- , attaching to the present stem: *phir-ar-* 'make walk, guide', often with a palatal, thus: *phirj-ar-* or *phil-ar* ; a change of -r- to -l- also appears in *kel-ar-* , the causative of *ker-* .

The suffix -av- is added to the present stem. Synchronically -av- is a transitivizing suffix, as the bases are intransitive verbs only. The derived transitives sometimes have a causative meaning, but many of them are lexicalized:

(31)   *Linde   la   dur themende,   ačh-av-de   la*
       took:3PL her:OBL far countries:LOC stay-CAUS-PRET3PL her:OBL
       ko   gurbeti
       PREP away:from:home
       'They took her to places far away, made her stay far away from home'
(32)   *Trrrt, baš-av-ela   ek tani   ril!*
              be noisy-CAUS-3SING one piece fart
       'Trrt, he farts once'

The transitive derived from *baš-* 'to make noise' is lexicalized as 'to fart'. In the dialect of the Kalderaš the same verb is lexicalized as 'to make music':

(33)   *Vov da arakh-av-elas   i   guruven*
       he   too find-CAUS-3SING.PAST ART cattle:OBL
       'He too herded the cattle'

The transitive verb derived from *(a)rakh-* 'to find', is lexicalized as 'to herd, to guard'.

Many two-syllable Romani verbs consist of a primary verb stem plus the inherited causative suffix -av-, such as *sikh-av-* 'to show', *ax-av-* 'to understand', or *gil-av-* 'to sing', the primary verbs being lost in most dialects. These two syllable stems containing -av- are derived with -ker- only:

(34) *Šun,   ti   axav-ker-av*   *tut*   *lačhes!*
      listen:IMP COMP understand-CAUS-1SING you:OBL.SING well
      'Listen, that I make this understandable for you!'
(35) *I   čhajen   tuke   gilav-ker-esa*
      the girls:OBL you:DAT .SING sing-CAUS-2SING
      'You let the girls sing for you'

Loanwords are causativized with *-ker-* . The loanverb suffix *-in-* is replaced by *-is-*. It is not clear whether the latter is an alternation of *-in-* , or an entirely different suffix, resembling *-iz-* of Greek origin. The latter is applied to loanverbs in other Balkan dialects (e.g. Bugurdži; cf. Boretzky 1993): *mislizava* 'to think'. Example (36) shows Turkish *bekle-* , Romani *beklet-in-* 'to wait', causative *beklet-is-ker-* 'to make/let s.o. wait'; in (37) we have Greek παντρεύω, Romani *prand-in-* 'to marry', causative *prand-is-ker-* 'to give in marriage':

(36) *Trin sahatja beklet-isker-dan*   *man,   akana*
      three hours   wait-CAUS-PRET2SING me:OBL now
      so mangesa?
      what want:2SING
      'You let me wait for three hours, what do you want now?'
(37) *Manglarde leske ekhe čhaja, prand-isker-de*   *les*
      wooed:3PL him:DAT a girl:OBL marry-CAUS-PRET3PL him:OBL
      'They wooed a girl for him and gave him in marriage'

The derived loanverbs have a general causative meaning; unlike causatives in *-av-*, they are rarely lexicalized. The process is very productive. For some intransitive Greek loanverbs derivation with *-ker-* results in non-causative transitives. In these cases *-ker-* has the same function as the suffix *-av-* with indigenous verbs. Thus in (38) we have Greek γλυτώνω, Romani *glut-in-* 'to save oneself', causative *glut-is-ker-* 'to save s.o.':

(38) *Čobano, jala,   glut-isker   man!*
      shepherd come here save:CAUS me:OBL
      'Shepherd, come and save me!'

Causatives are chosen whenever a situation of force, ordering or permission is expressed. An analytic causative construction is not in use. Examples (39)-(40) show force:

(39)   *'Tuj   hemen   i   derjavakoro pampuri*
        youSING right away ART sea:GEN   steam:engine
        ka-našavkeres   les.'   džikaj
        FUT-runCAUS:2SING him:OBL said:3SING
        '"You'll hijack the ship right away" said he'
(40)   *Zorisar   ka   xavkerelas   ja ka*
        force:INSTR PART eatCAUS:3SING.PAST or PART
        pijavkerelas   amen o   taratori!
        drink:CAUS:3SING.PAST us   ART garlic-mix
        'He urged us to eat or drink the garlic-vinegar-mix'

The following (41)-(42) are examples of order, while (43-45) show permission:

(41)   *Dešuduj phralen therava   ti   kerdarav   tuke*
        twelve brothers have:1SING COMP make-CAUS:1SING you:DAT
        po   lači angrušni!
        COMPAR good ring
        'I have twelve brothers to have a much better ring made for you!'
(42)   *Trin far   xutlardas   man   katar ko*
        three times jumpCAUS:PRET:3SING me:OBL PREP PREP
        bašne opral
        cocks above
        'Three times he made me jump over the cocks'
(43)   *Na   mangena ti   sovdaren   i   čhaven   ko*
        NEG want:3PL COMP sleepCAUS:3PL ART children:OBL PREP
        süneti
        circumcision
        'They do not want to let the boys sleep after the circumcision'
(44)   *Soske ti   džuvdarav   i   džamba ?*
        why COMP liveCAUS:1SING ART frog
        'Why should I let the frog live?'
(45)   *I   romni na   parundiskerdas   i   dades*
        ART wife NEG buryCAUS:PRET3SING ART father:OBL
        'The wife did not allow that the father was buried'

Causativation with *-ker-* is very productive, as it is the only suffix applicable to loanverbs. In other Balkan dialects, such as Erli from Sofia, *-ker-* causatives exist, but they are rare. In the dialect of Ajia Varvara they are unknown. It is noteworthy that in Sepečides-Romani indigenous verbs frequently take the suffix *-ker-* affixed to *-av-* or *-ar-* . Morphologically these forms represent double causatives. For some verbs suffixation with *-av-ker-* or *-ar-ker-* is obligatory to obtain a causative. Primary forms with *-av-* or *-ar-* are not in use. Example (46) shows the root *beš-* 'to sit', with the causatives *beš-av-ker-* and *bešl-ar-* 'to let someone sit', and the root *pi-* 'to drink', with the causative *pij-av-ker-* 'to make drink':

(46) *Lena   les   ko   kahve-hani, beš-av-ker-ena   les,*
      take:3PL him:OBL PREP café   sit-CAUS-CAUS-3PL him:OBL,
      pij-av-ker-ena   les
      drink-CAUS-CAUS-3PL him:OBL
      'They take him to the café, make him sit down and drink'

Example (47) has the root *putr-* 'to open', with the causative *putr-a(v)-ker-* 'to make s.o. open s.th.'. Again, there is no alternative to this double causative form:

(47) *O   patišaji putr-av-ker-ela   odova kher*
      ART king   open-CAUS-CAUS-3SING that   house
      'The king has that house opened'

Many other verbs have one causative with *-av-* or *-ar-* plus a second one with *-av-ker -*, or *-ar-ker-*. With a few exceptions, all these are synonymous forms: The second causative, containing two causative suffixes, does not differ semantically from the first one. The following examples illustrate the use of the different suffixes for the same word within one utterance. In (48) *xut-* 'to jump' appears with the causatives *xutl-ar-* and *xutl-a(r)-ker-* 'make s.o. jump':

(48) *'Trin far   ka-xutl-ar-ker-es   i   gerales!'*
      three times FUT-jump-CAUS-CAUS:2SING ART bald man
      Lindas   i   gerales, jek xutl-ar-das,   adže
      took:3SING ART bald man once jump-CAUS-PRET3SING again
      xutl-ar-das.
      jump-CAUS-PRET3SING
      '"Three times you'll make him jump!" He took the bald man, he made him jump once, he made him jump again ...'

Hübschmannová & Bubeník (this volume) describe similar phenomena for Hungarian Romani. Triggered by the contact language, in Hungarian Romani multiple causativization is possible. Suffix accumulation appears, such as *kalj-ar-el* 'make black', further derived as *kalj-ar-avel* 'have s.th. made black' (see their example (10), this volume). We find a similar situation in the dialect of the Austrian Lovara: The variety with Hungarian as a contact language (until 1956) has productive causativation with *-av-*: root *xa-* 'to eat', first causative *xa-xav-* 'to feed', second causative *xa-xav-av-* 'make s.o. feed'. In the dialect of the group which had German as a contact language for about 150 years, forms such as *xaxavel* 'he feeds s.o.' still exist, but further morphological causativation is unproductive. Suffix combinations and accumulations as described above are possible in Sepečides-Romani involving *-ker-* , but mostly there is no semantic difference between single and double causative forms. An exception is the verb *tordjava* 'to stand'. A first causative is formed with *-ar-*, *tordj-ar-ava* 'to stop'; the second one is *tordj-a(r)-ker-ava* 'let someone wait'.

Causativization is a common process in Turkish. There are several suffixes (some of them with two allomorphs) attaching to different verb roots. Similar to the situation of Hungarian Romani, the productivity of causativization in the language of the majority has triggered the process in Romani, where we find a large inventory of often synonymous causative verb forms.

4.2 Inchoative intransitives

Inchoatives are intransitive verbs derived from nouns. They denote a transition from one state into another, in the sense of 'begin' or 'become full of' or 'turn into'. The suffixes *-ndiv-* or *-aliv-* are combined with a noun to obtain an inchoative verb. These forms are unknown in other dialects. In the Kalderaš dialect as well as in Lovari there are inchoatives in *-ajvav* derived from adjectives: *šukajvav* 'become beautiful', *lašajvav* 'become better, turn good', *ratvajvav* 'turn bloody'. To derive inchoatives from nouns, an analytic construction with *avav* 'to become' is used: *avav rom* 'I turn into a man' (Sepečides Romani: *romandivava*); in Lovari: *kerǧovav rom* . Even the Arli of Prilep express inchoative meaning analytically with *ovava* 'to become', whereas in Sepečides Romani the derivational process is very productive for both indigenous nouns and loanwords. Thus Prilep has *ovava rom*, while Sepečides Romani has *romandivava*, both meaning 'turn into a man'. Further examples:

(49)   *O   sastri but   izgurjalivola* (from *izguri* 'rust')
        ART iron   much rustINCH:3SING
        Turkish: *demir çok   pas-lan-ıyor*
                 iron   much rust-INCH-3SING
        'The iron is becoming rusty'

(50) *I   rakli džuvljandivola*   (from *džuvli* 'woman')
ART girl   womanINCH:3SING
Turkish: *kız ergen-len-iyor*
        girl mature-INCH-3SING
'The girl matures/becomes a woman'

(51) *Ka   makhjandivona   o   xumerja,   furatin   len!*
when flyINCH:3PL   ART dough:PL   throw:away:IMP them:OBL
(from *makhi* 'fly, mosquito')
Turkish: *hamurlar   sinek-len-iyorlar*
        dough:PL   fly-INCH-3PL
'When the dough is full of maggots, throw it away!'

4.3 Double phrases

Double phrases are common in narrative speech. Some of them also exist in other dialects, like Kalderaš and the dialect of the Arli from Prilep. Due to Turkish influence the phrase has locative instead of ablative case:

(52) *Mo dat   sevlja   kerelas,   gav-gaveste   phirenas*
my father baskets made:3SING village-village:LOC travelled:3PL
o   Roma.
ART Roma
'My father made baskets, the Roma travelled from village to village'

Further examples are *mos-moste* 'from mouth to mouth', Turk. *ağız-ağıza*; *dum-dumeste* 'back to back', Turk. *omuz-omuza*; *kher-khereste*: 'from house to house', Turk. *evden-eve*; *rom-romeste*: 'from man to man'.
    In Sepečides Romani new such phrases are formed quite easily:

(53) *Drakh-drakhate   dikhela,   kaljola.*
grape-grape:LOC look:3SING turn black:3SING
'Man learns from man.' (literally: 'Looking from grape to grape one turns black.')

This phrase has a Turkish model, known as an old Ottoman proverb:

(54) *Üzüm üzüme   baka-baka   kararır.*
grape grape:DAT look-look:GERUND turn:black:3SING
'The grape, constantly looking at another grape, turns black'

As double phrases are very typical of Turkish, many expressions have been adopted by Sepečides Romani, closely following the Turkish formation. This leads to irregular morphological forms of indigenous Romani words. Some examples: *beši-beši* 'permanently sitting', Turkish *otura-otura; šuni-šuni* 'permanently listening', Turkish *duya-duya; rovi-rovi* 'permanently crying', Turkish *ağlıya-ağlıya*.

(55) *Ti   phiras xani, beši-beši   mi bul   šuvlili!*
      COMP walk a:little sit-sit-GERUND my bottom swollen:F
      'Let us walk a little, from sitting permanently my bottom is swollen!'

(56) *Ma   ker   javer   masali, šuni-šuni   čalilom!*
      PROH make:IMP another tale   hear-hear-GERUND fed:up:1SING
      'Don't tell another tale, I am fed up with listening!'

(57) *Dikhi-dikhi   šuvlardan   man   opral, telal!*
      see-see-GERUND swellCAUS:PAST2SING me:OBL above below
      'With your intensive looks you make me swell above and below!'

These forms do not exist in any other dialect. They are unique to Sepečides Romani, but were noted by Miklosich (1880) for the Greek Gypsies. The verb stem takes the suffix *-i*. Miklosich explained the forms as indigenous, corresponding to the absolute in some neo-Indic languages. Semantically the latter denote durative, concomitant actions or events, similar to the Romani phrases. At the same time the Romani phrases strongly resemble old Turkish gerunds in *-i* , where the verb stems are also suffixed with *-i*. Especially the doubling of the gerund is typical of Turkish. Like the Romani expressions the Turkish gerunds denote durative concomitant actions, but as such they are unknown in modern Turkish, where duration is expressed by gerunds in *-e, -a*. The formation of the Romani expressions with *-i-* , if not indigenous, would thus indicate an old Turkish influence. Less competent speakers of Sepečides Romani use the double phrases with *-e* , copying modern Turkish gerunds.

4.4 Genitive adjectives

A further characteristic of Sepečides Romani is the abundance of genitives used as nouns or adjectives. Genitives, very often with an *-ipe* derivation, are frequently used in everyday talks and especially in biographical stories as it is customary to create nicknames for almost every member of the closer family. Nicknames or names denoting certain features of persons usually are combined with an adjective. Inflection of this adjective is somewhat odd, as it need not necessarily have oblique case. Nominalized genitives are common in the Arli dialect of Prilep too; they also occur in Sinti, as in *khelipaskoro* 'dancer', *vešeskro* 'forester', *štaxlengro* 'hedgehog' and many more (Holzinger 1993:40ff.). In Sepečides-Romani they are an important means of compounding: *ratjakoro čiriklo* 'bat' (night:GEN bird), *sapeskoro mačho* 'eel' (snake:GEN fish), *derjavakoro pampuri* 'steamer' (sea:GEN steam-engine), *kokalaskiri džamba* 'turtle' (bone:GEN frog), *thudeskere phrala* 'bloodbrothers' (milk:GEN brothers), *thudeskiri daj* 'nurse' (milk:GEN mother).

Nicknames are frequently used to address other people of one's own group or to describe them directly: *buljakoro, buljakiri*: 'Someone greedy and hungry when the smell of food gets in his/her nose.' Turkish *götçü* (Argot), *kovle buljakoro* 'Lame-ass', *bare pelengoro* 'having long balls', *kukumaka šoroskoro* 'having a head like an owl', *bokhalo jakhakoro* 'scrounger', *džimlamo jakhengoro* 'having sleepy eyes' (Turkish *çapaklı gözlü*).

5. Conclusion

Sepečides Romani represents a rather conservative dialect in phonology and morphology, deeply influenced by Turkish at the semantic (as well as idiomatic) level. It is rich in derivational processes and expressive in the lexicon. Unfortunately the use of this dialect has rapidly declined in the area of Izmir within the last 35 years. Full language competence has disappeared among the middle-aged generation to a large extent, and completely vanished among the younger people. Most of the Sepečides from Izmir regard assimilation to the majority as essential for their economic welfare. The traditional social structure of their society collapsed when the families left the villages and moved into the urban environment. Basket weaving disappeared, but no equivalent profession took its place. Many young people have difficulties to find and keep a job altogether, because there are no more traditional professions among this group. Their half-way integration has not resulted in more economic welfare but in poverty. Both group identity and self esteem are very low. Typical Romani traditions concerning birth, marriage and feasts are declining. Compulsory school attendance and the low image of Roma among the Turks favor the use of Turkish. Consequently the young generation is not taught Romani any more. We have no information about the Sepečides of Mersin and other settlements in the East of Turkey, but we can expect a similar situation.

In Volos, on the other hand, the situation is different. When basket weaving lost its economic value, the Greek Sepečides replaced their traditional profession by another one of the same kind. Like basket weaving, the carpet trade comprises the manufacturing and the selling of the products by the group members. Whereas the men used to make the baskets and their wives had to sell them, in the carpet trade the women produce the carpets (in factories) and their husbands sell them. The young people grow up with this profession and take over, when they have to support their own families. As the Roma work in the carpet business as a group and not as single workers scattered in various jobs among non-Gypsies, Romani is spoken by all members of the group at home and at work, although the children attend school and talk Greek there. Presently Sepečides Romani seems to survive in Greece, while it is about to die out in Turkey. In the Heinschink Collection there exist only a few recordings of the Greek variant, therefore a detailed analysis is still wanting, but in progress.

Endnotes

1. A survey on Roma groups within Turkey is found in Andrews (1989) as well as Duyğulu (1994); cf. also discussions of Gypsy groups of the Balkans and Turkey in Sinclair (1908), Halliday (1922), Bairacli Levy (1952), and Arnold (1967). For the Turkish/Greek influenced Gypsies see Igla (1996).
2. For the derivational status of causatives and inchoatives see Cech (1996).

References

Andrews, Peter A., ed. 1989. *Ethnic Groups in the Republic of Turkey*. Wiesbaden: Reichert.
Arnold, Hermann. 1967. 'Some observations on Turkish and Persian Gypsies'. *Journal of the Gypsy Lore Society* 46:3-4. 105-122.
Bairacli Levy, Juliette de. 1952. 'The Gypsies of Turkey'. *Journal of the Gypsy Lore Society* 31:1-2. 5-13.
Boretzky, Norbert. 1993. *Bugurdži. Deskriptiver und historischer Abriß eines Romani-Dialekts*. Wiesbaden: Harrassowitz.
Cech, Petra. 1996. 'Inflection/Derivation in Sepečides-Romani'. *Acta Linguistica Hungarica* 43:1-2. 67-91.
---- & Mozes F. Heinschink. 1997. *Sepečides-Romani*. Munich: Lincom.
Duyğulu, Melih. 1994. 'Čingeneler'. *Istanbul Ansiklopedisi* Vol. 2:18. 294-297.
Fennesz-Juhasz, Christiane. 1996. 'Tondokumente europäischer Roma. Die Sammlung Heinschink im Phonogrammarchiv der Österreichischen Akademie der Wissenschaften'. In: J.S. Hohmann, ed. *Handbuch zur Tsiganologie*. Frankfurt: Peter Lang. 272-281.
Friedman, Victor A. 1991. 'Case in Romani. Old grammar in new affixes'. *Journal of the Gypsy Lore Society* 5:1-2. 85-102.
Halliday, W.R. 1922. 'Some notes upon the Gypsies of Turkey'. *Journal of the Gypsy Lore Society* 1:4. 163-189.

Heinschink, Mozes. 1989. 'Language and culture of the Izmir Basket-Weavers'. In: S. Balić et al., eds. *Jezik i Kultura Roma*. Sarajevo: Institut za Proucavanje Nacionalnih Odnosa. 103-111.

Holzinger, Daniel. 1993. *Das Rómanes: Grammatik und Diskursanalyse der Sprache der Sinte*. Innsbruck: Institut für Sprachwissenschaft.

Igla, Birgit. 1996. *Das Romani von Ajia Varvara. Deskriptive und historisch-vergleichende Darstellung eines Zigeunerdialekts*. Wiesbaden: Harrassowitz.

Miklosich, Franz von. 1880. *Über die Mundarten und die Wanderungen der Zigeuner Europas*. Part X. Wien: Karl Gerold's Sohn.

Paspati, Alexandre G. 1870 [1973]. Études sur les Tchinghianés ou Bohémiens de l'Empire Ottoman. Constantinople: Koroméla. [Osnabrück: Biblio].

Sinclair, Albert T. 1908. 'The Oriental Gypsies'. *Journal of the Gypsy Lore Society* 1:3. 197-211.

LINGUISTIC FORM AND CONTENT IN THE ROMANI-LANGUAGE PRESS OF THE REPUBLIC OF MACEDONIA

VICTOR A. FRIEDMAN
University of Chicago

0. Introduction

The Republic of Macedonia has one of the most significant Romani populations in Europe. According to the 1994 census 43,732 people or 2.3% of the total population declared themselves to be of Romani nationality (Nova Makedonija 15.IX.94:1). The figures were 52,103 and 2.7% in the 1991 census.[1] Romani nationality thus constitutes the fourth largest in the Republic after Macedonian, Albanian, and Turkish. The figures for the relationship of declared nationality to first or other language are not yet available, but given discrepancies in the categorization of nationality and language (e.g. Muslim constitutes a nationality category but not a linguistic one), it is not unreasonable to assume that -- despite the fact that some individuals declaring Romani nationality will have a non-Romani first language -- the total number of Romani speakers is higher than available figures indicate.[2]

The fact remains that Romani is both statistically and legally a significant language in Macedonia. It was one of the six languages used in the 1994 census and is the language of television and radio broadcasts coming out of Skopje, Tetovo, and Kumanovo. Like other languages of Europe that have emerged as vehicles of public life during the past two centuries, Romani in the Republic of Macedonia (as in other countries) has been the subject of efforts at literary standardization. Unlike the case with some other languages, however, the standardization of Romani is taking place in both a national and a transnational context. On the one hand, there have been efforts such as Jusuf and Kepeski's *Romani gramatika* (1980, henceforth, RG), which, while having in mind that transnational context, was nonetheless directed primarily at the Romani audience in Macedonia, as evidenced not only by the choice of dialects but also by the fact

that it was published bilingually in Romani and Macedonian. Similarly, the standardization conference of November 1992 sponsored by the Board of Education
of the Republic of Macedonia and the University of Skopje, while explicitly
aware of the efforts at creating an international Romani literary language as
specifically mentioned in the resulting document, nevertheless had as its goal a
standardization of Romani as a language of study in schools in the Republic of
Macedonia (see Friedman 1995).

On 17 November 1993 the first issue of a Romani monthly newspaper,
Romani Sumnal/Romski Svet 'Romani World' (hereafter RS), was published in
Skopje under the editorial leadership of Oskar Mamut, who is also employed in
the Romani-language division of Radio-Television Skopje.[3] The newspaper is
bilingual, with all material in both Romani and Macedonian. The issue of the
codification of a Romani standard language is explicitly addressed on the first
page of the first number, where the editorial board states that one of the tasks
they have set themselves is contributing to the development and use of literary
Romani. As such, the paper can be taken as a measure of the progress and ongoing concerns of the standardization of Romani in the Republic of Macedonia.
The role of the mass media is potentially of great importance in language standardization. Taking as its background RG (cf. Friedman 1985), the Skopje
Standardization conference of 1992 (cf. Friedman 1995), and international efforts such as the standardization conferences of 1971 and 1990 (cf. Kenrick
1981, Cortiade et al. 1991), this paper will examine issues of RS's orthography,
phonology, morphology, syntax and lexicon as they relate to on-going problems
and discussions in the standardization of Literary Romani in the context of the
Romani dialectal situation in the Republic of Macedonia with passing reference
to other countries, e.g. Romania, the Czech Republic, Bulgaria, and member
states of the EU.[4]

1. Orthography and phonology

1.1 Orthography

Choice of orthography is often connected with ethnic and political symbol-
ism. The choice among the Arabic, Greek, and Latin alphabets was a key issue
in the quest for Albanian unity at the beginning of this century (cf. Skendi
1967:366-90). In Croatia, Franjo Tudjman's decree that bialphabetical
Latin-Cyrillic signs be replaced by monoalphabetical Latin ones helped alienate
the Serbian population of Croatia on the road to subsequent war (Glenny
1992:14). In Macedonia, the specification of the Macedonian language and its

Cyrillic alphabet as official at the federal level in article 7 of the constitution has led to conflicts over public signs, particularly with the Albanian minority (Nova Makedonija 94.07.28, Rilindja 94.08.03, Flaka e vëllazërimit 94.08.13).

In the case of Romani, there are at present a variety of competing trends in those publications utilizing Romani and aimed at whole or in part at Romani audiences (cf. Friedman 1985, §1.0). The international orthography approved at the Fourth World Romani Congress held in Warsaw in 1990 (Cortiade et al. 1991), which uses the IPA yogh (ȝ) for the voiced dental affricate and the acute for the strident palatals, is currently in use in publications funded by organizations such as the Commission of European Communities (e.g., Hill 1994, and the newsletter *Interface*).[5] The magazine *Patrin* resembles the Fourth World Romani Congress in its use of the acute accent where most Latin-based orthographies use a haček, but in other respects its orthography resembles the First World Romani Congress (Kenrick 1981) orthography. In the Czech Republic, a Czech-based orthography, similar to that proposed at the First World Romani Congress (Kenrick 1981), is in use (e.g. Hübschmannová et al. 1991), while in Bulgaria there are several orthographies: one based on Cyrillic (e.g. Malikov 1992, Kjučukov 1993b, Marushiakova and Popov 1994), one using English spelling conventions (e.g. Kjučukov 1993a), and one similar to Kenrick (1981; e.g. Marushiakova and Popov 1994). As has been noted elsewhere, the problem with the Fourth World Romani Congress orthography is that in other East European orthographies (notably Polish and former Serbo-Croatian), the acute is used to indicate mellow palatals (cf. de Gila Kochanowski 1994:81, who has proposed an orthography based on the standard transliteration of Devanagari into the Latin alphabet but without diacritics, in which the palatals are represented by sh, zh, c, j). RS follows standard East European practice of using the wedge (*haček*, *čiriklo*) to indicate the strident palatals (š, ž, č, dž). In this it continues the standard Latinization practice for Macedonian and other Slavic languages.

1.2 Schwa

Schwa (used here as a cover term for central vowels ranging in realization from the low ă to high î) is a marginal phoneme in many Romani dialects and is generally restricted to words of foreign origin (cf. discussion in Friedman 1985, §1.1). It is excluded from the Fourth World Romani Congress orthography as well as the document produced at the 1992 Skopje conference (Friedman 1995), although RG proposed <ä> (Kjučukov 1993a uses <w>). In RS, schwa is indicated in the same manner as in Macedonian orthography -- where it is also marginal -- by means of an apostrophe: *g'ndinaja* 'we think', *s'kldiba* 'care, concern', *c'knide* 'nettles', *sak'zi* 'chewing gum'. In the case of schwa plus sonorant (or vocalic sonorants), there is hesitation between zero and the apostrophe: *s'kldiba, frdingje* 'directed, sent, led', *prčo* 'goat', but *v'rda* 'wagons', also *gndinela* as well as *g'ndinela*. These can to some extent be treated as loan-vowels in the same manner as <ü> and <ö> in those dialects that have borrowed unadapted lexical items from languages such as Albanian, Turkish, and Hungarian.

1.3 The palatal quality of velars/dentals

The palatalization or palatal mutation of dentals and/or velars before front vowels and /j/ (cf. Friedman 1985, §1.4), continues to be problematic. In the Fourth World Romani Congress orthography, the problem is obviated in case endings (treated there as postpositional clitics), which are represented by the morphophonemic symbols 'q' and 'θ', although the same phenomena occur elsewhere. Thus for example, the same variation found in phonetic realizations of the dative suffix '-ke' occurs in roots such as *ker-* 'do' (cf. Friedman 1995). In RS, there is considerably less inconsistency in the representation of velars and dentals before front vowels and jot than in RG. Thus, although the principle of phonetic versus phonemic versus morphophonemic spelling is not consistently applied throughout RS, there is a tendency for certain lexical items and endings to follow one or another principle. For example, the verb *vaker-* 'say' is consistently spelled with <kj>, while the root *ker-* is generally spelled <kj> but also <k>, e.g. *kerel* and *kjerel* 'does'. Aspirated <kh> is never combined with <j>: either aspiration is not indicated or <j> is not written, e.g. *khere* 'at home', *khelela* 'plays' but *mukjen* 'they leave' vs *mukhel pes* 'he is left', *dikhlo* 'seen', *dikhljam* 'we saw', *dikhena* 'they see [long form]' but *dikjen* 'they see [short form]'.

The voiced variant of the dative suffix shows variation, e.g. *amenge ~ amengje*, but the voiceless variant and all other case affixes as well as roots only rarely indicate a palatal, palatalized, or jotated quality in spelling: *lengere, gelo*, etc., but *muzikakjere* 'musical/of music' ~ *anglunipaskere* 'progressive/of progress', The root *kin-* 'buy' is consistently spelled *kjin-*, but the root *gil-* 'sing/song' occurs as both *gil-* and *gjil-*, similarly *mangela* 'wants' but *mangjin-dor* 'while wanting'. Elsewhere fronting before /i/ is not indicated, e.g. *lakiri* 'her', *ki Republika Makedonija*, etc.. The morphophonemic fronting of dentals before jotation is consistently spelled out: *buti -bukja* 'work sg/pl', *rat - rakja* 'night sg/pl', *kjerdi - kjergja* 'done - did'. Elsewhere, there is no graphic indication of fronted dentals. Thus the orthographic treatment of these phenomena, while gradually standardizing, remains problematic.

1.4 Jotation in feminine substantives

Romani dialects show variation in the jotation of oblique and plural forms of feminine stems, especially those with the nominative singular ending in a consonant (cf. Friedman 1985, §2.1). Moreover, oblique feminine stems in *-a(j)* frequently show contraction, e.g. *dajake ~ dake* 'mother (dat.)'. RS is consistent in the jotation or nonjotation of individual lexical items, e.g. *čhib* 'tongue' is regularly jotated (*čhibjakiri* '[F.gen])' while *jak* 'eye' is not (*jakha* [pl]). RS is also consistent in its use of uncontracted obliques of stems in *-a(j)*, e.g. *dajakiri čhib* 'mother tongue' (f. gen.), *ple čhajaja* 'with his own daughter'.

1.5 The opposition i/j

Although RS displays more consistency than RG in distinguishing vocalic /i/ from non-vocalic /j/, there is still some confusion (cf. Friedman 1985, §1.3). Thus, *duj* 'two' is consistently spelled but *šai* occurs alongside *šaj*. Vocalic /i/ is spelled in *leindor* 'while taking', *deindor* 'while giving', *roipe* 'weeping', *sasoitne* 'social' but *leibe ~ lejbe* 'taking', *asajbe* 'laughter/humor', *hajbe* 'food/nourishment'.

1.6 The opposition h/x

The etymologically unmotivated distinction between /h/ and /x/ (cf. Friedman 1985, §1.2) is not made in Arli or Burgudži, although it occurs in Džambaz, e.g. *has-* 'laugh', *xas-* 'cough'.[6] While RG prescribes the distinction, it is not consistently followed, e.g. both *hiv* and *xiv* 'hole'. RS reflects Arli practice using only the letter /h/, e.g. *hajlovela pes* 'it is understood/of course' (< h), *hošinel* 'feel, please' (< Tk. *hoş*), *hevja* 'holes' (< x), *ha* (< *xa*) 'eat'. Only the root *xram-*, e.g. *xramovipe* 'writing', *xramone ~ hramone* 'written'(< *hram-* < Gk. *gram-*, cf. Boretzky & Igla 1994) occurs, but this may be an editorial oversight. Macedonian influence seems to appear in some items in the loss of /h/ or its passage to /v/ intervocalically: *asala* 'laughs' (< *hasala*), *hovaven* (< *xoxaven*) 'deceive'. Note also the loss of intervocalic /v/ as in Macedonian in *sikloibe* alongside *siklovibe* 'studying'.

1.7 r / ř (rr, R, etc.)

As in most Macedonian Romani dialects, the distinction between plain /r/ and marked /r̆/ (long, uvular, etc.) is not present and therefore not indicated. This is the practice in RS as well as RG and Kenrick (1981) (cf. also Friedman 1995), but not in Cortiade et al. (1991) where <rr> is used for the marked member.

1.8 Clear, dark, and palatal /l/

In Macedonian Romani dialects, as in Macedonian, /l/ is clear before front vowels and dark elsewhere (cf. Friedman 1985, §1.5). It also contrasts with palatal /l'/. Unlike RG, where <lj> is sometimes used for clear and elsewhere for palatal /l/, in RS the sequence <lj> is reserved for palatal or jotated /l'/, e.g. *lil* 'letter', *lel* 'one takes', *leljum* 'I took', *milje* 'thousand', *sikljovibe* 'study', *sikljiljum* 'I studied'. The graphic combination <ll> for final dark /l/, e.g. *dell* 'gives' occurs as if in imitation of Albanian graphic conventions, however these are probably simply errata. The form *moll* (pl. *molla*) 'value/price' is apparently a Vlaxism (i.e. a word recently borrowed from a Vlax dialect for purposes of vocabulary enrichment).

1.9 Aspiration

As Boretzky (1993) observes, there is some variation in the realization of aspiration in individual lexical items, and it is generally neutralized word finally. This neutralization is generally reflected in spelling in RS: *jek* 'one' but *jekhipe* 'unity', *jekhfar* 'once', *jak* 'eye' but *jakha* 'eyes', etc. Some roots, however, display inconsistency, e.g. *pučen - phučava* 'ask' (2 pl. imp. - 1 sg), *lači - bilačhi/bilači* 'good - harmful', *mukha·* 'we leave' ~ *mukjen* 'they leave' (cf. 1.3 above). There are also several Indicisms written with unadapted voiced aspirates as in RG: *bhagja* 'consciousness/awareness', *dhamkjeribe* 'threat', *labhakjeren* 'use', *adhinel* 'depend'.

1.10 Intervocalic -s- in grammatical affixes

The treatment of original intervocalic /s/ and final /s/ in affixes (cf. Friedman 1985, §1.3)[7] is consistently modeled on Arli, i.e. with two exceptions

/s/ is generally lost, and in intervocalic position the resulting hiatus is spelled with <j> medially: *mangaja* 'we want', *šunaja* 'we hear', *kasetaja* 'with a cassette', *ple čhajaja* 'with his own daughter', *Ačhoven Devleja* 'Good-bye', *nijameja* 'with justification' (the lack of /j/ in *e čhavea* 'with the child' could be simply a typographical erratum) finally: *dikha* 'we see', *kjergja* 'he did', *ka la* 'we will take', *Džanena romane* 'they know Romani', *Me dikhava e manuše sar manuš* 'I look at a person as a person', *isi o le ~ ole ~ le* 'he/it has'. The first of the two exceptions is *isi* 'is, there is' (cf. the foregoing example). Although there is an alternative form in Arli without /s/, viz. *i*, only *isi* is used in RS. The other exception is original final /s/ in the reflexive accusative pronoun *pes*, which is important in the formation of various types of intransitives (on the model of Macedonian *se*). In RS, this final <s> is spelled with considerable inconsistency: *hajlovela pes* 'it is understood/of course', *džanela pes* 'it is known', *bistrela pes* 'is forgotten' but *kjergje pe* 'they pretended', *g'ndinela pe* 'it is thought of', *kamela pe* 'is liked, is wanted'. The three numbers of RS that appeared in 1993-94 displayed an apparent difference in editorial policy. Final <s> tended to be spelled with great frequency in the first number, omitted in the second, and spelled again in the third, although omission was not uncommon.[8]

1.11 The combination n+s at morpheme boundaries

The affixation of the instrumental *-sa[r]* to the oblique plural stem in *-n* results in a delayed release perceived as /t/ resulting in spellings such as *manušencar* 'with people', *lencar* 'with them' etc. Elsewhere, however, the combination /ns/ is spelled although it may be pronounced [nts], e.g. *sansara* 'peace'.

1.12 Combinations of preposition + definite article & obl. 3 sg. pronouns

In the Fourth World Romani Congress orthography, prepositions are connected to definite articles by means of a hyphen, as in Romanian, e.g. *k-o, k-i, tar-o, tar-i, baš-o, p-o* 'to the' (masc., fem.), 'from the' (masc., fem.), 'about the', 'on the' (cf. Friedman 1985, §2.3). In some orthographies, an apostrophe is used in place of a hyphen. The typical Arli initial *o-* and third person oblique pronouns are written together if at all: Fourth World Romani Congress orthography *olesqe, olaqe, olenqere*, etc. RS follows the practice of RG: prepositions of postpositional origin as well as underlying *p[e]* 'on' write the article with the preposition as one word: *ko Roma* 'to the Roms', *ki Japonija* 'in Japan', *taro tiknipe* 'from childhood', *tari dar* 'from fear', *dži ki kasarna* 'toward the bar-racks', *dži ko gav* 'toward the village'.

The tendency is to write initial third person pronominal *o-* separately, espe-cially in the genitive. Elsewhere there is some hesitation, e.g. *ola ~ o la* 'her, them', *uzal olende* 'besides them' but *mashkar o lende* 'among them', *Kjeren o leja lafi thaj pučen ole akala pučiba* 'Talk with him and ask him these questions', *O čhavo valjani te ovel o le plo than* 'The child should have its own place'. Although this *o-* is etymologically part of the pronoun (see Sampson 1926:161-63), it is sometimes interpreted as a type of definite article. This not only affects orthographic representation, but sometimes even results in grammat-ical reinterpretations, e.g. *baš i lakiri kariera* 'about her career' (see 2.3).

2. Morphology

2.1 Nominative third person pronouns

The shape of the third person nominative pronouns (Friedman 1985, §2.3) is consistently Arli: *ov, oj,* and *ola ~o la* 'he, she, they', which latter is used for both genders, e.g. in reference to masc. pl. nouns such as *manuša*, as opposed to masc. pl. *on*, which occurs only rarely. In other dialects, the shape can be *vov, voj*, etc. (Džambaz, Gurbet, Kalderaš) or *jov, joj,* etc. (central and north-ern Europe).

2.2 The nominative plural definite article

The nominative plural definite article (Friedman 1985, §2.4) is consistently the Arli *o* rather than *e* as found in other dialects, e.g. *o Roma* 'the Roms'.

2.3 The genitive marker

The long forms of the genitive (*-koro, -kiri, -kere*; cf. Friedman 1985, §2.3) are used with almost complete consistency: *baš i lakiri kariera* 'about her career', *baš o lakere učipa* 'about her heights', *baš o lakoro feniks* 'about her phoenix', *partijakere liderija* 'party leaders', *e romane poezijakoro dad* 'the fa-ther of Romani poetry', *duje čhavengiri daj* 'mother of two children', *o leskiri antropologikani, socijalakiri, thaj kulturakiri dimenzija* 'its anthropological, so-cietal and cultural dimension', *e minoritetengeri dživipaskeri praktika ko Balkani* 'the reality (practicality) of life of minorities in the Balkans'. The one short genitive in -ki also shows a different shape in the internal vowel of a long form: *E civilzacijakeri asimilacijaki balval* 'the civilizing wind of assimilation'; cf. also *ki belgradeskeri TV*. The form *ko kher e Sakipengo* 'at the house of the Sakips' is the only other short genitive.

2.4 Possessive pronouns

The singular possessive pronouns or Romani (Friedman 1985, §2.2) show a variety of shapes, among which the most common in the Balkans are (taking the masculine first person as exemplary): *miro, mlo, mro, moro, mo* (for details, see Boretzky and Igla 1994:388). Of these, the first two are markedly Arli, the third is Burgudži, the fourth is shared by Burgudži and Džambaz (Gurbet), while the last is common throughout Macedonia. Nonetheless, RS is distinctly Arli in its favoring forms of the type *mlo* and makes infrequent concessions by occasionally using forms of the type *mo*, e.g. *Dikhindor ma te našaven plo muj, našavgje pi bul* 'Taking care to save their face, they lost their butt.'

2.5 Aorist person markers

The shape of the first person aorist marker (Friedman 1985, §2.5) is a diagnostic feature separating the so-called Vlax from the Non-Vlax dialects of Romani.[9] The former are characterized by -*em*, the latter by a back rounded vowel, -*om* or -*um*. All three endings occur in the Romani dialects of Macedonia, in Džambaz, Burgudži, and Arli, respectively. RS consistently uses the Arli -*um*, e.g. *ačhiljum* 'I remained', *bistergjum* 'I forgot', *geljum* 'I went', *khelgjum* 'I danced', *leljum* 'I took' *g'ndingjum* 'I thought'. There is not much dialectal variation in the markers of the other persons (aside from 2 sg -*al* (vs -*an*) in Sinti and some other dialects of former Austria-Hungary).[10] RS, however, has a peculiar first person plural aorist marker, viz. -*em* rather than the expected -*am*, e.g. *bašalgjem* 'we played', *gelem* 'we went', *giljavgjem* 'we sang', *kjergjem* 'we did', *lelem* 'we took', *manglem* 'we wished', *vakjergjem* 'we spoke', *dikhlem* 'we saw'. On rare occasion, the expected -*am* is used: *ačhiljam* 'we remained', *dikhljam* 'we saw'. In the conjugated forms of 'be', which constitute the historical source of these affixes, RS consistently has the expected 1 sg *sijum* and 1 pl *sijam*. This may be an attempt to incorporate a Džambaz feature with an altered meaning, but at present it remains unclear.

2.6 Imperfect/Pluperfect

RS is consistently Arli in its formation of the imperfect (Friedman 1985, §2.5) adding the analytic preterit auxiliary *sine* (functioning as a particle) rather than by suffixing *-as* to the conjugated present:[11] *Ko adava vakti kjerela sine pes vakti [sic! = lafi] baš o but love, a oj mi čhorori na džanela sine te čhorel.* 'At that time it was said that it was a matter of a lot of money, but she, poor thing, did not know how to [= would not have thought of] steal.' *A sako dive o la avena sine ko pobaro numero, pa akhal avilo pes dži ko adava o la te čhiven pes ki privatikane khera.* 'But every day they came in greater numbers, and thus it came to this: they had to be put [up] in private houses.' *Sa džala sine šukar dži na agorkjergjum o fakulteti.* 'Everything went/was going fine until I finished college.'

2.7 Long versus short present tense forms

RS almost always follows the practice articulated in RG of limiting short present forms (Friedman 1985, §2.5) to modal constructions *sensu largo*, i.e. subordination to the future marker *ka* and the modal (conjunctive/subjunctive/ optative/conditional) marker *te*. The following examples are typical: *na mangaja te vakera* 'we don't want to talk', *tergjola thaj ka tergjol* 'it remains and will remain'. The following two sentences constitute exceptions to this practice: *Te perena tumare bala masirinen o la loneja a pali odova thoven o len sar sakana.* 'If your hair is falling out, rub it with salt and then wash it as usual'. *Ja ka ačhava bašijaver mlo dikhibe - bi cenzurakoro.* 'But I will leave my uncensored view for another time'. The first of these is explicable either as a progressive (Šaip Jusuf, pc) or as conditional versus conjunctive (Boretzky and Igla 1994:402).

2.8 Adjective comparison and agreement

This is an area of grammar in which RS reflects dialectal compromise (cf. also Friedman 1985, §2.2). The comparative is formed using the Arli/Burgudži prefix *po-* (from Macedonian) while the superlative is formed using the Džambaz prefix *maj-* (from Romanian, as opposed to Arli *naj-* [< Macedonian] or *em-* [<Turkish]), e.g. *baro, pobaro, majbaro* 'big, bigger, biggest'. The one remnant of the old synthetic comparative in *-eder* is the item *pobuter* 'more' (<*but* 'very'), which is used more frequently than *pobut*. RS shows ordinary adjective agreement, except for borrowings from Macedonian, which are taken over in the

Macedonian neuter, which looks like the Romani masculine (-*o*) but are then treated as indeclinables in RS, e.g. *socijalno buti* 'welfare' (literally 'social work', in which *buti* is feminine. If the adjective were made to agree, it would be *socijalni* [which would be identical to the Macedonian plural].)

2.9 Derivation of abstract nouns

RS uses both -*be* and -*pe* for the derivation of abstract nouns from verbs and adjectives (Friedman 1985, §2.1). It appears that -*be* is restricted to deverbal nouns, while -*pe* is used for both deverbal and deadjectival nouns: *akharipe* 'invitation', *bipakjavipe* 'distrust', *čačipe* 'truth, reality', *manušipe* 'humanity', *nanipe* 'destitution', *šajdipe* 'possibility', *dikhibe* 'view', *fiksiribe* 'establishment', *khelibe* 'playing', *pučibe* 'question, *s'kldiba* 'cares', *prandiba* 'weddings', *mariba* 'wars', *hardzhiba* 'expenses'. In at least one instance, the affixes are used to distinguish meaning in a single stem, viz. *mang-* which has such diverse but related meanings as 'want, wish, love, seek, beg, need, demand' etc., whence *mangipa* 'needs' but *mangibe* 'desire'; cf. also *namangibe* 'hatred'.

3. Syntax and lexicon

3.1 Modal constructions

RS consistently uses the Arli modal construction of *te* + aorist to express fulfillable hypothetical conditions: *Te gelem ničeja, ka džana kaj sa o džijanija, uzal e religiengere anava isi len specifikane anava* 'If we go in order, we will discover that all peoples, alongside religious names, have [their] particular names'; *Te phirgjem hari ki historija ka dikha o darhija e komplekseskere tari hari moll,* 'If we go a little into history, we will see the roots of the inferiority complex', *Te g'ndingja pes hari pohor, pakjava kaj ka vakjeren: Amen sijam...* 'If one thinks a little deeper, I believe that they will say: We are...'

On rare occasion, *te* plus long present is used: *Te perena tumare bala masirinen o la loneja a pali odova thoven o len sar sakana* 'If your hair is falling out, rub it with salt and then wash it as usual'. Otherwise *te* + present or *kana* express fulfillable expectative conditions: *kana šaj ov, soske našti me?/kana šaj ov, soske me te našti?/Kana šaj ov, thaj me ka kjerav adava/kana šaj o la, soske na amen* 'if he can, why can't I/If he can, why can't it be me/If he can, then I will do this/if they can, then why not us?'

194 VICTOR A. FRIEDMAN

The borrowed Slavic conditional marker *bi* also occurs for fulfillable conditions, but only rarely: *Salde na bi mangaja te ovel kaj sijam majbare Romane Don Kihotija.* 'Only we would not like it to be the case that we become the greatest Romani Don Quixotes'. Macedonian *ako* is extremely rare although the partial calque *thaj ako* 'although' does occur.

3.2 'be' and 'have'

Unlike many other problematic areas of dialectal variation, where RS shows some hesitation, albeit not as much as in RG, in matters of the copula RS shows great editorial consistency despite the great dialectal variation (cf. Boretzky and Igla 1994:403-406). The paradigm of the present copula is strictly Arli, of the Baruči type (Figure 1):

	sing.	pl.
1.	*sijum*	*sijam*
2.	*sijan*	*sijen*
3.	*isi*	*isi*

Figure 1: The RS copula

The 3 sg./pl. past tense is *sine*, which also functions as marker for all other past forms (see 2.6 above). The possessive/existential is always formed with *isi*, and the negative possessive/existential is consistently the general Non-Vlax *nane*, e.g. *Sakoja dujto diz isi la pli "Roma Union" numa, o la nane len nisave vjavaharija* 'Every second town has its "Romani Union", but (literally 'only') they have no connection with one another'. *Mujal akija klasično socijalno arka isi panda jek taro 1992-to berš pendžardi sar programa baš e dživdipaskoro standardeskoro arakhibe* 'Beside this classic welfare, there has been (lit. 'is') a program since May 1992 for the protection of the standard of living'. The third person present copulative functions of 'be', including passive participle constructions, are consistently rendered by *tano/tani/tane*: *o gendo e manušengoro so pherena o usulija baši socijalakoro arakhibe tano sa majbaro* 'the number of people fulfilling the conditions for social welfare is greater than ever', *xramone tane bigjende rigore* 'numberless pages have been written'.

3.3 Negation

Expressions of negation is an area where RS shows dialectal compromise. The negative existential *nane* and the distinction between the modal negator *ma* and the indicative negator *na* are all consistent with Non-Vlax (Arli, Burgudži) usage. The negative pronouns, however, *khanšik* 'nothing', *khonik* 'no one', as well as negative adverbs such as *nikana* 'never' reflect Vlax usage, as opposed to Arli *ništo* 'nothing', *niko* 'nobody' etc. RS also uses *čipota* 'nothing', which appears to be a Džambaz treatment of a Hellenism (Greek *tipota* 'nothing').

3.4 Vocabulary

The vocabulary of RS displays many of the trends in current efforts to establish literary Romani in Macedonia: the use of neologisms, Indicisms such as *raštra* 'state', *sansara* 'peace' (cf. also 1.9), 'internationalisms', calques on Macedonian, etc. In terms of vocabulary choice within the everyday lexicon of the various Romani dialects of Macedonia, as in grammar, RS tends to favor Arli but makes occasional compromises by selecting from the other dialects. Thus, for example, the following consistently uses Arli *oja* 'yes' (vs. Džambaz and Burgudži *va*), Arli *javer* 'other' (vs. *aver*), Arli *tajsa* 'tomorrow' (vs. *tehara* or *javine*), Non-Vlax *lafi* 'word' (vs. Vlax *vorba*) but also non-Arli *thaj* 'and' (vs. Arli *[h]em*) and Vlax *lungo* 'long'. In some cases synonymous items from different dialects are used, e.g. Arli *agjaar, akhal* and Džambaz *agaja* 'thus', Arli *bizo* 'without' but also the more widespread *bi*, Non-Vlax *salde* 'only' but also Vlax *numa*. Motivations for individual choices varies, thus for example *thaj* is apparently preferred to *[h]em* because the former is Indic whereas the latter is from Turkish, but *bizo* is influenced by Slavic whereas *bi* is not. Both *salde* and *numa* are borrowed (from Turkish and Romanian, respectively), but the same situation holds for *lafi* and *vorba*.

The name of the newspaper itself is peculiar. *Sumnal* in the Vlax dialects of Romani means, among other things, 'holy'. The Macedonian word for 'holy' is *svet*, which is homonymous with the word for 'world'.[12] In the meaning 'world' Macedonian *svet* is derived from an original meaning of 'light'. The semantic equation of 'light' and 'world' was calqued from South Slavic into Romanian, where the word for 'world' is *lume* (definite *lumea*). The Romanian word was borrowed into the Vlax Romani dialects, whereas Non-Vlax dialects in the Balkans use other borrowings such as the Turkism *dunya*. The use of *sumnal* to mean 'world' is based thus on a complex of misunderstandings.

4. Conclusion

In its basic principles, RS represents a development in the direction described by the decisions reached at the 1992 Skopje conference and indicated in RG, namely an Arli base with elements from other dialects using a Latin orthography of the type in wide use in Eastern Europe, including RG, and recommended at the 1971 standardization conference (cf. also Hancock 1993, 1995). Nonetheless, specifics of the solutions reached by RS differ from those seen elsewhere. Taken as a whole, RS clearly represents a step forward in the standardization of Romani in the Republic of Macedonia. The editors are aware of standardization issues and are attempting to make concrete contributions towards a consistent and usable norm.

Endnotes

1. According to Svetlana Antonovska, head of the Bureau of Statistics of the Republic of Macedonia, the difference in the 1991 and 1994 figures is due primarily to the fact that in 1991 Yugoslav citizens residing abroad for more than one year were included in the census figures, while in the 1994 Macedonian census -- in keeping with international norms -- citizens residing abroad for more than one year were not included (personal communication).
2. Because *nationality* and *mother tongue* (first language) constitute separate census categories, it is possible, for example, for an individual to declare Romani nationality but Turkish mother tongue or vice cersa.
3. Although the newspaper was intended as a monthly, it has so far appeared only thrice: 17 November 1993, 10 December 1993, and 1 April 1994.
4. We are accepting here as a useful heuristic device the distinction between the so-called Vlax and Non-Vlax dialects of Romani. Although the Romani dialectal situation in the Republic of Macedonia is quite complex, the majority of speakers use dialects of a Non-Vlax type that are described by the self-ascriptive cover term *Arli* (< Turkish *yerli* 'local'). Next in importance for Macedonia is Džambaz (< Turkish *cambaz* 'acrobat, horse-dealer', known elsewhere as Gurbet, related to Kalderaš, Lovari, Čurari, Mačvano, etc.), which is a Vlax type dialect that has undergone Non-Vlax influence. Also of significance for Macedonia is *Burgudži* or *Bugurdži* (< Turkish *burgucu* 'gimlet-maker', also known as Rabadži [< Turkish *arabacı* 'drayman']) or Kovačja (< Slavic *Kovač* 'blacksmith', a name which is also used for other groups including the non-Romani speaking *Gjupci* of southwestern Macedonia), which is also a Non-Vlax dialect. The term Vlax refers to the fact that speakers of these dialects sojourned in Romania and have a number of Romanian lexical elements in their vocabularies. See also Boretzky (1995) and Boretzky and Igla (1994).
5. This orthography is also used in Sarău (1991, 1992).
6. This phonemic distinction is not inherited from an earlier distinction (see Sampson 1926:47, 49-51).
7. The change of Roamni /s/ to /h/ (with subsequent loss or realization as /j/) in general or in certain restricted grammatical environments is well known in certain Romani dialects including Sinti and Bosnian Gurbet (Ventcel' & Čerenkov 1976:285-88). In Arli this

change is restricted to a few grammatical morphemes, and the phenomenon does not occur in the other dialects of Macedonia.

8. It is not clear what the motivation was for this apparent shift in editorial policy, but given the dialectal saliency of this feature, it seems to represent a vacillation between diactal compromise (presence of /s/) and a more consistent Arli base (lack of /s/).

9. On the dialectal disnction, see note 4. Following Paspati (1870), I use the term *aorist* to refer to the simple preterit based on the particpial stem.

10. There is considerable variation in the third person endings in all of Romani, a topic beyond the scope of this paper (see Matras 1995). For additional details see Friedman and Dankoff (1991) and Boretzky and Igla (1994:355-56).

11. Although not occurring in RS, the pluperfect is formed in the same manner in each dialect as its respective imperfect, but with the aorist rather than the present as the base.

12. The homonymy is a coincidence of historical development. The /e/ of *svet* 'holy' is from a Common Slavic front nasal, whereas the /e/ of *svet* 'world, light' is from a Common Slavic *ē.

References

Boretzky, Norbert. 1993. *Bugurdži. Deskriptiver und historischer Abriß eines Romani-Dialekts*. Wiesbaden: Harrassowitz.

---- 1995. 'Interdialectal interference in Romani'. In: Yaron Matras, ed. *Romani in contact: The history, structure, and sociology of a language*. Amsterdam: Benjamins. 69-94.

---- & Birgit Igla. 1994. *Wörterbuch Romani-Deutsch-Englisch*. Wiesbaden: Harrassowitz.

Cortiade, M. et al. 1991. 'I alfabèta e standardone Rromane ćhibăqiri: Décizia I Rromani alfabèta'. *Informaciaqoro Lil e Romane Uniaqoro* 1-2. 7-8.

de Gila-Kochanowski, Vania. 1994. *Parlons tsigane: Histoire, culture et langue du peuple tsigane*. Paris: L'Harmattan.

Friedman, Victor A. 1985. 'Problems in the codification of a standard Romani literary language'. In: Joanne Grumet, ed. *Papers from the fourth and fifth annual meetings: Gypsy Lore Society, North American Chapter*. New York: Gypsy Lore Society. 56-75.

---- 1995. 'Romani standardization and status in the Republic of Macedonia'. In: Yaron Matras, ed. *Romani in contact: The history, structure, and sociology of a language*. Amsterdam: Benjamins. 177-188.

---- & Robert Dankoff. 1991. 'The earliest text in Balkan (Rumelian) Romani: A passage from Evliya Çelebi's Seyāḥat-nāme'. *Journal of the Gypsy Lore Society* (Fifth Series) 1:1. 1-20.

Glenny, Misha. 1992. *The fall of Yugoslavia: The Third Balkan War*. London: Penguin.

Hancock, Ian. 1993. 'The emergence of a union dialect of North American Vlax Romani, and its implications for an international standard'. *International Journal of the Sociology of Language* 99. 91-104.

---- 1995. *A handbook of Vlax Romani*. Columbus: Slavica.

Hill, Eric. (trans. by O. and B. Galiuś et al.) 1994. *O Rukun ʒal and-i skòla*. Paris: Rromani Baxt-C.E.E.

Hübschmannová, Milena, Šebková, Hana & Žigová, Anna. 1991. *Romsko-český a česko-romský kapesní slovník*. Praha: Státni pedagogické nakladatelství.

Jusuf, Šaip & Krume Kepeski. 1980. *Romani gramatika - Romska gramatika*. Skopje: Naša Kniga.
Kenrick, Donald. 1981. 'Romano alfabeto'. *Loli Phabaj* 1. 3-4.
Kjučukov, Hristo. 1993a. *Učeben bălgarsko-romski rečnik*. Sofia: UNICEF.
---- 1993b. *Nasoki za ezikovo obučenie v I i II kl. po majčin romski ezik*. Sofia: Ministerstvo na naukata i obrazovanieto.
Malikov, Jašar. 1992. *Cigansko-bălgarski rečnik*. Sofia: Fondacija Otvoreno obštestvo.
Marushiakova, Elena & Vesselin Popov, eds. 1994. *Studii Romani*. Sofia: Club '90.
Matras, Yaron. 1995. 'Verb evidentials and their discourse function in Vlach Romani Narratives'. In: Yaron Matras, ed. *Romani in contact: The history, structure, and sociology of a language*. Amsterdam: Benjamins. 95-123.
Paspati, Alexandre G. 1870 [1973]. Études sur les Tchinghianés ou Bohémiens de l'Empire Ottoman. Constantinople: Koroméla. [Osnabrück: Biblio].
Sampson, John. 1926 [1968] *The dialect of the Gypsies of Wales*. Oxford: Clarendon.
Sarău, Gheorghe. 1991. *Limba romaní*. Bucharest: Editura didactică şi pedagogică.
---- 1992. *Mic dicţionar rom-român*. Bucharest: Kriterion.
Skendi, Stavro. 1967. *The Albanian national awakening*. Princeton: Princeton University Press.
Ventcel', T. V. & L. N. Čerenkov. 1976. 'Dialekty ciganskogo jazyka'. In: N. I. Konrad, ed. *Jazyki Azii i Afriki I*. Moscow: Nauka. 283-332.

GEORGE BORROW'S ROMANI

IAN F. HANCOCK

University of Texas, Austin

0. Introduction

George Borrow (1803-1881) has stood as the acknowledged source of inspiration for countless Romanophiles (as well as Romanophobes) ever since his literary heyday in the 19th century; in fact Brian Vesey-Fitzgerald saw himself as quite "unfashionable" (1944:x) because he was one of the few who *didn't* make his "first acquaintance with [Gypsies] in the pages of George Borrow". From Prosper Merimée, who "drew from Borrow his inspiration for Carmen" (Ridler 1996:55), to criminologist Detective Samuel Haines whose monograph on American Gypsy crime relied largely on the *Romano La Volil* (sic; 1989:2), George Borrow's writings have stimulated the creative muse for innumerable writers about Gypsies for more than a century and a half.

Borrow spent the greater part of his life studying languages, a love which was kindled while he was a boy learning Latin and Greek at Norwich Grammar School, and he was already able to translate some twenty as diverse as Armenian and Middle Welsh "with facility and elegance" by the end of his teen years (Ridler 1996:451-453). By the time of his death at the age of 78, he had dealt in greater or lesser detail with eighty more (op. cit., 427).

As one of two sons of a military family, he moved about England with his father's regiment and developed a love for the British countryside and its inhabitants later reflected so elegantly throughout his writings. So strong indeed was the lure of rural England, that instead of pursuing the legal education his father had intended for him, he left his parents to take up with Traveller families on the roads, acquiring a taste for the Romani language which he subsequently took with him to Spain, Hungary, Romania, Russia and elsewhere.

Few figures in Romani Studies have been so roundly praised nor yet so heartily criticized as George Borrow, or have prompted such extremes of reaction. His all-consuming interest in Gypsies condemned him to serve as a prime example of "feebly inhibited genetic development" in a report by the Director of the U.S. Department of Experimental Evolution, for example, while on the other hand John Sampson, the greatest scholar of Romani ever to have lived, was moved to dedicate his monumental grammar of Welsh Romani to Borrow. His inscription, in Devanagari script, reads *ki Borrow, kai but beršendi dudyerdas m'o drom akai, ta akana asala 'pre mande peske brišindeskeriate* ('to Borrow, who for many years lit my way here, and who now smiles at me from his rainbow') (1926:iv). And while Audrey Shields, in her study of the Gypsy stereotype in Victorian literature believed that Borrow's idealization "did as much harm as writers who denigrated Gypsies" (1993:167), a sentiment echoing that of British Member of Parliament John Wells, one of the few government representatives sympathetic to the Romani situation, who claimed that "George Borrow has done more harm to the cause of those of us who wish the Gypsy community well than almost anyone else" (quoted in Reid 1962:37),[1] John Geipel more recently lauded him as the "savant ... who provided posterity with its largest single source of information on the Indian roots of the 'secret' language of the gitanos" (1995:112). That he has prompted such widely differing responses probably accounts for the fact that the study of the man and his life remains so intriguing to this day; and it was his involvement with the Romani people and language in particular which has left the most indelible mark.

1. George Borrow and the Romani language

Three features in particular characterize George Borrow's relationship with Romani: firstly, that his knowledge of its structure was surprisingly poor, given his acquaintance with so many other languages; secondly, that he freely mixed dialects, and thirdly, that he was not above creating lexical entries and grammatical forms of his own.

True to his style, Borrow spared no pains in cloaking the origins of Gypsies and the Romani language in mystery, a mystification which in fact was forced, at least in one respect, for he was aware of the Indian identity of the Roma by the time that he published his work *The Zincali* in 1841, being already familiar with the works of Grellmann, Whiter, Marsden and Richardson, which also contains the vocabulary collected by Bryant. He had even seen Andrew Boorde's book, which he mentions in *The Romany Rye* — though he seems to have missed the Romani it contained. So on page 104 of the second volume of *The Zincali*, (1841) he stated quite plainly that "Gypsies... are the descendants of a tribe of Hindus, who, for some particular reason, had abandoned their native country".

Despite already being aware of this, he asked in *Lavengro*, published ten years later in 1851 (in Chapter 17), "Rommany Chals! ... whence did they come originally? ah! there is the difficulty", and the concluding statement of *The Romany Rye*, which appeared six years later in 1857, clearly gives the impression that the Indian connection had only at that moment occurred to him: "I shouldn't wonder", said I as I proceeded rapidly along a broad causeway, in the direction of the east, "if Mr. Petulengro and Tawno Chickno came originally from India. I think I'll go there."

Nowhere in those two books is the Sanskrit origin of Romani discussed, although there and elsewhere Borrow does compare other languages with Sanskrit, for example Welsh, in *Wild Wales* (1862:599-600). Even in the *Lavo-Lil* (1874:4), his final work, he did not elaborate upon his observation that "the Gypsy language... [is] decidedly of Indian origin, being connected with the Sanscrit or some other Indian dialect", although he did wonder in *Lavengro* (p. 316) whether it was perhaps "the mother of all languages in the world". Angus Fraser has suggested to me that this notion may have had its origin in Whiter (1800:xxvij; see also Grosvenor 1908; Fraser 1995; and Ridler 1996), who himself believed that Romani "as it is now spoken, may probably be considered as the most ancient form of Speech, which is at present extant in the world", and whom he toasts in the same book in Chapter 24.[2]

2. *Borrow's knowledge of Romani*

Because of his penchant for embellishment, and because so many of his samples are transparently of his own creation (though he was by no means such a sprucer as was his contemporary Leland), it would be useful to ascertain the extent of his knowledge of Romani, as well as the degree of its accuracy.

Perhaps his first exposure to it took place according to his own account about 1810, when he was seven years old, and when he met Jasper and his family for the first time. The words he heard during that initial encounter were *bengui* 'devil' *tawny* 'young', *sap* 'snake', *sap-engro* 'snake-charmer', *Romans* (sic) 'Gypsies', *gorgeous* 'non-Gypsy' and the non-Romani Cant word *mumper*. Although he didn't recognise the language being spoken around him, he knew enough to say "it wasn't French". He was not to meet Jasper again after this for nearly ten years.

Although this episode was described in *Lavengro*, which was published in 1851, it was not the first time that Borrow had introduced Jasper, whom he had already mentioned ten years before in an appendix to the second volume of the second edition of *The Zincali*. In those pages he provided vocabularies and texts in British Romani, and compared it with the dialects spoken in both Spain and Hungary. Jasper Petulengro and his brother Tawno Tickno were, in real life, Ambrose and Fāden Smith; but changing the names of people and places, or sometimes hiding them behind initials, was part of Borrow's mystifying style. Furthermore, while Jasper is presented in the stories as being older than George Borrow, he was in fact one year younger.[3]

Borrow visited Russia in 1833 when he was thirty, and remained there for two years. After a period of time spent back in England, he left again for Spain, and between 1836 and 1840 made three visits to that country. In 1844, he took an extended trip through Hungary and Romania to Turkey, in each place seeking out Gypsies and collecting linguistic material from them. It was clear that he recognized the linguistic unity of Romani, thinking of it as one language consisting of many dialects differing by more or less retention of the original vocabulary and original grammar. Perhaps this is why he felt at liberty to mix them so freely, though it is more likely that he in fact believed that his readers would be unable to distinguish one dialect from another. Thus in *Wild Wales* (Chapter 98) he had Romanichals speaking Hungarian Romani, and elsewhere he put Spanish Romani in the mouths of Transylvanian Roma (e.g. the entries *busno* and *errai* in Winstedt 1952), and British Romanichals; the very first Romani word in *Lavengro*, 'bengui', in fact, has the Spanish Caló spelling and pronunciation rather than the British Romani *beng*. This means, of course, that he was not reporting accurately, which seriously diminishes the value of his material — referred to by Thomas Acton (in p.c.) as "deeply unauthentic" — for Romanologists, a number of whom in the 19th century based their own work at least partially upon it. Smart & Crofton remarked upon this in their own book, referring to "... the intrinsic evidence in his writings that many of his words have been procured from various and wide-spread sources" (1875:xij). This is evidenced by the fact that well over half of the ca. 120 words they give as unattested in English Romani (op. cit., 157-163) are listed as having originated in the works of Borrow.

3. The creation of Roma and Romani

In a paper I wrote some years ago (1980:14-15), I made reference to Douglas' notion of Bongo-Bongoism, the practice of some scholars of faking or misrepresenting data with the assumption that their audience knew nothing about the topic, and was therefore not in a position to challenge their claims. Borrow was especially guilty of this, although he should not be judged too harshly for that. Approaching his work on Romani as linguists may be frustrating and disappointing, or even amusing sometimes, but coming to it from the point of view of the literary critic is something else entirely. Borrow's writings are widely enjoyed precisely for their ponderous and self-involved style; he had a particular fondness for this, and modelled his prose upon the numerous 18th century works his library contained. He was, after all, writing for a particular audience. Helyear sums this up very well when she says (1972:82) that Borrow "complied, consciously or not, with the requirements of Victorian society, to the detriment of realism. He obviously sought literary success, and consequently had to satisfy his public's tastes and suit its intellectual esthetics".

Victorian readers relished being titillated by tales of the savage and the exotic in the Sunday afternoon safety of their drawing rooms, and Borrow's writings typified very well the popular middle class literature of the period. In fact he tended to overdo it, and was criticised in the press for being too prone to philosophizing and flights of moralistic fancy. In retrospect, we might reproach Borrow for presenting the Romani population in too romanticized and idealized a light — Helyear points out that nowhere does he "drop a single hint about the hardship of their life", instead sustaining the more attractive image of "picturesque outsider". Like Frederick Ackerley, whose only observation in his review of Potra's volume on the enslavement of Gypsies in Romania (1942:69-71) was that it was a pleasure and a delight to read and that it gave him a chance to practice his Romanian, Borrow too had nothing to say about that ultimate violation of humanity. Although he visited Romania while slavery was still everywhere in effect, for example, he was not moved sufficiently to comment upon it:

> I visited Wallachia with the express purpose of discoursing with the Gypsies, many of whom I found wandering about, the men supporting themselves by smithery, and the women by telling fortunes, but the generality [were] employed in the brick-fields making bricks like the Ishmaelites of old in Egypt (in Knapp 1899, ii:44).

Although *Lavengro* and *The Romany Rye* were not especially well received at the time of their publication, and Shields (1993:113) believed that in particular it was the "long, virulent diatribe against Scotts and Catholics ... that readers found excessive", and that the "picaresque style, lacking moral earnestness, was less fashionable than it had been in the previous century", they nevertheless had a singular effect upon both contemporary and later writers.

Lavengro appeared in 1851, the year of the Great Exhibition in London, when the British Empire was enjoying the height of its power on every continent. *The Romany Rye* was published in 1857, only two years after the appearance of Gobineau's *Essay On the Inequality of the Human Races* and two years before Darwin's equally influential *Origin of the Species*. Colonialism and new ideas about evolution and racial superiority stimulated a particular interest in foreign, and especially non-western, peoples and cultures. Readers' imaginations did not need to be transported to Borneo or Zululand or Nepal, when this dark and mysterious eastern population occupied their very doorstep. The *Illustrated London News* (1873:503) drew attention to this. Describing a Gypsy community "within an hour's walk of the royal palace", it urged "a few serious reflections upon social contrasts at the centre and capital of the mighty British nation, which takes upon itself the correction of every savage tribe in South and West Africa and Central Asia".

Ideas about these "savage tribes" and the superiority of the colonizing powers gave rise in time to the kind of racist dogma expounded by Houston Chamberlain (1899) and specifically elaborated upon against Roma by Alfred Dillmann (1905), in a document which laid the foundation for the National Socialists' concept of Gypsies as subhumans vis-à-vis the German master race, and which later paved the way for the racial policy of ethnically cleansing the Third Reich by attempting to exterminate the entire Romani population — adopted in modified form since the Holocaust by Ceauşescu in Romania into the 1980s (Hancock 1993:27).

The Industrial Revolution (ca. 1730-1850) had also brought tremendous changes to urban society by the time of Victoria's reign, having created a foul and unhealthy mechanized environment vividly described in the works of Dickens and others. But Borrow's idealized Gypsies lived apart from all this and above it, noble savages untouched by civilization, representatives of a vanishing rural era who had refused to relinquish it for the sake of progress. This has been well discussed by Wilson (1986:33-39). Shields (1993:113) calls Borrow's attitude towards his Romani acquaintances "preachy and condescending", and says that he was "worried that their aspirations to gentility [would] corrupt them". That the real experience of British Romanies didn't mirror the literary descriptions of it presented no dilemma, since those who obviously didn't match the idealized image were simply dismissed as being "not real Gypsies", but mumpers, diddicais, pikeys, people with little or no Romani ancestry who got the "True Romanies" a bad name (see in particular Mayall 1988). Here again, the particular devaluation of individuals regarded as being genetically mixed between Gypsy and white was to re-emerge in a frightening way in Hitler's Germany half a century later. Although many authors before Borrow's time incorporated Romani characters into their works, it was not until the appearance of George Borrow's books, as Fraser states (1993:15),

> that the literary and dramatic clichés received a clear and credible challenge. Borrow conveyed something of the real nature of Gypsies and their life-style, language and attitudes, and provided a picture that offered an exciting alternative to the previous hackneyed views.

But Fraser was choosing his words carefully when he referred to Borrow's exposition of *"something* of the real nature of Gypsies", for his writings are an exasperating mixture of fact and fancy, and separating the two is not easy. Borrow clearly imagined that he had some special status, reflecting what Shields has appropriately called "the rye phenomenon" (1993:164). For Borrow this provided something of a conflict because, as Helyear says, "he mingled with ruffians and people of the road, but insisted upon his being [regarded nevertheless as] a scholar" (1972:82). It might say something of his aloofness that he missed entirely learning of the existence of inflected Romani in Wales — a discovery which would have been of tremendous importance to him — despite his exploration of that country and the book resulting from it. Ken Lee brought my attention to the information in Jarman & Jarman's book *The Welsh Gypsies* (1991:151), that

> George Borrow missed the opportunity of hearing this language when he was in Bala, for he drank in the front room of the inn, while the local Wood family of Gypsies drank in the rear room with the rest of the ordinary Welsh people of the town.

To be fair to Borrow, he spent only three days in Bala altogether, and there is no evidence that the Woods were in the inn while he was there, or that they were even in the district. Nevertheless during his entire stay in Wales, he encountered Gypsies only once, and those were Boswells, from England.

Despite his rather distant behaviour, he regarded himself as a "brother", at least on his own terms, almost certainly a self-designation just as his status as a *rye* was. We shall never know whether his Romanichal acquaintances saw him as he saw himself, but Mrs. Hearne's attempt to murder him with a poisoned cake (*Lavengro*, Chapter 71)[4] is a good indication of their general attitude. Allingham (1934:5) came to realise what seemed never to have occurred to Borrow, despite his being told repeatedly and in many ways to mind his own business: "I decided to steal out of London as quietly and as quickly as possible and join the Gypsies. That the Gypsies would not be too keen to have me, did not then occur to me."

This perception of Gypsies simply as sources of data, as objects of study, rather than as people with sensibilities of their own, was one characteristic of the early ryes. Describing his visit to the Baltic lands in 1908, for example, Gilliat-Smith (1909:154) wrote: "I could see clearly five or six black tents pitched on the left side of the road under some birches. I would fain have stopped, waked the *Baro*, and there and then collected material of interest for the Gypsy Lore Society."

Like some modern ryes, Borrow was not above giving others the impression that he was himself a Gypsy; in *Lavengro* (Chapter 110), when asked by the man in black Reverend Fraser "are you then, a Gypsy?", he replied "what else should I be?". He has also been taken to task for putting far too cultured a brand of English in the mouths of the Romanichals (Helyear even calls it "pompous"). Pakomovna tells him, when she visits him in the dingle, "do you allow me to officiate upon your hair" — a hortative construction obsolete in English even by Borrow's day — while in the Book of Wisdom in the *Lavo-Lil*, the heavily class-marked pronoun 'one' turns up in his list of homilies in Romani, justifying the charge that "his Gypsies all spoke like bishops", thus *when yeck's tardrad yeck's beti tan oprey, kair'd yeck's beti yag ta nashed yeck's kekauvi...* ('when one's put one's little tent up, made one's little fire and hung up one's kettle...'). Equally transparent are the English origins of his translations, thus *the mush savo kek si les the juckni-wast oprey his jib* 'the man who has not got the whip-hand of his tongue'. While calquing upon English idioms certainly characterizes Angloromani, constructions of this kind lack the ring of authenticity (see Tilford (1953) for a discussion of the English spoken by Borrow's Gypsies).

4. Borrow as Romani scholar

As a linguist, he was prone to exaggeration and sometimes quite impressive creativity; Ridler (1981:329), referring to Caló, relates how in a letter to the British and Foreign Bible Society Borrow wrote that within a day of having first arrived in Spain, he located some Gypsies and "we began conversing in the Spanish dialect [of Romani], with which I was tolerably well acquainted". It is significant that in his defence of *Lavengro*, which appeared as an appendix in *The Romany Rye*, he chided his critics for not having spotted his "deliberate" mistakes in the Armenian and Welsh samples in his books, but he did not mention Romani. It is possible that some of his errors in the latter language were likewise deliberate — certainly they have allowed us to spot plagiarism in the writings of others.

Ridler also remarked upon his ability to undertake a complete re-translation of his earlier version of *St. Luke* thirty years after having left Spain and any further contact with Caló speakers. Her implication is that much of his new version was in what we might call Borromani, a concocted dialect not actually spoken by anyone. Ridler goes on to provide examples of such created forms, e.g. his word for 'incense' for which he used the Spanish word *incienso* in the original version, and which became *usur-gudlo* in the new version, compounded from *usur* 'smoke' and *gudlo* 'sweet'. The first item, *usur* occurs only in Pott (1844), who got it from Borrow's *Zincali* in the first place; it isn't in any other Caló wordlist. And the second item, *gudlo*, has the English and not the Spanish

Romani form, which is *gulo*. Another example of lexical creation Ridler cites is *Brono Aljeñicato* for 'Pontius Pilate', or Pòncio Pilato in Spanish. To Borrow's ear, the name (in English moreso than in Spanish) sounded like *puente* and *pila*, which mean 'bridge' and 'fountain' in Spanish. According to Borrow, the Caló words for these are *brono* and *aljeñicato* respectively, and both have been listed in his *Zincali* lexicon as legitimate Caló, and were furthermore entered as such, like *usur*, without comment by Pott in his dictionary (1844-II:433); but in his correspondence with the British and Foreign Bible Society he indicated that he made up both words himself, from Sanskrit and Arabic.

The same creativity is evident in his English Romani versions. Thus in the appendix on this dialect in the second volume of *The Zincali*, he includes his translation of the Apostle's Creed; to the line "I believe in the Holy Ghost", he appends the following note: "The English Gypsies, having, in their dialect, no other term for ghost than mulo, which simply means a dead person, I have been obliged to substitute a compound word. Bavalengro signifies literally a wind thing, *or form of air.*"

This word, respelt as *bavol-engro*, then turns up as the only entry for 'ghost' in the *Romano Lavo-Lil*, published in 1874, while at the entry *mullo* in the same vocabulary, which is the *actual* English Romani word for both 'ghost' and 'dead', only the meanings 'dead man' and 'dead' are given.

While it would be possible to reconstruct the lexical and grammatical characteristics of the kind of British Romani Borrow was hearing, such an undertaking might be more usefully achieved by looking at the work of others, e.g. by Whiter or Vallancey, because of Borrow's tendency to mix dialects. But even from his own material it is clear to see that English Romani is a member of the Northern European dialect group, sharing much in common with Sinti (e.g. such items as *jin-, tikno, miro, grai, haier-, ma, chomoni, juvel, stif(o)-p(r)al, mukh* ('know', 'small', 'my', 'horse', 'understand', 'don't', 'something', 'woman', 'brother in law', 'let', — compare Southern Romani *jan-, tsino, mu(n)rro, gras, hatyer-, na, vareso, juvli, salo, mekh*).[5] Like Sinti, the infinitive seems to be modelled upon the third person singular indicative (Sinti *kamav te jal* 'I want to go' rather than *kamav te jav* — cf. Central Romani *kamav te jan*), although Welsh Romani, like Vlax, does not do this. Like Vlax but unlike the Central or Northern dialects, Welsh Romani negates 'is/are' as *nai*, recorded by both Borrow and Smart & Crofton for English Romani. Borrow correctly analyses this as *na + hi*, although unlike Northern and Central Romani, British (Welsh, Scottish and English) Romani, like Vlax, belongs to the /s/ group, thus *si, san, lesa, sår* rather than the /h/ group (*hi, hal, leha, har*, 'is/are', 'am', 'with it', 'like/as'). British Romani preserves the original negative construction with preverbal *na*, now lost in most dialects of Sinti, which has postverbal *ga(r)* (from German).

The most authentic Angloromani Borrow reproduces, i.e. recorded verbatim from Romanichals, is probably found in his "beti rockrapens" and to a lesser extent in his collection of English Gypsy songs in the *Lavo-Lil*, but even here, material of his own creation is quite evident. Thus in the section entitled "The English Gypsies", he includes a song called "Tugney Beshor" which contains the line *cauna volélan* 'when they fly', using the Spanish root for 'fly', an item he does not enter in his dictionary. In the same song is the word *artavàvam*, glossed as 'we'll forget'. His knowledge of Romani grammar seemed to have deserted him by 1874, since this is an aorist construction, not a future one, and he also appears to have forgotten its real meaning, which is 'forgive' rather than 'forget' (in English Romani *bister*), but even as early as 1844 he was confusing tense and number endings, listing *camenna* 'they (will) love' as 'I love' and *chorava* 'I (will) steal' as 'I have stolen' (Winstedt 1951).

In the dingle episode in *Lavengro* (Chapter 83) he is describing the manufacture of a horseshoe, and refers to the fire's 'tongues of flame' as *vagescoe chipes*, using the Caló word for 'tongues' (*vagescoe* is probably a misprint for *yagescoe* here, though the form is continental rather than British, which would be *yogeskro*), and to an 'anvil' as a *covantza*, a Slavic-derived item listed in his Hungarian Romani vocabulary (Winstedt 1951) and by Paspati (1870), and recorded by Smart & Crofton (1875, along with *volélan* and *artavàvam*) as only having been encountered by them in print in Angloromani, and in the works of Borrow.

Borrow was evidently influenced by the Romani he heard in Eastern Europe, for even Jasper's wife Sanspirella Heron was renamed with the Balkan-sounding *Pakomovna* in his stories. The same Continental influence is evident in three unusual words which occur in Chapter 26 of *Lavengro*, where Jasper Petulengro is muttering to himself about the weather: *dearginni* 'it thundereth', *villaminni* 'it flameth' (referring to the lightning) and *grondinni* 'it haileth'. With the exception of *vílamo* 'lightning' in Bohemian Romani (Ješina 1886), the items themselves turn up in no other recorded dialect,[6] though it is clear where Borrow found them, for their origins are, respectively, in Hungarian *dörgő* and *villám*, and Romanian *grindină*. It might now be possible to temper Winstedt's caution that 'it would be rash to attempt to define the precise dialect of Borrow's 'Czigány' (1951:49); the morpheme {-*in*-} is characteristic of Hungarian Lovari loanverbs (like {-*sar*-} in other Vlax dialects), and the athematic termination {-*i*} (more properly {-*ij*}) for third person singular {-*il*} is likewise indicative of Hungarian phonological interference in the Lovari Vlax spoken in that country and in Transylvania. Clearly these items were recorded during his visit to

Hungary and Romania in 1844, seven years before he wrote *Lavengro*, although only *rondíni* 'hail' turns up in his Hungarian Romani vocabulary (Winstedt 1951:56). The spellings both with and without initial /g/ may reflect trouble Borrow had in attempting to represent the Vlax voiced uvular fricative in this word. In Welsh Romani, 'thunder' is *devléski gódli* 'God's noise' and 'hail' is *brisindéske bára* 'rain stones;' 'lightning' is *molóna* (from Slavic)[7]. Smart & Crofton include all three of Borrow's words, but mark each of them as unattested; the fact that two of the items don't occur in Winstedt's list lends support to his suggestion (1951:47) that Borrow may have collected more material in Cluj than has so far been located.

One creation of Borrow's has become particularly widely repeated in subsequent literature: his *hokkano baro* or 'great lie'. But while this is first described in *Lavengro* it is not English Romani, which would be *bori huckiben* (cf. Welsh Romani *båro xoxiben*), either phonologically, semantically or syntactically; again, he seems to have been influenced by Continental dialects of Romani.

Borrow errs in his explanation of the plural morpheme, which he spells <-or> and which he sometimes applied to words indiscriminately and incorrectly (for example *bauor* 'mates', from English dialect *bor* 'chum')[8]. Because he spoke a non-rhotic dialect of English, /r/ was not articulated in his speech except before vowels; after vowels, it merely indicated length. This confusion is evident in such conflicting orthographic representations as both <*saulo*> and <*sorlo*> 'early', <*sap*> and <*sarp*> 'snake', <*villaminni*> and <*villarminni*> 'lightning-flashes' and so on. Thus what he wrote as <-or> in fact represents the sound '-aw', which corresponds to the Common Romani plural postconsonantal morpheme {-*a*} and reflects the regular phonetic shift of [a] to 'aw' (Sampson's <å>) in British Romani (e.g. his *shockor* 'cabbages' for Common Romani *šaxa* etc.). But on the basis of this non-existent /r/, Borrow assumes that the English Romani plural may be derived from the Romanian neuter plural {-*uri*}.[9]

It is possible, however, that by Borrow's day, an intrusive /r/ could have found its way into a number of words, since in Angloromani as spoken in North America, it is clearly present in such words as *gorjer*, *vonger*, *kekker* and so on (where in British Angloromani these are pronounced *gawja*, *vonga*, *kekka*, etc.). This behaviour of /r/ suggests that Borrow was dealing with south-eastern varieties of British Romani, since Welsh Romani is in the main rhotic (cf. *feder*, *určos*, *sår*, etc.). Rhotacism as a phonological feature of English began to disappear from the south-eastern dialects in the early modern period (1500-1700), but survives today in Welsh English and in the South-Western dialect area, in which the Kåle lived before moving into Wales.

That phonological changes in English should affect the phonology of Romani spoken in that country suggests not only a high degree of bilingualism, but that the population probably became English-dominant early on. A similar sound shift in English which has affected Romani is that of [er] to [ar] (cf. sartain, varsity, sergeant, clerk, etc.), thus the original [er] in *erti-* 'forgive, excuse' (< Romanian) becomes *ātav-* in Welsh Romani, also demonstrating loss of postvocalic /r/, which is Borrow's *artav*, [er] in *vērdō* 'waggon' (Common Romani *vurdon*) becomes Angloromani *vardo*, and *terno* 'young' becomes Angloromani *tawno* with loss of /r/ and shift of [a] to [aw], cf. Welsh Romani *tārnō*, Common Romani *terno*. This latter, which is characteristically British Romani, also reflects a soundshift which began in South-Eastern (but not South-Western) English in the early modern period, cf. [græs], [hæf], [læf] to [gra:s], [ha:f], la:f].

Other misinterpretations which bear comment are Borrow's assumption that the genitive postposition, legitimately a nominalizer in Central and Northern Romani, in its various forms (*-engro, -eskro*) is a free morpheme meaning 'thing' or 'fellow', thus *boro drom engroes* 'highwaymen', (*Lavengro*, 358), also listed with the same interpretation in his Hungarian Romani vocabulary (Winstedt 1951:110), and that the sociative postposition {*-sa*}, meaning 'with' or 'by', could be detached and made into a preposition: *come sar mande*, 'come with me'. It is entered as a separate word not only in his *Lavo-Lil* but also for Caló in the glossary in *The Zincali*, and turns up in Leland's *English Gipsy songs* and in Smart & Crofton. Sampson (1907:95) doubts that this ever existed as a separate preposition, suggesting that these various compilers, like Borrow himself, misinterpreted the postposition as they heard it.[10]

Borrow also treated the bound affix {*-i-sar*} (or {*-a-sar*}), a marker of loanverbs, as though it were a free morpheme, and entered it into his *Lavo-Lil* as the independent item *asarlas* 'at all'. However, his own example originates in the misanalysis of *we can't help asarlus*, which he glosses as 'we can't help at all', when the construction he heard was *we can't helpasar les*, 'we can't help it'. It is possible, however, that this development was in part a legitimate one in English Romani, since Smart & Crofton (1875:52-54) list many examples of *asár* meaning 'also' which clearly demonstrate a reinterpretation of earlier {*-i-sar*}. But it is not paralleled in Welsh Romani nor has the form and use seemed to have survived in modern Angloromani. This athematic morpheme is particularly characteristic of the Vlax group of dialects, and is used with loanverbs in Welsh Romani too, though with one exception only in imperative constructions (Sampson 1926:117-118). Another indication of Vlax influence is the non-final affix {*-n-*}, a marker of athematic adjective-derived adverbs, thus *drago, dragones, mundro, mundrones*, compared with thematic *baro, bares*, *tikno, tiknes,* without the {*-n-*}. Thus we have such Borromani forms as *weshenjugalogonæs, bolli-menggreskoenæs, dinnileskoenæs, dovodoiskoenæs* and so on. This last is compounded from *dovo* 'that', + *odoi* 'there', and is given to mean 'in that way', while that item and the two before it include *-(e)sko,* which consists of the singular masculine oblique nominal morpheme {*-es*} plus the Vlax genitive {*-ko*} (rather than the Northern Romani {*-k(e)ro*}), and followed by the adverbial {*-es*} linked with non-athematic {*-n-*}. In actual Angloromani, *dovodoi* is a legitimate determiner meaning 'that there', but not even in inflected British Romani could it combine with grammatical particles meant for nouns and adjectives. Yet such forms are presented as "genuine Gypsy... clear-sounding and melodious, and well-adapted to the purposes of poetry" (*Lavo-Lil*, page 11).

George Borrow probably never dreamt that his work would come under scrutiny a century and a half after it appeared; but at the time it was written, interest in Gypsies and the Romani language was marginal, and remained so until almost the end of the 20th century. His writings were evaluated by his contemporaries not at all for the Romani they contained, but for his observations and descriptions and opinions in other areas. Those few individuals, such as Pott (1844), Ascoli (1865), Paspati (1870) Miklosich (1872) and Colocci (1889) who had an academic interest in Romani, on the other hand, used his material uncritically, and were scarcely interested in his writings otherwise.

5. Conclusion

Fifteen years ago, Angus Fraser summed up a talk he gave on George Borrow at The University of East Anglia[11] with the words "I wish I could feel sure that a new generation of Borrovians is growing up". His wish has clearly been fulfilled; there is now a society and a journal dedicated wholly to Borrow's life and works, and an international conference on the man has become an annual event. As specialists in Romani, we must be careful to separate our judgement of Borrow's linguistic expertise in that language from our judgement of him as a prose writer and raconteur. In the latter role, he holds a special place; and even as a linguist dealing with other languages, as Ridler (1996) has so magnificently documented, he demonstrated a remarkable genius. It is all the more puzzling, therefore, that he dealt so inadequately with the one language for which he is remembered best of all.[12] As a student of Gypsies, he must only be regarded as prime example of the term he himself created, a *Romany Rye* — for today, the word has been taken back by Gypsies, and is a term of disdain. It is no coincidence that Kalderash Roma in Europe and America use the word *rai* for a policeman or an authority figure, meanings also shared in England by the present-day descendants of George Borrow's Romani brothers and sisters.

Endnotes

1. The original is in Hansard (see Wells 1961).
2. Borrow's observations on the Iranian element in Romani (1841(ii):111-112) are worth reproducing (as an adjunct, for example, to Hancock 1995a):

   Still more abundant ... than the mixture of Greek, still more abundant than the mixture of Sclavonian, is the alloy in the Gypsy language, wherever spoken, of modern Persian words, which circumstance will compel us to offer a few remarks on the share which the Persian has had in the formation of the dialects of India, as at present spoken.

   The modern Persian, as has been already observed, is a daughter of the ancient Zend, and, as such, is entitled to claim affinity with the Sanscrit, and its dialects. With this language none in the world would be able to vie in simplicity and beauty, had not the Persians, in adopting the religion of Mahomet, unfortunately introduced into their speech an infinity of words of the rude coarse language used by the barbaric Arab tribes.

3. The age and identity of Jasper is the topic of an article by Fraser (1996:7-12).
4. Borrow was probably poisoned not by "Mrs. Hearne" (Martha Boss in real life) but by her daughter Joni (Borrow's "Leonora"). See Fraser (1996:7-12).
5. Scottish Romani on the other hand appears to have entered Britain via Scandinavia rather than from the northern European coast; see Hancock (1984b).
6. In Kalderash Vlax these words are *trézneto* or *rróndžeto* for 'thunder' and *bábica* for 'hail,' both from Romanian, and *strélica* for 'lightning,' from Slavic; no Lovari Vlax wordlist contains Borrow's three items.
7. The same metaphorical compounding, especially typical of Northern Romani, is found in Sinti, thus 'thunder' is *devleskero čiro* ('God's noise'), and 'lightning' is *devleskeri jakh* ('God's eye').
8. *Bor* (from Old English *būr*, and retained in the word 'neighbour') is listed by Wright (1898-I:345) as meaning 'a term of familiar address' and localized to Cumberland, East Anglia and Essex. Borrow's created plural should have been **boror* rather than 'bau-or.'
9. The Rumanian-derived plural morpheme {-uri} does, however, seem to have made its way into British Romani otherwise; see Hancock (1984a:103 and 1995b:30).
10. Sampson (1907) demonstrated convincingly that *sar* in British Romani was a literary creation, though Peter Bakker (in p.c.) points out that this may not be the case for Caló, referring to texts collected by de Luna (1951) in which *sar* is used prepositionally. Norbert Boretzky has also documented its prepositional use in some Balkan Romani dialects.
11. "George Borrow: The romance and the reality", lecture given at the University of East Anglia, June 12st, 1981.
12. This would suggest strongly that he worked best from written materials, and perhaps had a photographic memory; Romani was the only language in his working repertoire for which he had no access to a comprehensive grammatical description.

References

Ackerley, Frederick G. 1942. Review of Potra, Gheorghe. 1939. *Contribuţiuni la Istoricul Ţiganilor dîn România. Journal of the Gypsy Lore Society* 21:1. 68-71.
Allingham, P. 1934. *Cheapjack*. New York: Frederick Stokes.
Ascoli, G.J. 1865. *Zigeunerisches*. Halle: Julius Fricke.
Boorde, Andrew. 1547. *The fyrst booke of the introduction of knowledge*. London: Copland.
Borrow, George. 1841. *The Zincali, or an account of the Gypsies of Spain*. London: John Murray.
---- 1843 [1947]. *The Bible in Spain*. London: Dent.
---- 1851 [1910]. *Lavengro: Scholar, Gipsy, priest*. London & Glasgow: Collins.
---- 1857 [1924]. *The Romany Rye: A sequel to Lavengro*. London: Murray.
---- 1862. *Wild Wales*. London & Glasgow: Collins.
---- 1874 [1910] *Romano lavo-lil, word book of the Romany or, English Gypsy language*. London: Murray.
---- 1874 [1982]. *Romano lavo-lil, word book of the Romany or, English Gypsy language*. London: Sutton.
Bryant, Jacob. 1785. 'Collections on the Zingara or Gypsey language'. *Archæologia* 7. 387-394.
Chamberlain, Houston Stewart. 1899. *The foundations of the nineteenth century*. London: John Lane.
Colocci, Adrian. 1889. *Gli zingari: Storia d'un popolo errante*. Turin: Loescher.
de Luna, José Carlos. 1951. *Gitanos de la Bética*. Madrid: Ediciones y Publicaciones Españolas S.A.
Dillmann, Alfred. 1905. *Zigeuner-Buch*. Berlin: Widsche.
Fraser, Angus. 1993. 'Authors' Gypsies'. *Antiquarian Book Monthly* 20:2. 10-17.
---- 1995. 'Borrow, the Palgraves, and the Worships'. *The George Borrow Bulletin* 9. 10-20.
---- 1996. 'The parallel universe of Borrow's Gypsies'. *The George Borrow Bulletin* 11. 7-12.
Geipel, John. 1995. 'The 'secret' language of the Gypsies of Spain'. In: Peter Burke & Roy Porter, eds. *Languages and jargons: Contributions to a social history of language*. Cambridge: Polity Press. 102-132.
Gilliat-Smith, Bernard. 1909. 'Russian Gypsies in Lithuania, July 1908'. *Journal of the Gypsy Lore Society* 3:2. 154-155.
Gobineau, Arthur Compte de. 1855. *Essai sur l'inégalité des races humaines*. Paris: Vactreau & Cie.
Grellmann, Heinrich M.G. 1787. *Disseration on the Gipsies*. (Matthew Raper translation). London: Elmsley.
Grosvenor, Lady Arthur. 1908. 'Whiter's 'Lingua Cingariana'. *Journal of the Gypsy Lore Society* 2:2. 161-179.
Haines, Samuel M. 1989. *The Travelers*. [Privately-circulated report]. Swindle Section, Dallas Police Department.
Hancock, Ian. 1980. 'Talking back'. *Roma* 6:1. 13-20.
---- 1984a. 'Romani and Angloromani'. In: Peter Trudgill, ed. *Languages in the British Isles*. Cambridge: Cambridge University Press. 367-383.
---- 1984b. 'The social and linguistic development of Angloromani'. In: Donald Kenrick & Thomas Acton, eds. *Romani rokkeripen to-divvus*. London: Romanestan Publications. 89-122.

---- 1993. 'Antigypsyism in the new Europe'. *Roma* 39. 17-35.
---- 1995a. 'On the migration and affiliation of the Dōmba: Iranian words in Rom, Dom and Lom Gypsy'. In: Yaron Matras, ed. *Romani in contact. The history, structure, and sociology of a language.* Amsterdam: Benjamins. 29-59.
---- 1995b. *A handbook of Vlax Romani.* Columbus: Slavica.
Helyear, Annick. 1972. *The British Traveller: The Romani civilization, its mythical presentation in the English literature, and the social problems today.* Diplôme d'Etudes Supérieures d'Anglais, Université d'Aix en Provence.
Jarman, A., & Eldra Jarman. 1991. *The Welsh Gypsies: Children of Abraham Wood.* Cardiff: University of Wales Press.
Ješina, P. Josef. 1886. *Romáñi Čib, oder die Zigeunersprache.* Leipzig: List & Francke.
Knapp, William I. 1899. *Life, writings and correspondence of George Borrow, derived from official and other authentic sources.* London: Murray.
Leland, Charles G., J. Palmer & E. Tuckey. 1875. *English-Gipsy songs.* London: Trübner.
Mayall, David. 1988. *Gypsy-Travellers in nineteenth century society.* Cambridge: Cambridge University Press.
Miklosich, Franz. 1872-1881. *Ueber die Mundarten und die Wanderungen der Zigeuner Europa's.* Vienna: Karl Gerold's Sohn.
Paspati, Alexandre G. 1870. *Études sur les Tchinghianés ou Bohémiens de l'Empire Ottoman.* Constantinople: Koroméla.
Pott, August F. 1844. *Die Zigeuner in Europa und Asien.* Halle: Heynemann Verlag.
Reid, Alastair. 1962. 'The Travellers'. *The New Yorker* August 18th. 37-40.
Ridler, Ann M. 1996 [1983]. *George Borrow as linguist: Images and contexts.* Ph.d. dissertation, Oxford University. 1983. [Published by the author for private circulation as *George Borrow as a linguist: Images and Contexts*].
Sampson, John. 1907. 'sar, 'with',' *Journal of the Gypsy Lore Society* 1, 95-96.
---- 1926. *The dialect of the Gypsies of Wales.* Oxford: Clarendon.
Shields, Audrey C. 1993. *Gypsy stereotypes in Victorian literature.* Ph.d. dissertation, New York University.
Smart, Bath C. & Henry T. Crofton. 1875. *The dialect of the English Gypsies.* London: Asher & Co.
Tilford, J.E. 1953. 'A note on Borrow's bookish dialogue'. In: T.B. Strong & S.A. Stondemire, eds. *South Atlantic studies for Sturgis E. Leavitt.* Washington: Scarecrow Press. 199-206.
Vesey-Fitzgerald, Brian. 1944. *Gypsies of Britain: An introduction to their history.* London: Chapman & Hall.
Wells, John. 1961. [Comments regarding Borrow]. *Hansard* (Commons), Vol. 650. cols. 829-830.
Whiter, Walter. 1800. *Etymologicon Magnum.* Cambridge: Hodson.
Wilson, Nerissa. 1986. *Gypsies and Gentlemen.* London: Columbus Books.
Winstedt, Eric Otto. 1951. 'Borrow's Hungarian-Romani vocabulary'. *Journal oj the Gypsy Lore Society*, 29:1-2. 46-54, 103-115; 30:1. 50-61.
Wright, Joseph. 1898. *The English Dialect Dictionary.* London: Henry Frowde.

INDEX OF NAMES

INDEX OF SUBJECTS

LIST OF CONTRIBUTORS AND EDITORS

Peter Bakker
Institut for Lingvistik
Aarhus Universitet
Nordre Ringgade 1
8000 Aarhus C
Denmark

Norbert Boretzky
Sprachwissenschaftliches Institut
Ruhr-Universität Bochum
Universitätsstraße 150
44780 Bochum
Germany

Vít Bubeník
Department of Linguistics
Memorial University of Newfoundland
St John's, Newfoundland A1B 3X9
Canada

Petra Cech
Phonogrammarchiv der Österreichischen
Akademie der Wissenschaften
Liebiggasse 5
1010 Wien
Austria

Viktor Elšik
Indologický ústav, Filosofická fakulta
Universita Karlova
Celetná 20
11000 Praha 1
Czech Republic

Victor A. Friedman
Department of Slavic Languages
University of Chicago
1130 E. 59th Street
Chicago, Ill. 60637
U.S.A.

Ian F. Hancock
Department of Linguistics
University of Texas
Austin, Texas 78723
U.S.A.

Mozes F. Heinschink
Phonogrammarchiv der Österreichischen
Akademie der Wissenschaften
Liebiggasse 5
1010 Wien
Austria

Milena Hübschmannová
Indologický ústav, Filosofická fakulta
Universita Karlova
Celetná 20
11000 Praha 1
Czech Republic

Birgit Igla
Deutsche Philologie
St. Kliment Ohridski University
Car Osrobaditel 15
1000 Sofia
Bulgaria

Hristo Kyuchukov
Loznitsa 3
9200 Provadia
Bulgaria

Yaron Matras
Department of Linguistics
University of Manchester
Oxford Road
Manchester M13 9PL
United Kingdom

In the CURRENT ISSUES IN LINGUISTIC THEORY (CILT) series (edited by: E.F. Konrad Koerner, University of Ottawa) the following volumes have been published thus far or are scheduled for publication:

1. KOERNER, Konrad (ed.): *The Transformational-Generative Paradigm and Modern Linguistic Theory.* 1975.
2. WEIDERT, Alfons: *Componential Analysis of Lushai Phonology.* 1975.
3. MAHER, J. Peter: *Papers on Language Theory and History I: Creation and Tradition in Language.* Foreword by Raimo Anttila. 1979.
4. HOPPER, Paul J. (ed.): *Studies in Descriptive and Historical Linguistics. Festschrift for Winfred P. Lehmann.* 1977.
5. ITKONEN, Esa: *Grammatical Theory and Metascience: A critical investigation into the methodological and philosophical foundations of 'autonomous' linguistics.* 1978.
6. ANTTILA, Raimo: *Historical and Comparative Linguistics.* 1989.
7. MEISEL, Jürgen M. & Martin D. PAM (eds): *Linear Order and Generative Theory.* 1979.
8. WILBUR, Terence H.: *Prolegomena to a Grammar of Basque.* 1979.
9. HOLLIEN, Harry & Patricia (eds): *Current Issues in the Phonetic Sciences. Proceedings of the IPS-77 Congress, Miami Beach, Florida, 17-19 December 1977.* 1979.
10. PRIDEAUX, Gary D. (ed.): *Perspectives in Experimental Linguistics. Papers from the University of Alberta Conference on Experimental Linguistics, Edmonton, 13-14 Oct. 1978.* 1979.
11. BROGYANYI, Bela (ed.): *Studies in Diachronic, Synchronic, and Typological Linguistics: Festschrift for Oswald Szemérenyi on the Occasion of his 65th Birthday.* 1979.
12. FISIAK, Jacek (ed.): *Theoretical Issues in Contrastive Linguistics.* 1981. Out of print
13. MAHER, J. Peter, Allan R. BOMHARD & Konrad KOERNER (eds): *Papers from the Third International Conference on Historical Linguistics, Hamburg, August 22-26 1977.* 1982.
14. TRAUGOTT, Elizabeth C., Rebecca LaBRUM & Susan SHEPHERD (eds): *Papers from the Fourth International Conference on Historical Linguistics, Stanford, March 26-30 1979.* 1980.
15. ANDERSON, John (ed.): *Language Form and Linguistic Variation. Papers dedicated to Angus McIntosh.* 1982.
16. ARBEITMAN, Yoël L. & Allan R. BOMHARD (eds): *Bono Homini Donum: Essays in Historical Linguistics, in Memory of J.Alexander Kerns.* 1981.
17. LIEB, Hans-Heinrich: *Integrational Linguistics. 6 volumes. Vol. II-VI n.y.p.* 1984/93.
18. IZZO, Herbert J. (ed.): *Italic and Romance. Linguistic Studies in Honor of Ernst Pulgram.* 1980.
19. RAMAT, Paolo et al. (eds): *Linguistic Reconstruction and Indo-European Syntax. Proceedings of the Colloquium of the 'Indogermanischhe Gesellschaft'. University of Pavia, 6-7 September 1979.* 1980.
20. NORRICK, Neal R.: *Semiotic Principles in Semantic Theory.* 1981.
21. AHLQVIST, Anders (ed.): *Papers from the Fifth International Conference on Historical Linguistics, Galway, April 6-10 1981.* 1982.
22. UNTERMANN, Jürgen & Bela BROGYANYI (eds): *Das Germanische und die Rekonstruktion der Indogermanischen Grundsprache. Akten des Freiburger Kolloquiums der Indogermanischen Gesellschaft, Freiburg, 26-27 Februar 1981.* 1984.
23. DANIELSEN, Niels: *Papers in Theoretical Linguistics. Edited by Per Baerentzen.* 1992.
24. LEHMANN, Winfred P. & Yakov MALKIEL (eds): *Perspectives on Historical Linguistics. Papers from a conference held at the meeting of the Language Theory Division, Modern Language Assn., San Francisco, 27-30 December 1979.* 1982.
25. ANDERSEN, Paul Kent: *Word Order Typology and Comparative Constructions.* 1983.
26. BALDI, Philip (ed.): *Papers from the XIIth Linguistic Symposium on Romance Languages, Univ. Park, April 1-3, 1982.* 1984.

27. BOMHARD, Alan R.: *Toward Proto-Nostratic. A New Approach to the Comparison of Proto-Indo-European and Proto-Afroasiatic. Foreword by Paul J. Hopper.* 1984.

28. BYNON, James (ed.): *Current Progress in Afro-Asiatic Linguistics: Papers of the Third International Hamito-Semitic Congress, London, 1978.* 1984.

29. PAPROTTÉ, Wolf & René DIRVEN (eds): *The Ubiquity of Metaphor: Metaphor in language and thought.* 1985 (publ. 1986).

30. HALL, Robert A. Jr.: *Proto-Romance Morphology.* = *Comparative Romance Grammar, vol. III.* 1984.

31. GUILLAUME, Gustave: *Foundations for a Science of Language.*

32. COPELAND, James E. (ed.): *New Directions in Linguistics and Semiotics.* Co-edition with Rice University Press who hold exclusive rights for US and Canada. 1984.

33. VERSTEEGH, Kees: *Pidginization and Creolization. The Case of Arabic.* 1984.

34. FISIAK, Jacek (ed.): *Papers from the VIth International Conference on Historical Linguistics, Poznan, 22-26 August. 1983.* 1985.

35. COLLINGE, N.E.: *The Laws of Indo-European.* 1985.

36. KING, Larry D. & Catherine A. MALEY (eds): *Selected papers from the XIIIth Linguistic Symposium on Romance Languages, Chapel Hill, N.C., 24-26 March 1983.* 1985.

37. GRIFFEN, T.D.: *Aspects of Dynamic Phonology.* 1985.

38. BROGYANYI, Bela & Thomas KRÖMMELBEIN (eds): *Germanic Dialects:Linguistic and Philological Investigations.* 1986.

39. BENSON, James D., Michael J. CUMMINGS, & William S. GREAVES (eds): *Linguistics in a Systemic Perspective.* 1988.

40. FRIES, Peter Howard (ed.) in collaboration with Nancy M. Fries: *Toward an Understanding of Language: Charles C. Fries in Perspective.* 1985.

41. EATON, Roger, et al. (eds): *Papers from the 4th International Conference on English Historical Linguistics, April 10-13, 1985.* 1985.

42. MAKKAI, Adam & Alan K. MELBY (eds): *Linguistics and Philosophy. Festschrift for Rulon S. Wells.* 1985 (publ. 1986).

43. AKAMATSU, Tsutomu: *The Theory of Neutralization and the Archiphoneme in Functional Phonology.* 1988.

44. JUNGRAITHMAYR, Herrmann & Walter W. MUELLER (eds): *Proceedings of the Fourth International Hamito-Semitic Congress.* 1987.

45. KOOPMAN, W.F., F.C. Van der LEEK , O. FISCHER & R. EATON (eds): *Explanation and Linguistic Change.* 1986

46. PRIDEAUX, Gary D. & William J. BAKER: *Strategies and Structures: The processing of relative clauses.* 1987.

47. LEHMANN, Winfred P. (ed.): *Language Typology 1985. Papers from the Linguistic Typology Symposium, Moscow, 9-13 Dec. 1985.* 1986.

48. RAMAT, Anna G., Onofrio CARRUBA and Giuliano BERNINI (eds): *Papers from the 7th International Conference on Historical Linguistics.* 1987.

49. WAUGH, Linda R. and Stephen RUDY (eds): *New Vistas in Grammar: Invariance and Variation. Proceedings of the Second International Roman Jakobson Conference, New York University, Nov.5-8, 1985.* 1991.

50. RUDZKA-OSTYN, Brygida (ed.): *Topics in Cognitive Linguistics.* 1988.

51. CHATTERJEE, Ranjit: *Aspect and Meaning in Slavic and Indic. With a foreword by Paul Friedrich.* 1989.

52. FASOLD, Ralph W. & Deborah SCHIFFRIN (eds): *Language Change and Variation.* 1989.

53. SANKOFF, David: *Diversity and Diachrony.* 1986.

54. WEIDERT, Alfons: *Tibeto-Burman Tonology. A comparative analysis.* 1987

55. HALL, Robert A. Jr.: *Linguistics and Pseudo-Linguistics.* 1987.

56. HOCKETT, Charles F.: *Refurbishing our Foundations. Elementary linguistics from an advanced point of view.* 1987.
57. BUBENIK, Vít: *Hellenistic and Roman Greece as a Sociolinguistic Area.* 1989.
58. ARBEITMAN, Yoël. L. (ed.): *Fucus: A Semitic/Afrasian Gathering in Remembrance of Albert Ehrman.* 1988.
59. VAN VOORST, Jan: *Event Structure.* 1988.
60. KIRSCHNER, Carl & Janet DECESARIS (eds): *Studies in Romance Linguistics. Selected Proceedings from the XVII Linguistic Symposium on Romance Languages.* 1989.
61. CORRIGAN, Roberta L., Fred ECKMAN & Michael NOONAN (eds): *Linguistic Categorization. Proceedings of an International Symposium in Milwaukee, Wisconsin, April 10-11, 1987.* 1989.
62. FRAJZYNGIER, Zygmunt (ed.): *Current Progress in Chadic Linguistics. Proceedings of the International Symposium on Chadic Linguistics, Boulder, Colorado, 1-2 May 1987.* 1989.
63. EID, Mushira (ed.): *Perspectives on Arabic Linguistics I. Papers from the First Annual Symposium on Arabic Linguistics.* 1990.
64. BROGYANYI, Bela (ed.): *Prehistory, History and Historiography of Language, Speech, and Linguistic Theory. Papers in honor of Oswald Szemérenyi I.* 1992.
65. ADAMSON, Sylvia, Vivien A. LAW, Nigel VINCENT and Susan WRIGHT (eds): *Papers from the 5th International Conference on English Historical Linguistics.* 1990.
66. ANDERSEN, Henning and Konrad KOERNER (eds): *Historical Linguistics 1987.Papers from the 8th International Conference on Historical Linguistics,Lille, August 30-Sept., 1987.* 1990.
67. LEHMANN, Winfred P. (ed.): *Language Typology 1987. Systematic Balance in Language. Papers from the Linguistic Typology Symposium, Berkeley, 1-3 Dec 1987.* 1990.
68. BALL, Martin, James FIFE, Erich POPPE &Jenny ROWLAND (eds): *Celtic Linguistics/ Ieithyddiaeth Geltaidd. Readings in the Brythonic Languages. Festschrift for T. Arwyn Watkins.* 1990.
69. WANNER, Dieter and Douglas A. KIBBEE (eds): *New Analyses in Romance Linguistics. Selected papers from the Linguistic Symposium on Romance Languages XVIIII, Urbana-Champaign, April 7-9, 1988.* 1991.
70. JENSEN, John T.: *Morphology. Word structure in generative grammar.* 1990.
71. O'GRADY, William: *Categories and Case. The sentence structure of Korean.* 1991.
72. EID, Mushira and John MCCARTHY (eds): *Perspectives on Arabic Linguistics II. Papers from the Second Annual Symposium on Arabic Linguistics.* 1990.
73. STAMENOV, Maxim (ed.): *Current Advances in Semantic Theory.* 1991.
74. LAEUFER, Christiane and Terrell A. MORGAN (eds): *Theoretical Analyses in Romance Linguistics.* 1991.
75. DROSTE, Flip G. and John E. JOSEPH (eds): *Linguistic Theory and Grammatical Description. Nine Current Approaches.* 1991.
76. WICKENS, Mark A.: *Grammatical Number in English Nouns. An empirical and theoretical account.* 1992.
77. BOLTZ, William G. and Michael C. SHAPIRO (eds): *Studies in the Historical Phonology of Asian Languages.* 1991.
78. KAC, Michael: *Grammars and Grammaticality.* 1992.
79. ANTONSEN, Elmer H. and Hans Henrich HOCK (eds): *STAEF-CRAEFT: Studies in Germanic Linguistics. Select papers from the First and Second Symposium on Germanic Linguistics, University of Chicago, 24 April 1985, and Univ. of Illinois at Urbana-Champaign, 3-4 Oct. 1986.* 1991.
80. COMRIE, Bernard and Mushira EID (eds): *Perspectives on Arabic Linguistics III. Papers from the Third Annual Symposium on Arabic Linguistics.* 1991.
81. LEHMANN, Winfred P. and H.J. HEWITT (eds): *Language Typology 1988. Typological Models in the Service of Reconstruction.* 1991.

82. VAN VALIN, Robert D. (ed.): *Advances in Role and Reference Grammar.* 1992.
83. FIFE, James and Erich POPPE (eds): *Studies in Brythonic Word Order.* 1991.
84. DAVIS, Garry W. and Gregory K. IVERSON (eds): *Explanation in Historical Linguistics.* 1992.
85. BROSELOW, Ellen, Mushira EID and John McCARTHY (eds): *Perspectives on Arabic Linguistics IV. Papers from the Annual Symposium on Arabic Linguistics.* 1992.
86. KESS, Joseph F.: *Psycholinguistics. Psychology, linguistics, and the study of natural language.* 1992.
87. BROGYANYI, Bela and Reiner LIPP (eds): *Historical Philology: Greek, Latin, and Romance. Papers in honor of Oswald Szemerényi II.* 1992.
88. SHIELDS, Kenneth: *A History of Indo-European Verb Morphology.* 1992.
89. BURRIDGE, Kate: *Syntactic Change in Germanic. A study of some aspects of language change in Germanic with particular reference to Middle Dutch.* 1992.
90. KING, Larry D.: *The Semantic Structure of Spanish. Meaning and grammatical form.* 1992.
91. HIRSCHBÜHLER, Paul and Konrad KOERNER (eds): *Romance Languages and Modern Linguistic Theory. Selected papers from the XX Linguistic Symposium on Romance Languages,University of Ottawa, April 10-14, 1990.* 1992.
92. POYATOS, Fernando: *Paralanguage: A linguistic and interdisciplinary approach to interactive speech and sounds.* 1992.
93. LIPPI-GREEN, Rosina (ed.): *Recent Developments in Germanic Linguistics.* 1992.
94. HAGÈGE, Claude: *The Language Builder. An essay on the human signature in linguistic morphogenesis.* 1992.
95. MILLER, D. Gary: *Complex Verb Formation.* 1992.
96. LIEB, Hans-Heinrich (ed.): *Prospects for a New Structuralism.* 1992.
97. BROGYANYI, Bela & Reiner LIPP (eds): *Comparative-Historical Linguistics: Indo-European and Finno-Ugric. Papers in honor of Oswald Szemerényi III.* 1992.
98. EID, Mushira & Gregory K. IVERSON: *Principles and Prediction: The analysis of natural language.* 1993.
99. JENSEN, John T.: *English Phonology.* 1993.
100. MUFWENE, Salikoko S. and Lioba MOSHI (eds): *Topics in African Linguistics. Papers from the XXI Annual Conference on African Linguistics, University of Georgia, April 1990.* 1993.
101. EID, Mushira & Clive HOLES (eds): *Perspectives on Arabic Linguistics V. Papers from the Fifth Annual Symposium on Arabic Linguistics.* 1993.
102. DAVIS, Philip W. (ed.): *Alternative Linguistics. Descriptive and theoretical Modes.* 1995.
103. ASHBY, William J., Marianne MITHUN, Giorgio PERISSINOTTO and Eduardo RAPOSO: *Linguistic Perspectives on Romance Languages. Selected papers from the XXI Linguistic Symposium on Romance Languages, Santa Barbara, February 21-24, 1991.* 1993.
104. KURZOVÁ, Helena: *From Indo-European to Latin. The evolution of a morphosyntactic type.* 1993.
105. HUALDE, José Ignacio and Jon ORTIZ DE URBANA (eds): *Generative Studies in Basque Linguistics.* 1993.
106. AERTSEN, Henk and Robert J. JEFFERS (eds): *Historical Linguistics 1989. Papers from the 9th International Conference on Historical Linguistics, New Brunswick, 14-18 August 1989.* 1993.
107. MARLE, Jaap van (ed.): *Historical Linguistics 1991. Papers from the 10th International Conference on Historical Linguistics, Amsterdam, August 12-16, 1991.* 1993.
108. LIEB, Hans-Heinrich: *Linguistic Variables. Towards a unified theory of linguistic variation.* 1993.
109. PAGLIUCA, William (ed.): *Perspectives on Grammaticalization.* 1994.

110. SIMONE, Raffaele (ed.): *Iconicity in Language*. 1995.
111. TOBIN, Yishai: *Invariance, Markedness and Distinctive Feature Analysis. A contrastive study of sign systems in English and Hebrew*. 1994.
112. CULIOLI, Antoine: *Cognition and Representation in Linguistic Theory. Translated, edited and introduced by Michel Liddle*. 1995.
113. FERNÁNDEZ, Francisco, Miguel FUSTER and Juan Jose CALVO (eds): *English Historical Linguistics 1992. Papers from the 7th International Conference on English Historical Linguistics, Valencia, 22-26 September 1992*.1994.
114. EGLI, U., P. PAUSE, Chr. SCHWARZE, A. von STECHOW, G. WIENOLD (eds): *Lexical Knowledge in the Organisation of Language*. 1995.
115. EID, Mushira, Vincente CANTARINO and Keith WALTERS (eds): *Perspectives on Arabic Linguistics. Vol. VI. Papers from the Sixth Annual Symposium on Arabic Linguistics*. 1994.
116. MILLER, D. Gary: *Ancient Scripts and Phonological Knowledge*. 1994.
117. PHILIPPAKI-WARBURTON, I., K. NICOLAIDIS and M. SIFIANOU (eds): *Themes in Greek Linguistics. Papers from the first International Conference on Greek Linguistics, Reading, September 1993*. 1994.
118. HASAN, Ruqaiya and Peter H. FRIES (eds): *On Subject and Theme. A discourse functional perspective*. 1995.
119. LIPPI-GREEN, Rosina: *Language Ideology and Language Change in Early Modern German. A sociolinguistic study of the consonantal system of Nuremberg*. 1994.
120. STONHAM, John T. : *Combinatorial Morphology*. 1994.
121. HASAN, Ruqaiya, Carmel CLORAN and David BUTT (eds): *Functional Descriptions. Theorie in practice*. 1996.
122. SMITH, John Charles and Martin MAIDEN (eds): *Linguistic Theory and the Romance Languages*. 1995.
123. AMASTAE, Jon, Grant GOODALL, Mario MONTALBETTI and Marianne PHINNEY: *Contemporary Research in Romance Linguistics. Papers from the XXII Linguistic Symposium on Romance Languages, El Paso//Juárez, February 22-24, 1994*. 1995.
124. ANDERSEN, Henning: *Historical Linguistics 1993. Selected papers from the 11th International Conference on Historical Linguistics, Los Angeles, 16-20 August 1993*. 1995.
125. SINGH, Rajendra (ed.): *Towards a Critical Sociolinguistics*. 1996.
126. MATRAS, Yaron (ed.): *Romani in Contact. The history, structure and sociology of a language*. 1995.
127. GUY, Gregory R., Crawford FEAGIN, Deborah SCHIFFRIN and John BAUGH (eds): *Towards a Social Science of Language. Papers in honor of William Labov. Volume 1: Variation and change in language and society*. 1996.
128. GUY, Gregory R., Crawford FEAGIN, Deborah SCHIFFRIN and John BAUGH (eds): *Towards a Social Science of Language. Papers in honor of William Labov. Volume 2: Social interaction and discourse structures*. 1997.
129. LEVIN, Saul: *Semitic and Indo-European: The Principal Etymologies. With observations on Afro-Asiatic*. 1995.
130. EID, Mushira (ed.) *Perspectives on Arabic Linguistics. Vol. VII. Papers from the Seventh Annual Symposium on Arabic Linguistics*. 1995.
131. HUALDE, Jose Ignacio, Joseba A. LAKARRA and R.L. Trask (eds): *Towards a History of the Basque Language*. 1995.
132. HERSCHENSOHN, Julia: *Case Suspension and Binary Complement Structure in French*. 1996.
133. ZAGONA, Karen (ed.): *Grammatical Theory and Romance Languages. Selected papers from the 25th Linguistic Symposium on Romance Languages (LSRL XXV) Seattle, 2-4 March 1995*. 1996.
134. EID, Mushira (ed.): *Perspectives on Arabic Linguistics Vol. VIII. Papers from the Eighth*

Annual Symposium on Arabic Linguistics. 1996.
135. BRITTON Derek (ed.): *Papers from the 8th International Conference on English Histori-cal Linguistics.* 1996.
136. MITKOV, Ruslan and Nicolas NICOLOV (eds): *Recent Advances in Natural Language Processing.* 1997.
137. LIPPI-GREEN, Rosina and Joseph C. SALMONS (eds): *Germanic Linguistics. Syntactic and diachronic.* 1996.
138. SACKMANN, Robin (ed.): *Theoretical Linguistics and Grammatical Description.* 1996.
139. BLACK, James R. and Virginia MOTAPANYANE (eds): *Microparametric Syntax and Dialect Variation.* 1996.
140. BLACK, James R. and Virginia MOTAPANYANE (eds): *Clitics, Pronouns and Move-ment.* 1997.
141. EID, Mushira and Dilworth PARKINSON (eds): *Perspectives on Arabic Linguistics Vol. IX. Papers from the Ninth Annual Symposium on Arabic Linguistics, Georgetown Univer-sity, Washington D.C., 1995.* 1996.
142. JOSEPH, Brian D. and Joseph C. SALMONS (eds): *Nostratic. Sifting the Evidence.* n.y.p.
143. ATHANASIADOU, Angeliki and René DIRVEN (eds): *On Conditionals Again.* 1997.
144. SINGH, Rajendra (ed): *Trubetzkoy's Orphan. Proceedings of the Montréal Roundtable "Morphophonology: contemporary responses (Montréal, October 1994).* 1996.
145. HEWSON, John and Vit BUBENIK: *Tense and Aspect in Indo-European Languages. Theory, typology, diachrony.* 1997.
146. HINSKENS, Frans, Roeland VAN HOUT and Leo WETZELS (eds): *Variation, Change, and Phonological Theory.* 1997.
147. HEWSON, John: *The Cognitive System of the French Verb.* 1997.
148. WOLF, George and Nigel LOVE (eds): *Linguistics Inside Out. Roy Harris and his critics.* 1997.
149. HALL, T. Alan: *The Phonology of Coronals.* 1997.
150. VERSPOOR, Marjolijn, Kee Dong LEE and Eve SWEETSER (eds): *Lexical and Syntacti-cal Constructions and the Construction of Meaning. Proceedings of the Bi-annual ICLA meeting in Albuquerque, July 1995.* 1997.
151. LIEBERT, Wolf-Andreas, Gisela REDEKER and Linda WAUGH (eds): *Discourse and Perspectives in Cognitive Linguistics.* n.y.p.
152. HIRAGA, Masako, Chris SINHA and Sherman WILCOX (eds): *Cultural, Psychological and Typological Issues in Cognitive Linguistics.* n.y.p.
153. EID, Mushira and Robert R. Ratcliffe (eds): *Perspectives on Arabic Linguistics Vol. X. Papers from the Tenth Annual Symposium on Arabic Linguistics, Salt Lake City, 1996.* 1997.
154. SIMON-VANDENBERGEN, Anne-Marie, Kristin DAVIDSE and Dirk NOËL (eds): *Reconnecting Language. Morphology and Syntax in Functional Perspectives.* 1997.
155. FORGET, Danielle, Paul HIRSCHBÜHLER, France MARTINEAU and María-Luisa RIVERO (eds): *Negation and Polarity. Syntax and semantics. Selected papers from the Colloquium Negation: Syntax and Semantics. Ottawa, 11-13 May 1995.* 1997.
156. MATRAS, Yaron, Peter BAKKER and Hristo KYUCHUKOV (eds): *The Typology and Dialectology of Romani.* 1997.